With Liberty
and JUSTICE
for Some

The Bible, the Constitution, and Racism in America

SUSAN K. WILLIAMS SMITH

Foreword by Iva E. Carruthers

JUDSON PRESS
PUBLISHERS SINCE 1824
VALLEY FORGE, PA

Interior design by Crystal Devine.
Cover design by Wendy Ronga, Hampton Design Group.

Library of Congress Cataloging-in-Publication data

Names: Smith, Susan K. Williams, 1954- author.
Title: With liberty & justice for some : the Bible, the constitution, and
   racism in America / Susan K. Williams Smith.
Other titles: With liberty and justice for some
Identifiers: LCCN 2020004986 (print) | LCCN 2020004987 (ebook) | ISBN
   9780817018139 (paperback) | ISBN 9780817082123 (epub)
Subjects: LCSH: African Americans. | Racism--Religious
   aspects--Christianity. | Racism--United States. | Race
   relations--Religious aspects--Christianity. | United States--Race
   relations. | African Americans--Civil rights.
Classification: LCC E185.61 .S656 2020 (print) | LCC E185.61 (ebook) |
   DDC 305.800973--dc23
LC record available at https://lccn.loc.gov/2020004986
LC ebook record available at https://lccn.loc.gov/2020004987

Printed in the U.S.A.

First printing, 2020.

Contents

Foreword

The personal journey and passion that drove Rev. Dr. Susan Smith to write this book is evident. Indeed, this is a response to questions she has held since childhood—questions that have persisted for her as a pastor, as a justice activist, and as a follower of Jesus Christ. Her interrogation of the foundational documents of this nation is undertaken through this experiential lens, along with her critique of some of the most historical racialized moments in this nation's path toward "equality and justice for all."

From the outset, the author offers a disclaimer: "I am not an historian but am, rather, a student of history. That said, I hope you who read this will take the nuggets of historical fact in this book and explore them more deeply yourselves." The book provides much fodder for extraction, exploration, and explication. Rev. Smith introduces this resource when the United States of America needs all the ideational momentum it can produce to strengthen the conviction that the arc of the universe bends toward justice and to further the forward movement of our nation toward that ideal.

Smith relates factual and historical vignettes about these foundational documents, weaving that history together with her interpretations of the content and evolution of those documents. Her incisive analysis, in juxtaposition of America's racial and religious histories, contributes to the essential work of demythologizing notions of this nation's exceptionalism, delusions about a divine destiny of hegemony, and dare we say its entangling "roots" in the gospel of Jesus Christ.

With this book, Susan Smith has stepped beyond her past writings of award-winning theological, meditative, and biographical genres. Her historiography is heuristic in nature. The window to two significant, but often ignored, questions are opened. The first interrogates the iconography of Jesus in early American history, and the second explores the relationship of African spirituality and religion to early Christianity. Her arguments are grounded in four key assumptions: (1) to be a Christian, one must know and follow the words and commandments of Jesus the Christ; (2) many who call themselves Christians ignore Jesus' ministry as it relates to social justice; (3) Jesus is conceived of differently by those who refer to the Gospels and those who do not; and (4) Americans have *never* had a monolithic view of Jesus nor of Christianity.

In her last chapter, "Moving On," Smith declares, "The country is slipping into an abyss, led by this president, and it is slipping largely because racism still exists and too many churches are still more aligned with the state than they are with a God of equality and egalitarianism, even as governments are still influenced by people who say their concept of a God who sanctions white supremacy is the only God."

In the age of Black Lives Matter, COVID-19, and the demands for African American reparations, when the nakedness of America's racism lays bare, Smith's work has unearthed and exposed a bedrock of truth that offers a foundation on which this generation's fiercest prophets may stand and sound off, piercing the silence of hegemonic history for such a time as this.

Rev. Iva E. Carruthers, PhD
General Secretary
Samuel DeWitt Proctor Conference
Chicago, IL

Introduction

*In the beginning, when God created the heavens and
the earth, the earth was a formless void and darkness
covered the face of the deep.* —Genesis 1:1-2

*In the beginning was the Word and the Word was with
God, and the Word was God. He was in the beginning
with God. All things came into being through him and
without him not one thing came into being.*
—John 1:1-3

It was from our Sunday school teachers that we, little Black children, first learned about the presence of God and about the goodness of God.

Holding onto and reading from well-used and somewhat tattered copies of the King James Bible, they read to us on Sunday mornings in deep, reverent voices, full of awe and respect. "In the beginning," they read to us, "God created the heaven and the earth. And the earth was without form, and void; and darkness was upon the face of the deep. And the Spirit of God moved upon the face of the waters. And God said, Let there be light; and there was light" (Genesis 1:1-3, KJV).

This was the best story ever told, I felt. The images that our teachers painted for us with their voices as they read the words inspired in us the same awe they seemed to have. Who was this God? Whoever he was, God was magnificent, with enormous power. This God had been sitting in nothingness which was dark and cavernous and chilly, when he finally decided (only masculine pronouns were used when I was in Sunday school) that he wanted more. And so, the Bible said, God created light, calling it day, and the darkness, which he called night. He created the firmament, which he called heaven, and bodies of water and dry land. He created grass and "herb yielding seed," the sun, which would rule the day, and the

1

moon, which would rule the night. He made the stars and moving creatures and huge whales, winged fowl, and cattle and insects and beasts (Genesis 1). Our teachers read the Creation story out of the Bible, which they treated as though it was a rare and precious jewel. Even the way they turned the thin pages said to us that the Bible was not an ordinary book.

It was from the Creation story that we learned that everything God created God said was "good." And so we had no reason to doubt that we, as human beings, were special and "good," because God had created us, just as God had created Adam and Eve. The sacred book which told the sacred story of how we had come to be said we were "good," and we believed it.

I don't remember at what age I was introduced to the United States Constitution, but I was quite young when I learned how it had come to be, forged out of the fight for freedom from a country which had treated its people poorly. We learned the words of the Declaration of Independence, "all men are created equal, and are endowed by their Creator with certain unalienable rights," and we again believed it. By this time, we were learning that being Black in America was a problem; the story of our ancestors having been enslaved was a sobering one, and bit by bit, at least in my house, we learned about racism and how it was something with which we would have to deal for the rest of our lives. That made me sad, but the fact that these two sacred texts—the Bible and the US Constitution—existed made me believe that no matter how bad racism was, we were protected and loved by God and by man. God had created us when God created everyone else, and the famous man who would one day become president, Thomas Jefferson, had written the words about our being equal which we regarded as holy, as holy, perhaps, as were the words in the Creation story.

But as time went on, it became apparent to me that neither the Bible nor the Constitution protected me or any African Americans from the evil of racism. That was confusing to me because both the Bible and the Constitution had taught me that God had created African Americans during the same creative process in which he had created everything else. And Thomas Jefferson, it seemed to me, had understood the heart and spirit of God when he made the declaration that we were all equal to each other. But it turned out that though there was one Bible and one Constitution, there was not one way of reading and interpreting those texts. White and Black people in this country did not live in community but rather in conflict, and both groups used and read the sacred documents in ways that supported their beliefs and their needs. Why were they, in my mind, sacred? Because they had been created with their notion of God and goodness at the center. The Bible was written precisely and specifically to bring God to the people and the people closer to God. The Constitution was written by men who had a sense of justice, though skewed, that they derived from God. Because of God being at their cores, they had the power to squash and ultimately destroy the problem of racism in this country, but that very power was diluted by two groups of people who professed to love God and country but in two remarkably different ways. The divide has never disappeared. Racism still stands as an important piece of this country which professes to be a Christian nation. It is as though it is Christian, however, without Jesus.

Diametrically Opposed Belief Systems

If it was puzzling to me how, in spite of the presence of God and the Bible there could be such racism, I was comforted to learn that I was not the only one. The history of this country was one in which there always seemed to be a pro-slavery and an anti-slavery way of looking at both God and country. America had been established in a seabed of hypocrisy. Throughout history, the pro-slavery and anti-slavery proponents argued their cases for their points of view. The pro-slavery proponents believed that God had created and sanctioned slavery, while the anti-slavery proponents believed quite the opposite. A good God, argued the anti-slavery advocates, could not possibly approve of how Africans were being treated, but pro-slavery champions went to passages in the Bible to "prove" that God did in fact approve of the institution. In *Frederick Douglas*, David Blight wrote that "Douglass loved the Declaration of Independence, but since its principles were *natural* rights, like the precious ores of the earth, he refused to argue for their existence or their righteousness against the claims of pro-slavery ideologues. 'What point in the anti-slavery creed would you have me argue?' he asked in his famous Fourth of July speech. 'Why must he prove that the slave is human?' Rather, Douglass claimed his authority *from two great scriptures*, 'the Constitution and the Bible'"[1]

Much later, Howard Thurman, the great spiritualist, described the inherent and indigenous tension in the United States. In spite of both the Bible and the Constitution, Thurman noted that "for a long time the Christian Church has profoundly compromised with the demands of the Gospel of Jesus Christ, especially with respect to the meaning and practice of love."[2] The Bible and the Constitution notwithstanding, Thurman wrote that "it was taken for granted that the very existence of law was for the protection and the security of white society."[3]

It seemed that Black and white society had two diametrically opposed belief systems when it came to how to treat not only Black people but also all people, since, as the Creation story taught us, everyone was made by God. Douglass, Thurman, and so many others based their beliefs on how God intended for people to be treated on the Great Commandment, found in all three Synoptic Gospels, which said that humans were to love the Lord their God with all their hearts, minds, and souls, and their neighbors as themselves.[4] Many white Christians, however, used as their guide the words found in the Great Commission, found in Matthew 28:19: "Go therefore and make disciples of all nations, baptizing them in the name of the Father and of the Son and of the Holy Spirit." They viewed it as their godly duty to civilize people whom they believed were inferior to them; God gave them the mandate, they believed, to exercise dominion over all the creatures of the earth, including people of color. That way of interpreting the Bible was the foundation of the concept of Manifest Destiny, the nineteenth-century belief that the expansion of the United States, which included subjugating people and their cultures, was the will of God, based on the words of the Great Commission. In the present day, Christian nationalists believe that it is a "God-given responsibility to moralize the world through the use of force."[5] One group of people sees the primary command of Jesus as it being necessary to love one another and build community, while the other group believes the duty of Christians is to exercise dominion over others and to gain political power, something we will examine later. Both groups call themselves Christian. Both read the same Bible and both are made up of American citizens, but neither group sees or interprets the Bible or Constitution in the same way.

Some Assumptions in This Book

This book is laid out upon a few assumptions. First is that in order to be a Christian, one must read, know, and follow the words and commandments of Jesus the Christ. I am making the case that calling oneself Christian does not make it so. Celebrating Christmas and Easter does not qualify one for Christian status. It is Jesus the Christ who teaches us, in the Sermon on the Mount and throughout the Gospels, that love is or should be the foundation of all that we do. One of the sources of the gospel is that Jesus is shown to have not only talked with, healed, and fellowshipped with society's outcasts—the "least of these" (Matthew 25:40)—but that he did so in spite of being severely opposed and challenged by the powers that be both in the church and in the state. For this writer, it is in the Gospels, specifically the Sermon on the Mount found in Matthew 5–7, that the primary and central message is found. Jesus' command to love our enemies, to pray for those who do us wrong, and to forgive (not once but for as long as we need to) are the foundation, this book will argue, of the Christian faith. Reading the Synoptic Gospels leads one to a belief that Jesus is a proponent of social justice.

The second assumption is that many who call themselves Christian ignore much of Jesus' Sermon on the Mount and reject that Christianity is about social justice. We will show how some religious lawmakers criticized the Gospels, thinking the lessons taught therein made a person weak. Conquerors did not back down; they fought until they won their battles. This group of Christians believes that their purpose, as laid out by the Christ, is to conquer others and to be advisors to political leaders. Their foundational Scriptures are not any found in the Gospels but rather in portions of the Pauline epistles. Ironically, it seems that many conservatives look at religion not as religion per se but as a political system, and we will examine how that view may have deposited a mindset in those who founded this country and wrote the United States Constitution. (When I refer to conservatives in this book, I will be talking about religious and political conservatives. These are people who want to hold on to traditional policies and practices, which tend to be racist and sexist and supportive of discrimination in general, and who use their version of Christianity to justify their beliefs.) Always, we will show, there was wrangling about what to do with the Negro, in spite of this country's apparent commitment to justice for all people, and always there seemed to be no dominant agreement as to what the Christ meant to be the blueprint for all people.

In *The Power Worshippers*, Katherine Stewart quotes Ralph Drollinger, a well-known and respected figure among conservative evangelical Christians, who said, "Nowhere does God command the institutions of government or commerce to fully support those with genuine needs," and says that "social welfare programs have no basis in scripture."[6] Drollinger goes so far as to say that some liberals "reject the Jesus of Scripture."[7] As their foundational Scriptures, Drollinger and others refer to 1 Timothy 2:1-2,4 and Romans 13:1-2. In these Scriptures, Paul, who was a Roman citizen who converted to Christianity, tells believers to respect the state—something he would have been required to do in order to save his own life, as disloyalty to the state was an offense punishable by death. He writes in 1 Timothy 2:1-4: "First of all, then, I urge that supplications, prayers, intercessions, and thanksgivings be made for everyone, for kings and all who are in high positions, so that we may lead a quiet and peaceable life in all godliness and dignity. This is right and is acceptable in the sight of God our Savior, who desires everyone to be saved and to come to the knowledge of the truth." In Romans 13:1-2, former US Attorney General Jeff Sessions brought us to the foundational belief of his faith: "Let every person be subject to the governing authorities; for there is no authority except from God, and those authorities that exist have been instituted by God. Therefore whoever resists authority resists what God has appointed, and those who resist will incur judgment." For this group of believers, the words of Jesus have been marginalized and peripheralized, but it is clear that they are heavily invested in converting the government to a force which will do the will of God as they see it, because, they will and do say, "It's in the Bible."

A third assumption that will underlie all that is in this book is that the person of Jesus is conceived differently by groups who use the words of Jesus as found in the Gospels and by those who do not. According to Rita Nakashima Brock and Rebecca Ann Parker, authors of *Saving Paradise*, Jesus the Christ was militarized; to be a good Christian was to be a good soldier. Theologians of that time praised Charlemagne's conversion of the Saxons through violence: "a text from 777 . . . praised his 'conversion' of the Saxons by comparing his victory to Christ's defeat of death through his crucifixion, descent into hell, and resurrection. In their view, Charlemagne's military victories replicated divine salvation."[8] Brock and Parker say that "Charlemagne and his army jettisoned the Christian experience of this earth as being infused with divine presence and power."[9] In spite of the efforts of some to remind people that the Christ had achieved victory over death through love and humility, the militarized Christ gained a foothold in the Christian belief system that was never able to be eliminated. This image of the Christ as a warrior is far different than the one with which I grew up, that of a man, the Son of God, who stressed that love of and for others was stronger than the sword and was the way to bring people to God.

The fourth assumption of this book is that Americans have never had a monolithic view of Jesus, nor have they had a monolithic understanding of what Christianity is. In fact, so-called liberals and conservatives are miles apart when it comes to race. While it does not seem to be the case that evangelical conservative Christians are all Christian nationalists, what is clear is that conservatives have much in common with the beliefs of Christian nationalists, so much so that they have not, in history, railed against the presence of racism. Stewart says that "Christian nationalism looks backward on a fictionalized history of America's allegedly Christian founding."[10] Christian nationalists and some evangelical Christians adhere to the belief that "true Christians" have been commanded by God to gain control of the "seven mountains" of culture and influence: "government, business, education, the media, the arts and entertainment, family, and religion."[11] By referring to the Bible, they push the belief that what they are seeking is God's will, a will which has been muddied over time by the theology of liberals and others who, frankly, do not understand God.

This book will also show that, contrary to popular belief spouted over the airwaves, this is not a Christian nation. We will see that the founders were explicit in their determination that it should not be considered as such. Although the founders, for the most part, had all gone to church in their youth, many were uneasy with the tenets of Christianity and with the mystical components of

Jesus. They had rebelled against the intrusion into government by the church in England; they were determined that the same thing would not happen in the new government they were creating in the new world.

Why does any of this matter? Because living with the belief that there is one Christianity, one notion of who God is and what God requires, has caused this writer angst as the problem of racism in this country has never abated. How could it be that the God of my Sunday school lessons would be all right with the raw hatred, bigotry, and discrimination meted out to African Americans? How could some people call themselves Christian while not quoting or practicing the lessons of agape love, forgiveness, and mercy taught by the Christ? The contradiction was too great. It puzzled and then bothered me that so many people who called themselves Christian could lynch a Black person on a Saturday night and go to church the next morning—and possibly even serve communion?

Thinking about Racism

While the focus of this book is primarily the status of African Americans in this country in spite of the Bible and the United States Constitution, it is painfully true that neither of those documents has been successful in stopping the subjugation of other people as well. The Bible was and is patriarchal and sexist in its worldview. From the days of the first Puritan settlers in the British colonies to the westward expansion of America's homesteaders and pioneers, Native American peoples have been ruthlessly murdered in the name of Manifest Destiny, because European and Euro-American settlers have believed they were doing God's will.

But the story of racism in this country most strongly resonates around the story of white Americans and African Americans. The late Vincent Harding wrote in the foreword for Howard Thurman's *Jesus and the Disinherited* that African Americans were in search of and needed a "liberating spirituality."[12] Thurman, wrote Harding, "had a quest to bring the harrowing beauty of the African-American experience into deep engagement with what he called 'the religion of Jesus.'"[13] Do we dare posit that the "religion of Jesus" has failed because both the Bible and the United States Constitution have been so recklessly manipulated in order to support the worldview of the system called white supremacy? For this book, we posit exactly that.

A disclaimer: I am not a historian but am, rather, a student of history. That said, I hope you who read this will take the nuggets of historical facts in this book and explore them more deeply yourselves. The purpose of this book is not to give answers as to how to fix what I see as a failure of these two sacred documents but instead to engage others to think about our American problem in a deeper way. We are all products of American Christianity, which was given to us by the Puritans who settled here. And we have all likewise been trained to believe in the concept of American exceptionalism, which has compelled us to think of this country as the most advanced and forward-looking country in the world. But when it comes to racism, the whole world knows our story. Our dirty laundry has hung on the clotheslines of American history for generations. We have lived in the myth that this is a country which believes in and practices "liberty and justice for all," when we have always been a country which has practiced liberty and justice for some. We have lived within the safe bosom of the myth of America, even those who have suffered from bigotry. Perhaps this book will help us push through the myths to the core of who we really are as a nation with two sacred texts which have been sorely ignored. And with that realization, perhaps we can move forward with eyes wide open to a new world where both sacred documents are revered for what they were intended to be.

One final thought: though this book will be talking about race and its impact on how both the Bible and the United States Constitution have been read, interpreted, and applied, it is important to know that this is not about blaming white people. If there is blame to be assigned, it is against the system called white supremacy. Many, many white people abhor racism; they see what it does and has done. The immediate reaction when the word "racism" is used is defensiveness; people will say, "I didn't do that," or ask, "Why do people keep bringing it up?" It is easier to live in denial than to face the truth, no matter what the distasteful subject is before us.

But it is our very denial which has allowed the system to continue, challenged from time to time, but not eradicated. Rev. Dr. Martin Luther King said that it was the silence of so-called liberals that bothered him and made the situation worse, and the poet

Audre Lorde wrote that our silence does not and will not protect us. Even as she dealt with the fact that she was a lesbian, a Black woman, and, finally, a woman with breast cancer, she acknowledged that being silent about any of that, acting as though it were not her reality, did not change her reality. She wrote:

> I was going to die, if not sooner, then later, whether or not I had ever spoken myself. My silences had not protected me. Your silence will not protect you. But for every real word spoken, for every attempt I had ever made to speak those truths for which I am still seeking, I had made contact with other women while we examined the words to fit a world in which we all believed, bridging our differences. And it was the concern and caring of all those women which gave me strength and enable me to scrutinise the essentials of my living.[14]

Reni Eddo-Lodge wrote, in the preface of Lorde's book, "And yet, Audre lets us know that staying silent is betraying yourself, because nobody will speak up for you but you. Silence can be a survival strategy, but it can also be a way of giving up, saying nothing simply because there's too much to say, and you fear your intervention will make no difference."[15]

Our desire to remain silent and to ignore racism is understandable but not acceptable. It feels as though the God of us all beseeches us to do better.

I hope this book will help us all to do that.

NOTES

1. David W. Blight, *Frederick Douglass, Prophet of Freedom* (New York: Simon & Schuster, 2018), 233, italics added.

2. Howard Thurman, *The Luminous Darkness* (New York: Harper & Row, 1965), 3.

3. Thurman, *The Luminous Darkness*, 4.

4. The Great Commandment is found in Matthew 22:35-40, Mark 12:28-34, and Luke 10:27. Jesus quoted the words from the Shema, found in Deuteronomy 6:4-5.

5. Katherine Stewart, *The Power Worshippers: Inside the Dangerous Rise of Religious Nationalism* (New York: Bloomsbury Publishing, 2019), 5.

6. Stewart, 49.

7. Stewart, 39.

8. Rita Nakashima Brock and Rebecca Ann Parker, *Saving Paradise: How Christianity Traded Love of This World for Crucifixion and Empire* (Boston: Beacon Press, 2008), 229.

9. Brock and Parker, 230.
10. Stewart, 4.
11. Stewart, 25.
12. Howard Thurman, *Jesus and the Disinherited*, foreword by Vincent Harding (Boston: Beacon Press), 1976, 2.
13. Thurman, *Jesus and the Disinherited*.
14. Audre Lorde, *Your Silence Will Not Protect You* (UK: Silver Press, 2017), 2.
15. Lorde, iii.

1
How Did We Get Here?

*Then you will know the truth, and the truth will set you
free.* —John 8:32, NIV

In the slave castle in Elmina, Ghana, West Africa, there sits a Christian church, the first Christian church built in Africa, atop a dungeon where enslaved Africans, captured by European slave traders, were kept until it was time for them to be transported to the Americas. The structure, built in 1482 by the Portuguese, was a bastion of protection for the Portuguese as well as a place to store the metals they mined. When the Dutch overthrew the Portuguese in 1637, the storage rooms meant for gold were converted to dungeons and the Catholic church became Protestant. That church itself became Elmina's slave market. The dungeon below it was literally stuffed with Black bodies—hundreds in a space which should have had, at the most, only fifty. There were dungeons for men and for women; the women's dungeons could hold five hundred Africans, and up to one thousand men were "stored" in the men's dungeons.[1]

While church services were held, with people singing and praying, declaring that the church was "the only place where God lives; God lives here and nowhere else," the enslaved men below suffered. The conditions were so heinous that the captured humans could not sit or move around; there were no windows, so they had no light and no fresh air; they had a space in the middle of the floor where the men could eliminate, but obviously not everyone could get to that place. Thus, the dungeon, over which the church sat where people praised God, was hot, dark, with a horrific stench; men who died were often left there until some castle official felt like taking them out. While merchants came searching for precious metals, Christians came seeking to save the souls of human beings whom they considered to be inferior to themselves.[2] If the captives survived the dungeons, they walked to and then out of the "Door of No Return," getting on ships in which they would continue to live in barbaric and inhumane conditions as they traversed the Middle Passage. Gold brought good money, and so did enslaved Africans.

Much later, as slavery continued to thrive in the United States, slave traders, many of whom called themselves Christian, participated in the business of selling human beings. As the economy of the South was growing, more and more labor was needed, and so many enslaved Africans who lived north of the deep South were sought as laborers whose work would create the economy which grew as the country grew. Human beings were captured in Maryland and made to walk the nearly five hundred miles to South Carolina and beyond, chained together with metal collars around their necks and chains around their hands and feet. They were made to walk anywhere from ten to twenty miles a day. They were not allowed to bathe while they made the journey, so they were filthy, their bodies infested with lice and other pesky and dangerous insects. One route sometimes used in the trek to the Deep South took them past the US Capitol, that bastion which was supposed to represent the ideals and values of America.[3] It was embarrassing to lawmakers who saw them pass. Though they believed in and supported slavery, they did not like to see the raw evidence of their hypocrisy. It bothered them, as it did some religious leaders, but neither group was willing to eliminate the institution of slavery.

From our beginning as a nation, we were not one, and the church, as opposed to being a harbinger of justice and morality, showed itself to be incapable of preaching that God's love was inclusive of everyone. Both the church and the state, when it came to racism, were weak from the start.

The Word of God and the Qualities of God

We learned at an early age about the presence and about the magnificence of God. Our proof was the Bible, that sacred book which our parents and Sunday school teachers regarded as having been given to the human race by God. They believed God had written it with the divine hand. They knew nothing about it being a collection of many separate books, written over many thousands of years and finally joined together to make a single book. They also knew nothing about it having been written by many different people, not by God, in many different languages, and even if someone had told them those facts, they would not have cared, if they even believed it. This was "the Word of God," and one did not tamper with it. One accepted it and treasured it. In church and at home, the Bible was the penultimate sacred text.

It was from the King James Version of the Bible, many times tattered and worn, that they taught us. We learned that God was powerful: omnipotent, omnipresent, omniscient, and perfect. We learned that God was an artist, a genius, who created order out of chaos. None of us questioned anything that we were taught about how the world came into being. There was no mention of God having made different races and ethnicities and proclaiming that some were better than others. My siblings and I felt good about being the children of a God who had no favorites. We were precious in God's sight. That was a good lesson for us. I felt moved by the sheer brilliance of a God who knew how to make trees that grew toward the heavens, a God who created earth which contained life and produced more life.

I was moved by the fact that this God—our God—could create the colors that made the earth and the seas so glorious: flame-red flowers as brilliant as bright lilies, and seas so deep that they rivaled heaven's heights. This God was an artist, determining not only the colors but also the shapes of different flowers: red roses, purple lilacs, yellow daffodils. I wondered how God had figured out how to do all of that, but what I did not wonder about was God's intentionality in making everything. Who was this God who could make a zebra different from a donkey, a mule different from a horse, a sheep different from a goat? How did God do that? Who was this God who created warm-blooded and cold-blooded animals, and how did God decide what these two groups of living creatures needed in order to live? God figured out how to make lungs and hearts, brains and kidneys; hands and feet, fingers and toes. Nothing God did was a mistake. To the contrary, God had seemingly been an intentional creator.

And so, with the lessons of my Sunday school teachers deeply imbedded in my very spirit, I grew to love and respect God, whom

I believed to be the parent of us all. I believed that every single one of us mattered. As I got older, however, the ugliness of the world began to invade my consciousness, and my naïve God-consciousness began to be challenged in ways I could never have expected.

We worshiped the Bible; holding it was almost like holding the very hand of God. Our Sunday school teachers would have been shattered and perhaps unable to teach us had they been told that mere humans had written it. Our teachers needed to believe in the mystery of God, and thus they taught us to embrace that mystery. The word "sacred" meant God wrote it and that it had a higher status than did a book written by mere human beings. We didn't know the technical definition of the word "sacred," defined in one dictionary as "connected with God (or the Gods) or dedicated to a religious purpose and so deserving veneration." Anything sacred is, according to the *Cambridge English Dictionary*, "considered to be holy and deserving respect because of a connection with a God." Because we were taught that God had personally written every word in the Bible, we were not to question anything in the text, even if we did not understand or vehemently disagreed with what we read. The Bible as the Word of God was not to be tampered with. We were to accept it and everything contained therein. It was sacred.

The Bible brought God close to us. Through the words in that sacred text, we were convinced that God was near us. We did not know what God looked like, but it did not matter. God was God, and God was good. The presence of God was a comfort and a source of strength and for us. The biggest blessing of this God for us African Americans was that since God had created everyone and said his total creation was good, we were therefore loved by God in spite of the race-based hatred that was forever in our lives.

We, as African Americans, needed a good God, an inclusive God, and a loving God, and the Bible provided us that affirmation. We needed a God who did not discriminate against us and who advocated for us. Even as a child, I realized that we as African Americans were constantly fighting for our place in the world. We were frequently beaten down and beaten back, so the Bible was critically important for and to us in ways that our white brothers and sisters could not understand. We needed God to be close; we needed to be able to call on God's name and have the blessed assurance that God heard us. We needed the Creation story found in Genesis to remind us that "everything that was made was made by God," including us.

We needed the God we held onto to believe in us and in our worth. For many African Americans, the disconnect between what we held onto as the "God of goodness" about whom we learned in our Sunday school classes and the God we saw practiced by the religious people in America was almost too great to bear. We lived in a country which had owned and yet disowned us at one and the same time. We lived in a country where people called on the same Jesus of the Bible that we all read and shared, but whose practice of religion was deeply different than was ours. It was mind-boggling and troubling. Howard Thurman talked about the "three hounds of hell," that is, "fear, hypocrisy, and hatred,"[4] which truly challenged those who could see the contradiction between the print and the pragmatism of everyday life. The "disinherited" were not just African Americans but included people of color who lived in countries that had been colonized by the United States. We would learn that people of color were, in the eyes of white Christians, the bane of the earth, and for some, not even created by God.

We, the disinherited, were holding onto the Bible for dear life, but we were sinking in the sea of racism caused by white supremacy. Thurman made a distinction between the Christian religion practiced by white and Black people in this country. He called American Christianity a "strange mutation."[5] It was a mutation for many reasons which we will examine, but perhaps the biggest reason was because white American Christianity seemed to ignore the very words of Jesus the Christ. Jesus of Nazareth had embraced all people created by God—male and female, Jew and Gentile, rich and poor—but American Christianity had put in place some exceptions to the commands Jesus gave for our lives to be aligned with God and God's will as described in the Bible.

It was puzzling to Thurman and to many others why Christianity could not practice its own dictates. "Why is it that Christianity seems impotent to deal radically, and therefore effectively, with the issues of discrimination and injustice on the basis of race, religion and national origin?" Thurman asked.[6]

The Great Commandment

We had the answer in the book we said we loved; our beloved Bible gave us the Great Commandment, found in the Synoptic Gospels of Matthew, Mark, and Luke.[7] It is significant that these words are found in all three of the Synoptics, which indicates that they are the heart and soul of the Christian faith. In all three Gospels, Jesus the Christ is asked, "What is the most important commandment?" The Pharisees were trying to stop Jesus in his tracks, so in asking this question, they hoped he would answer it in a way that indicated either his knowledge or ignorance of the Law. In each Gospel account, Jesus answered, "'You shall love the Lord your God with all your heart, and with all your soul, and with all your mind.' This is the greatest and first commandment. And a second is like it: 'You shall love your neighbor as yourself.' On these two commandments hang all the law and the prophets."

It is hardly a difficult lesson and seems quite clear, yet many white Christians, using their sacred Bible, seemed for the most part to have been unable, and in many instances unwilling, to abide by it. In the practice of racism, Jesus seemed absent, his words ignored. It was puzzling. There was one Bible, one set of Gospels, and one Jesus, yet in the grip of racism, there were two radically different ways of internalizing and practicing—or not practicing—the same words.

It is that very contradiction which is part of the bedrock of this book. In spite of the obviously clear and simple lesson given by Jesus, taken right out of the sacred text, there was rampant hatred based on race. It seems that white people who considered themselves to be deeply religious created a God who is not bothered when people who say they are believers can and do kill, discriminate against, and hate people because of the color of their skin. These practicing white Christians do not direct their ire only at African Americans but against people of color in general—Asians, Hispanics, and other brown people—and against Jews, a puzzling reality in that Jesus was a Palestinian Jew. The problem comes from many sources, but one is the phenomenon of free will, which allows believers to make personal choices in keeping or not in keeping with what we call the Word of God. What's more, biblical interpretation is not a hard science; the words of Jesus are not a mathematical formula. In the creation of many different people, of many races, God did not create a spiritual mechanism for everyone to look at God in the same way. God apparently entertained no consideration of the impact of culture when God created the many races of people.

That there is such a phenomenon is troubling, for it goes against the thread of belief which says that God made everything and that everything God made was good. Yet from very early in the history of this country, preachers and theologians tried to make sense out of a Creation story with which they had issues. The presence of Black people was, to many, an anomaly, something that did not happen, as many would have liked to believe. They posited that Adam and Eve were white. Because Black people existed, there had to be another reason why and how. Even as they taught that Black people were destined to be ruled over for the duration of their lives (which we will deal with later on), they had to explain how Black people got here in the first place. Some taught that there was another God, a "pre-Adamic" God who created Black people first. They taught that when Adam and Eve were in the Garden of Eden, the serpent was a Black man who ended up seducing Eve and causing damnation of the human race.[8] In the quest of protecting and justifying white supremacy, the Bible was being manipulated. A religion was being created based on the Bible, but it wasn't what Thurman referred to as "the religion of Jesus." The belief in the supremacy of whites over all other people had to be supported, and that support came from manipulation of the Bible to make it appear that the "good" that God created was white.

But that was a problem, because the beauty and the power of Christianity is its message of inclusive, agape love. For Jesus, there was no "other." Instead, all people were worthy of being treated with dignity and honor. Jesus' ministry showed the people of God the power of loving each other; his work demonstrated how that love helped build community, which was the will of God. Those whom the world rejected Jesus embraced.

The power of his ministry and the reason Jesus was able to draw such large crowds was partly due to his healing ministry, but it was also due to the fact that he dared reach out to the unreachable, the undesirable, and the untouchables. He himself was a minority; he was a Palestinian Jew whose family was poor. He lived during the rule of the Roman Empire, which was no less brutal and race-, class-, and religion-conscious than our United States is today. Jesus knew what it was like to be one of the least, so he showed those who were willing to see how the world could be revolution- ized if the least were pulled into society instead of being pushed to the periphery. The God of "the Bible" created by white supremacist ideology was not the religion of Jesus that is found in the Gospels.

This break, this schism between "the Bible" and the gospel, is a fundamental reason why we are questioning the sacredness of the words of "the Bible" outside of the gospel. The Bible is filled with problem texts and stories: it is sexist and supports toxic masculin- ity, at the very least. The Gospels lead us to community, including acceptance of "the least of these," who were considered to be vital to the wholeness of Roman society although the Roman elite did not and would not admit it. Like Africans who were brought to the Americas, the Jews, and especially the poor ones, had strengthened the Roman economy. They were needed but not necessarily wanted, tolerated but not accepted. Jesus knew the pain of living life as a marginalized member of the society, and he also knew that God wanted people to live in community. Jesus talked about how he had not come to destroy the law but to fulfill it with the practice of lov- ing each other and thus community building (Matthew 5:17-30, the Sermon on the Mount).

The law was ineffective in fighting injustice, as ironic as that might sound. The law coupled with a love and respect for each other, however, was what would make God's kingdom a reality on earth. It is probably safe to say that the Romans did not care about God's kingdom on earth; in fact, they may have felt threatened by the very idea of that happening, but Jesus was clear about the work before him. The world could not survive if law and love were not integrated and balanced. Making and following the law without love was as problematic as loving each other without the law. Jesus wanted and needed the people to whom he was sent to understand the need for the balance between law and love. That balance would keep those who were interested only in the rule of law from becom- ing despots and criminals themselves, as they descended into nefari- ous ways to keep the law. However, the balance would help those who understood the concept of agape love to refrain from enabling people to do things that were not helpful to them or to the society.

So, it was simple in its proclamation: Love the Lord God with all your heart and with all your mind and with all your soul, and your neighbor as yourself. It was a simple command, not difficult to understand, but incredibly difficult for human beings to practice and master. Christians in general decided to love the Lord God in their own way, and white Christians in America were no different. People faltered and fell away from God and from God's intention that there be peace and community. People sought money and power, not God. The religion of Jesus was gone almost before Jesus was crucified. Monotheism taught that there was one God and that the one God had created everything and everyone, but God's children wrestled and fretted. In their spirits, they were not able to get past the human inclination to seek that which was important to them, too often at the expense of the least of these. Jesus came to earth, but at the end of his life and ministry, that which he had been sent to teach was still largely absent from God's world.

Two Religions: Community or Empire

Most of us were taught to regard God as an absolute, a God for all people, who we comfortably put into a box. When we think about it, such a view is naïve, especially as the Bible, our source of learning about God, was not a monolithically written book. Because it was, as we have already stated, written by many different people who spoke different languages, lived in many different countries, and who, because of their culture, were bound to look at life and God in their own culturally-influenced ways, it was bound to be interpreted differently by the cultures which embraced it. Wes Howard-Brook, in *"Come Out My People!"* states what should be the obvious, that the Bible does not present a single, unified perspective on what it means to be a "Jew or a Christian, . . . but rather what it means to be God's people."[9] Howard-Brook says religion is not about denominationalism; instead, it is about "binding people together."[10] Binding people together does not mean that our differences become unimportant or that they disappear, but rather that we learn from each other and learn to live with each other, differences included and respected. Religion seems to call more for integration than assimilation, and if we believe that God made "everything that was made" and was pleased with the differences that God created, it is not a stretch to believe that God would want integration, which would ultimately build community.

If community was God's will, then how did religion fail to create community but instead feed the development of divisiveness based on race, class, religion, and other factors? Even in Jesus' day, people recognized that there were two religions, each pulling in opposite directions.[11] Howard-Brook says that "all of history is the story of the interplay" between these two religions—one being the "religion of creation" and the other, the "religion of empire." He goes on to say:

> [W]e can understand one of the Bible's religions to be grounded in the experience of and ongoing relationship with the Creator God, leading to a covenantal bond between that God and God's people for the blessing and abundance of all people and all creation. The other, while sometimes claiming to be grounded in that same God, is actually a human invention used to justify and legitimate attitudes and behaviors that provide blessing and abundance for some at the expense of others.[12]

The fact that Howard-Brook can write that the Bible itself had two religions is jarring and insults the Sunday school experience of many of us, Black and white, who were taught that the Bible was about one God; therefore, when it came to Christianity, there was one religion. The thought that in our most sacred text there was from the beginning evidence of there being two religions at war with each other and that one was a "human invention" destroys the comfortable stories we have all carried with us about God, religion, and the Bible. This unwelcome thought flies in the face of some of the words in that Bible, notably that there is "one Lord, one faith, one baptism, one God and Father of all, who is above all, and through all, and in you all" (Ephesians 4:5-6, KJV).

As Paul writes in some of his epistles, we too might ask, "What, then?" Is the Bible sacred or not? Have we been foolhardy in regarding it as sacred if, as Howard-Brook says, it had from the beginning evidence of there being two religions? Whether it is or is not sacred, can it be trusted to guide people who are looking for God? And is it even possible for a sacred book that has two religions pulling at each other in opposition to present the notion of one God? If there is one God, whose God is it? Is it the God of the oppressed or the God of the oppressor? Finally, if there is more than one God, whose God is the father of Jesus the Christ? Is Jesus the son of the God the oppressor, the God who apparently looks the other way in the face of racial, sexual, and ethnic discrimination and hatred, or is Jesus the son of the God who desires community and who directs us to take care of the least of these?

NOTES

1. Stephen Nuwagira, "Ghana's Slave Castle, the Only Place Where God 'Lives,'" *The New Times* [English-language daily, Rwanda], January 12, 2013, https://www.newtimes.co/rw/section/read/105694.

2. Judith Graham, "The Slave Fortresses of Ghana," *New York Times*, November 25, 1990, section 5, 14, https://www.nytimes.com/1990/11/25/travel/the-slave-fortresses-of-ghana.html.

3. Edward E. Baptist, *The Half Has Never Been Told: Slavery and the Making of American Capitalism* (New York: Basic Books, 2014), 27–29.

4. Howard Thurman, *Jesus and the Disinherited*, foreword by Vincent Harding (Boston: Beacon Press, 1976), 6.

5. Thurman, 9.

6. Thurman, 1.

7. The Great Commandment is found in Matthew 22:34-30, Mark 12:28-31, and Luke 10:25-28.

8. Mason Stokes, "Someone's in the Garden with Eve: Race, Religion and the American Fall," *Autumn Quarterly* 50, no. 4 (1998): 718–44, quote on 718; www.jstor.org/stable/30042166.

9. Wes Howard-Brook, *"Come Out My People!": God's Call Out of Empire in the Bible and Beyond* (Maryknoll, NY: Orbis, 2010), 4.

10. Howard-Brook, 5.

11. Howard-Brook, 7.

12. Howard-Brook.

2
How Then Do We Proceed?

*The Spirit of the Lord G*OD *is upon me,*
*because the L*ORD *has anointed me;*
[the Lord] has sent me to bring good news to the oppressed,
to bind up the brokenhearted,
to proclaim liberty to the captives,
and release to the prisoners;
*to proclaim the year of the L*ORD's *favor.*

—Isaiah 61:1-2; Luke 4:18-19

In order to begin to get some understanding of which God the Bible represents, we may do well to look at some of the words in the text. One of the most notable things about the God of the Hebrew Scriptures is that this God is a warrior who supports war. That fact might bother those who think that the notion of a good God and that of a God who promotes and encourages war are contradictory. Though many of us grew up in churches singing "Onward Christian soldiers, marching as to war! With the cross of Jesus, going on before," it is probably safe to assume that while singing that song we did not think of God as a promoter of war. However, in the Hebrew Scriptures, God is involved in all kinds of wars, not as an observer but as an active participant. The concept of holy war exists in the study of religious warfare. Holy war is defined as an action in which the Lord is personally engaged and in which the people respond with zealous devotion.[1]

For example, in the Book of Deuteronomy, God, speaking through the prophet Moses, says to the Israelites, "The LORD your God will fight alongside you and help you win the battle . . . Whenever you capture towns in the land your God is giving you, be sure to kill all the people and animals" (Deuteronomy 20:4,16, Freedom

Bible [CEV]). What? God ordains that kind of mass murder? Is that who God is and what God stands for? In other parts of the Hebrew Scriptures, we see a God who causes or incites war.

From another favorite song taught to Sunday school children all over this country, we learn that "Joshua fit the battle of Jericho, and the walls came a'tumbling down." What was this battle of Jericho, and why was it fought? It seems that the people of Jericho were depraved beyond redemption because of their sexual promiscuity, child sacrifice, incest, and more. God had said to Abram that these people were so sinful that they "deserve to be punished" (Genesis 15:16, Freedom Bible [CEV]).[2] Jericho was the first city of the Promised Land to be attacked and conquered by the Israelites. If the words of the sacred text are to be believed, God called that war, which resulted in the deaths of many innocent women and children. Because the morality of Jericho's people was problematic, God decided that the solution was genocide. This God was so concerned about the sexual immorality in Jericho that he starts a war.

This God, who has the right to declare and decide who is living in God's will and who is not, is nonetheless one who thinks nothing of wiping out entire populations of people when things are not going his way. This is not to say that there are not instances in the Bible where God shows mercy and extreme patience, as, for example, when Abraham intercedes for the people of Sodom and Gomorrah (Genesis 18:23ff.), when God is about to destroy those cities. Abraham asks God, "Will you indeed sweep away the righteous with the wicked?" and what follows is a conversation where the text shows that God listens when intercession is made. But that does not change the fact that in the Hebrew Scriptures, God is depicted as wiping out, or sanctioning the elimination of, whole villages of people. When humans do that, it is called genocide, but when the good God does it, how is it labeled? Did God arrange and approve of the annihilation of ethnic and religious groups God did not approve of? Is it from the sacred text that we get the blueprint of how God's "chosen people" are permitted and encouraged to kill those who are different from themselves? Was God a proponent of the creation of religion of empire?

The Israelites were certainly the victims of conquest. In 586 BCE, when the Babylonian destruction of the temple was complete, the Israelites were exiled to a strange land and exposed to a religion different from their own. Although it seems that the Israelites were involved in plenty of wars, the first eleven chapters of Genesis were written as a rebuke of Babylonian religion. Walter Wink writes that "the religion of Babylon is the real religion of America"[3] and explains:

> We will discover that the religion of Babylon—one of the world's oldest, continuously surviving religions—is thriving as never before in every sector of contemporary American life, even in our synagogues and churches. It, and not Christianity, is the real religion of America. I will suggest that this myth of redemptive violence undergirds American popular culture, civil religion, nationalism, and foreign policy, and that it lies coiled like an ancient serpent at the root of the system of domination that has characterized human existence since well before Babylon ruled supreme.[4]

The Babylonian religious systems, and therefore Babylon's gods, came about as the result of wars between the Babylonian gods. The story of the *Enuma Elish* revealed how the Babylonians believed the world to have come into being not through the hands of a loving God but as the result of a horrible familial spat in which the children of the parent gods, Tiamet and Apsu, killed them. Tiamet had apparently devised a plan where some of his children would be killed, and some of them heard of his plot and told the others, including Marduk. Marduk killed Apsu, but Tiamet was yet alive and the siblings wanted her murdered, too. Marduk said he would do it if he were granted a palace in which to live; the spoil of his kill was Babylon. In order to serve the gods, the Babylonians had to serve Marduk, so it was expected that the Israelite exiles would worship Marduk, as well.[5] Wink says that "the implications are clear: humanity is created from the blood of a murdered god . . . We are the consequence of deicide."[6]

The Israelites, banished to Babylon during the Babylonian conquest of Jerusalem, knew the Babylonian myth of creation, and it was opposite to what they had grown up believing. They were appalled; they created the Creation story as found in Genesis 1 (written during the Babylonian exile, somewhere between 539–450 BCE and attributed to the Priestly [P] source) even as they remembered it, a majestic tale of how their God had created the earth and everything in it from nothing. In spite of some similarities to the *Enuma Elish*, this Creation story was meant to stand in opposition to the Babylonian story of creation in a way that said to their captors that their God was better. Their Creation story was mysterious and beautiful and awe-inspiring; it did not come about as a result of family conflict which had resulted in murder. At this point, the Israelites were establishing themselves as practitioners of the religion of creation, as opposed to the Babylonian religion of empire. The Israelites constructed not only their religion but also their God. Wes Howard-Brook noted that for the Babylonians, "only the city is sacred ground. But for the people of Genesis, all the heavens and earth are filled with God's creative presence and life."[7]

Hence, here we have the biblical creation of two gods and two religions, both of which did, in fact, live together in tension. It was during their seventy years in Babylon that the Israelites mourned what they experienced as the loss of the God they believed to be the true God, and the psalmist recorded their pain: "By the rivers of Babylon—there we sat down and there we wept when we remembered Zion. On the willows there we hung our harps. For there our captors asked us for songs, and our tormentors asked for mirth, saying, 'Sing us one of the songs of Zion!'" (Psalm 137:1-3).

The God of creation was conceived while the Israelites were in the cradle of oppression. The struggle between the two gods—one of the oppressed and one of the oppressors—might be said to have been born during the exile of 586 BCE, and it continues to this day.

The Religion of Empire and the Roman Empire

Thus, it appears that this idea of at least two gods is not a new idea, except that in this country, and perhaps in the world, we have lived inside of the myth that insists that there is only one God that we all worship. The state of the world, however, and the practice of religion, indicates something different. Even within Christianity itself, there are hundreds, if not thousands, of denominations all claiming to know the true message of Jesus the Christ. Now, as in ancient and pre-biblical days, we have a polytheistic system in which gods are competing with each other.

In addition to that, as much as we might want to claim that we all are practicing the religion of Jesus, or the religion of creation, the fact is that the religion of empire has permeated nearly every Christian sect in this country and in the world. Therefore, the religion of creation, which is described in the Creation story in Genesis, is still wrestling with the religion of empire.

As we make our way into the discussion of how Christianity and the Christian Bible have been ineffective in fighting and ending racism, we do well to consider, albeit briefly, the place and the role of racism and racist practices in early Christianity. Christianity developed in the bowels of the Roman Empire. Jesus the Christ was a Palestinian Jew in a place which touted a belief in the superiority of Romans, a belief and prejudice which had existed in Greek society and culture before the Romans conquered the Greeks. While there was no homogeneous servant group that was easily identified by skin color, the Romans disdained certain ethnic, racial, and geographic entities and believed that real Romans embraced the culture and belief system of their government. They had little time, patience, or respect for groups that resisted being assimilated into Roman life.[8] That put the Jews in a bad place, for they refused to bow down to the Romans, as they had refused to bow down to Nebuchadnezzar. Rather than offend their God, three Hebrew boys who lived in Babylon, Hananiah, Mishael, and Azariah, willingly went into the fiery furnace and escaped death because of their faithfulness to the Israelite God (Daniel 3).

In Jesus' time, the Jews lived in the empire but battled the empire at the same time. The socially and politically elite, including some church leaders and educators, found it alluring and tempting to yield to the demands of the empire and thus assimilate, while still trying to hold onto their Jewish heritage. It was advantageous for them to do so, but the Romans disliked and looked down on them, largely because of their refusal to abandon their God and their religious rituals. Conversion to Judaism by a Roman was considered to be a criminal act.[9] Romans were known to call people "barbarians" who were from a different geographical location. The Romans considered themselves to be superior to all other ethnic and racial groups, including the Greeks. However, they borrowed liberally from Greek culture, especially in the area of education, as well as from the Egyptians, from whose culture both they and the Greeks borrowed.

Church writers, scholars, and historians, including Origen and Augustine, moved further and further away from the seedbed of the religion of creation into the garden planted by the religion of empire. It was to their advantage to align themselves with the state, so they did, while at the same time writing documents that would be read and referred to for generations. The Christianity about which they wrote was infiltrated with the ideals and beliefs of the empire, so much so, says Howard-Brook, that they "generated a Christianity that almost inverted the Gospel of Jesus."[10]

The Religion of Empire in America

This discussion of how the religion of creation and the religion of empire were realities in Jesus' time and before is important because when America became a republic, these same two competing religions would come to exemplify white versus Black religious practices. White people, it seemed, did not know what to do with Black people. In the ancient Roman Empire, the Romans had established themselves as superior and had looked down upon Jews and people from other geographical areas, but this was a sense of superiority based largely on culture and religion, not race. As the global African presence grew, elsewhere but most especially in the United States, white people were confused about how Africans even came to be. As we have established, it seems that as soon as Black people became more numerous, white people did two things: try to figure out who they were and where they had come from, and decide that wherever Black people came from they were inferior to whites and worthy of being enslaved.

In *Stamped from the Beginning*, Ibram Kendi noted that "ethnic and religious and color prejudice existed in the ancient world," a fact we have already briefly discussed. Kendi writes that the "foundations of race and racist ideas [were] laid in Greco-Roman antiquity."[11] We have seen that the Romans believed in their superiority. Their sense of supremacy laid the groundwork for the racism that was to come. Their anti-Semitism was widespread, as was their disdain for the Egyptian people. Within the Roman Empire, slavery existed, but it had not started there; it in fact began much earlier. In our world, the master-slave construct has always existed.

But the mere presence of people with dark skin, in antiquity and beyond, seemed to do something to the minds of white people. They could not figure out how it happened that these strange and different people existed. White people were fascinated by people with Black skin, but it did not take long for their fascination to turn into a mindset which was at once toxic and ominous for Black people. By the time we get to the history of Blacks in America, white people are well-versed in the Bible. They know the Creation story as found in Genesis. They know the psalms which declare the sovereignty of God, but they have also already made the decision that Black people are an anomaly, a mistake. In creating everything, God had not created Black people, many religious leaders decided, and taught their church members the same. They negated the sovereignty of God, who had created everything out of nothing, and had decided that even though everything else had been created by God, Black people had not. Racism morphed into full-blown white supremacy, with white people insisting that they knew that almighty God had not created these abominable creatures.

They had to have proof, and so they turned to the Bible, the Word of the God whose sovereignty they were now questioning. The Black presence on the earth was the fault of Ham, a son of Noah, who had committed the gross sin of seeing his father naked. It was taboo in Israelite society for a child to see his father naked. Ham had not sinned intentionally; he had walked into his father's tent and seen him there, apparently in a drunken stupor, and then in horror had run out to tell his two brothers, Shem and Japheth. The two of them backed into their father's tent and covered him, and when Noah awakened and "knew what his youngest son had done to him, he said, 'Cursed be Canaan! The lowest of slaves shall he be to his brothers.' He also said, 'Blessed by the LORD my God be Shem; and let Canaan be his slave. May God make space for Japheth, and let him live in the tents of Shem; and let Canaan be his slave'" (Genesis 9:24-27).

White religious people grabbed hold of this story, which came to be called the Ham Doctrine, to justify the enslavement of Black people. Although religious teachers and slaveholders alike said in their lessons that God had cursed Ham, the text says that Noah cursed Canaan, whom some scholars say was the youngest son of Ham and others say was the youngest son of Noah. Regardless of whose son Canaan was, there were important details that the teachers of the narrative left out: that Noah, not God, did the cursing, and that the curse did not appear to be meant to last forever but would be punishment for the generation of children who were alive then.

The curse of Canaan convinced those who grabbed hold of this text that God was giving permission to enslave the people of Canaan, who were a despised people because of their alleged sexual practices and who presumably had darker skin. What was then called Canaan may have included parts of modern-day Israel, Palestine, Lebanon, Syria, and Jordan. Ham's descendants were darker-skinned Africans who lived in parts of Africa known as Cush, Egypt, Put (also known as Phut), and sections of Canaan. Ham's brothers, Shem and Japheth, were the progenitors of people who lived in other parts of the ancient world. Shem became the father of the Semitic people, who lived in a part of the land which later became Israel, and Japheth became the progenitor of people who later lived in Asia Minor. Noah, then, had three sons who became the progenitors of African, Jewish, and various Semitic people groups, as well as Asian and European people groups. Whites held that Ham and his descendants were marked by God (not Noah) to be slaves to the descendants of the other brothers for eternity. When challenged about their theory, the proponents of this idea begged innocence and recommended that people read Genesis 9 and 10.

Because of how this story of the curse was used and circulated, white people, who were bothered by Blacks' very presence in the world, comfortably decided that the curse was still active and that God had relegated descendants of Ham to the permanent status of slaves. Blacks were to be considered inferior in all ways to the people who enslaved them. By the time the Puritans came to America, fleeing religious persecution, they were indoctrinated as to the "rightness" of their disapproval of Black people. From England, they brought with them a firm desire for freedom from religious persecution and an equally firm conviction that Black people and Native Americans were inferior to them. They also believed that they had the blessing of God and permission to treat the so-called inferior people any way they wanted, including enslaving them.

The late historian, activist, and author Gayraud Wilmore wrote in Paul R. Griffin's *Seeds of Racism in the Soul of America* that he was disturbed when he heard Griffin indict New England Puritanism and Reformed theology as "the taproot of racism,"[12] even though he realized that Blacks had suffered immeasurably at the hands of white Christians for generations. Perhaps he, like so many of us, had never taken the time to think about the racism that was brought to this country from another land by America's first inhabitants. We tend to want to make racism a poison that emanated from the South in its most virulent forms, even though we acknowledge, grudgingly sometimes, that there was racism in the North. But to think that the persons who came here full of hope, love, and the Christian ethic had brought their ingrained racist beliefs with them, which proceeded to spread throughout New England and beyond, was troubling. It destroyed the myth that good people from England set a firm foundation upon which later Americans would build this country, a foundation based on Christian love as well as the principles of equality and justice for all.

Griffin writes that New England Puritans "promoted racism and slavery just as aggressively as did their southern counterparts."[13] What is troubling is that these new Americans were Christian but had minds that had been poisoned by belief in the inferiority of Black people. Therefore, while the new settlers could have made Black people (who already were in America) a part of their indentured servitude system, which would have meant they could serve for a period of time and then be released, they chose instead to relegate Blacks to perpetual servitude, that is, slavery. These Christians undoubtedly knew the Great Commandment but chose to ignore it and to manipulate the Scriptures they so loved to fit their racist ideological mindsets. They saw nothing wrong with what they were doing and certainly did not consider the possibility that they were putting ideology in front of theology. Instead, they called their belief "theology," a system of knowledge that they said expressed the will of almighty God.

Griffin notes that "translating racist ideas into acts of racism should have stood in stark tension with Puritan ideals." Puritans, he said, "were a devout people who on occasion acknowledged that slavery stood in gross contradiction to the religion of Jesus, in which the conscience is freed and all thoughts and deeds correspond to God's will."[14] But white supremacist ideology had pulled them into its web. They came to a place where they put the whole question of racism and slavery on God; they "rather mindlessly accepted slavery for Negroes and Indians, but not for white men."[15]

It is troubling that even these religious people did not respect the Creation story that said that God had created everything, including the first man and woman from whom all human beings came. They apparently saw no issue. They believed themselves to be the new chosen people of God, a self-affirmation not substantiated by any theological treatise. They believed that they were pure, even though they acknowledged that some within their ranks were impure. Following the Calvinist tradition, they believed that they were predestined to be the new "chosen people" and that "only those who could give visible proofs of their divine election by living a life of absolute purity could be members of this full covenant."[16] This way of thinking was an absolute rejection of "God made everything that was made," because it equipped and enabled the Puritans to exclude those whom they considered to be unworthy of the full presence of God. They believed and taught that God "had not made humanity equal."[17] What the Puritans did was establish America's foundation of white supremacy, which they said was the ultimate will of God. When Theophilus Eaton, the first governor of the state of Connecticut, said that he would "forever" hold slaves, he referred to Leviticus 25:45-46. Conditions and rules regarding slavery are listed in this chapter, including how long slaves could be kept and giving an end time for their term of servitude, namely, the Jubilee:

> You shall count off seven weeks of years, seven times seven years, so that the period of seven weeks of years gives forty-nine years. Then you shall have the trumpet sounded loud; on the tenth day of the seventh month—on the day of atonement—you shall have the trumpet sounded throughout all your land. And you shall hallow the fiftieth year and you shall proclaim liberty throughout the land to all its inhabitants. It shall be a jubilee for you: you shall return, every one of you, to your property and everyone one of you to your family. That fiftieth year shall be a jubilee for you: you shall not sow, or reap, . . . In this year of jubilee, you shall return, every one of you, to your property. (LEVITICUS 25:8-11,13)

Those who would benefit from being freed at the time of Jubilee were fellow Israelites who had become servants who had experienced economic crises. They were not to be made slaves; rather, they were to be "hired or bound laborers" who would serve until the year of the Jubilee (Leviticus 25:39-40). But aliens taken into servitude by an Israelite had no such guarantee of freedom—ever. The Israelites were told that they could "acquire them from among the aliens residing with you, and from their families that are with you, who have been born in your land; and they may be your property. You may keep them as a possession for your children after you, for them to inherit as property. These you may treat as slaves" (Leviticus 25:45-46).

In the Freedom Bible (CEV), Leviticus 25:44-46 stands out: "If you want slaves, buy them from other nations or from the foreigners who live in your own country, and make them your property. You can own them and even leave them to your children when you die."

White religious leaders, in the earliest days of their new country, referred to these Bible verses and others to justify their stance on slavery and to convince people that they were only doing what God had said they could do. Using the Bible, and specifically verses like these, "the Puritans of New England were the first Christians . . . to build a theological argument that God had created Black people innately inferior to other human beings."[18]

The Puritans relied upon the Calvinist theology to which they adhered, as well as the Bible, to justify their belief that God had created some human beings inferior to them. John Calvin taught that sin was hereditary; he also taught that an all-sovereign God determined who would and could be saved and granted the gift of eternal life, and who would be condemned to eternal damnation. The Puritan writings about the doctrine of Creation reveal that the Puritans were assured that they were correct in believing that some people were worthy of salvation but that others were not. Griffin writes:

> [T]heir central issue was that God had not created humanity equal. Human beings had been created hierarchically. This meant that there were levels of humanity, ranging from the highest to the lowest. "God Almighty, in His most holy and wise providence . . . hath so disposed of the condition of mankind

as in all times some must be rich, some poor, some high and
eminent in power and dignity, others mean and in subjection."[19]

The Puritans, then, were taught that it was God's will that they
were superior and that others, including Blacks, were inferior. It
was not only God's will, but it was God's doing. John Saffin was a
Boston Puritan who wrote the first systematic defense of slavery in
America, claiming that "Blacks have neither a divine right to liberty
and all outward comforts of this life because this would invert the
order that God hath set in the world."[20]

The proclamation of this belief that God had made Black
people inferior and that consequently white people were within
their divine right to oppress them played a significant role in lay-
ing the religious foundation for the doctrine of white supremacy in
America. It was the cornerstone which would prove to be so solid
that not even the cries of the oppressed would be enough to shake
those descendants of the Puritans who believed that racism and the
"thingification" of Black people (a term Dr. Martin Luther King
used to describe how Black people had been dehumanized) was in
alignment with the will of almighty God. Importantly, the men who
would write the Declaration of Independence and the United States
Constitution were descendants of people who had been taught a
biblical ideology on which racists leaned, some unconsciously, from
the time America was born.

NOTES

1. See the study note to Deuteronomy found in the NRSV.

2. It is interesting that the Freedom Bible, largely used by and referred to by evangelical Christians, says that the people of Jericho "deserve to be punished," while
the NRSV says, "for the iniquity of the Amorites is not complete." This is noteworthy
because it gives an understated reference to Canaan, named after the son of Ham
who was cursed by Noah; one may infer the Canaanites were guilty of the "sin of
Ham." This verse as found in the Freedom Bible gives tacit approval to kill Ham's
descendants.

3. Walter Wink, *Engaging the Powers: Discernment and Resistance in a World of
Domination* (Minneapolis: Fortress, 1992), 13.

4. Wink.

5. Wink, 14–16.

6. Wink, 5.

7. Wes Howard-Brook, *Empire Baptized: How the Church Embraced What Jesus
Rejected* (Maryknoll, NY: Orbis, 2016), 19.

8. Howard-Brook, 300; see also 82.

9. Howard-Brook, 19.

10. Howard-Brook, 27.

11. Ibram X. Kendi, *Stamped from the Beginning: The Definitive History of Racist Ideas in America* (New York: Nation Books, 2016), 18.

12. Paul R. Griffin, *Seeds of Racism in the Soul of America* (Cleveland: Pilgrim Press, 1999), x.

13. Griffin, 11.

14. Griffin, 14.

15. Griffin, 7.

16. Griffin, 16.

17. Griffin, 17.

18. Griffin.

19. Griffin.

20. Griffin, 19.

3
We Hold These Truths

If a conventional idea of God inspires empathy and respect for all others, it is doing its job. But the modern God is only one of the many theologies that developed during the three-thousand-year history of monotheism. Because "God" is infinite, nobody can have the last word. —Karen Armstrong

If nothing else, the Bible as sacred text is supposed to bring to us, its readers, truth—about God, about Jesus, and about the way God commands us to live. But the real truth is that the Bible does not lead to a monolithic understanding of its words, and therefore of a monolithic code of behavior.

Karen Armstrong writes in *The Case for God* that in spite of the fact that all of the world's faiths insist that "true spirituality must be expressed consistently in practical compassion,"[1] that rarely happens. The evidence of the shortcomings of those who profess to believe in God is clear and obvious, as, despite belief in God and belief in the moral supremacy of the Constitution, human behavior has not indicated a weddedness to a belief that God requires moral, compassionate, and empathetic behavior of human beings toward each other, especially when it comes to race.

Jemar Tisby, in *The Color of Compromise*, says that "from the beginning of American colonization, Europeans crafted a Christianity that would allow them to spread the faith without confronting the exploitative economic system of slavery and the emerging social inequity based on color."[2] Americans practice, he said, either a "courageous" or a "complicit" Christianity, and noted that "white complicity with racism isn't a matter of melanin; it's a matter of power."[3]

That is the truth about American Christianity, and the profound difference in the way Black and white people read, understand, and interpret the Bible has been and continues to be problematic. What is *the* truth? Whose interpretation is correct? The Rev. C. T. Vivian once said to me, "You cannot be racist and be Christian!" but many who practice a "complicit" Christianity believe the opposite, and they point to the Bible—the same Bible by which Rev. Vivian swears his allegiance to the Christ—to support their theology. For them, God not only allows racism; God created it.

Views of Slavery and Color: A Survey

By the time the sacred text of the United States, the Constitution, was being written, there was hardly a chance that it would not be contaminated by the poison of white supremacy. John Saffin, the Boston Puritan who in 1701 had argued that Black people had no right to liberty and dignity, relied upon the Calvinistic doctrines of sin and predestination to support his theses on the depravity of Black people. In 1844, after the Constitution had been written and ratified, a man named Josiah Nott offered his opinion that "since Canaan's descendants were white, then Africans must have different ancestors."[4] Cotton Mather, who has often been portrayed as a white more sympathetic to the cause of justice for Black people, was nonetheless brutal in his descriptions of Black people. He called enslaved Africans "the miserable children of Adam and Noah," adding that they were "the blackest instances of blindness and baseness and the most brutal creatures upon earth."[5] He, too, said that it was God who caused "Black people to fall into a dreadful condition of slavery, because they were created as vassals of Satan."[6]

The formation and solidification of the idea that Black people were depraved was happening not in the South but in New England, where the brutal attacks on Blacks were said to be worse than anywhere else in the country. Even worse, the opinion makers were Christian people who said they loved the Lord Jesus, yet they created, fertilized, and spread the damning narrative about Black people that would soon spread throughout the country. Clearly, the possibility of there being a different concept of God for white people than for Blacks had taken root in New England and would spread far and wide as the new nation grew. Forrest G. Wood pinned the blame of the spread of racism precisely on Christianity: "English North Americans," he said, "embraced slavery *because* they were Christians, not in spite of it."[7]

The Bible itself did not help eliminate the belief that God ordained and sanctioned slavery. In the first chapter of Exodus, there is a story about how Pharaoh was disturbed that so many Hebrew people lived in his kingdom. He wanted them gone, which is why he issued an order that all Hebrew baby boys be killed at birth. Furthermore, this Pharaoh ordered that these unwanted people be oppressed: "Now a new king arose over Egypt, who did not know Joseph. He said to his people, 'Look, the Israelite people are more numerous and more powerful than are we. Come, let us deal shrewdly with them, or they will increase and, in the event of war, join our enemies and fight against us and escape from the land.' Therefore they set taskmasters over them to oppress them with forced labor" (Exodus 1:8-11).

This was the "truth" supporting slavery coming right from the Bible. The men who would write America's founding documents and the writers of the Constitution would have known about it and have been affected by it. Although this dogma began in New England, Southerners were taking note. If, or since, slavery was in the Bible, how could anyone take issue with what they believed? Never mind that the slavery described in the Hebrew Scriptures was nothing like the chattel slavery of the United States. Slaves in biblical times could expect one day to be set free, and their enslavement was not based upon the color of their skin. Slavery in the Bible had nothing to do with white supremacy, but those points of truth were ignored. Along with the doctrine of Ham, whites began to make themselves believe that it was God's will that they enslave these dark creatures who were clearly inhuman and inferior to white people. In 1837, a woman noted that religion was being used in the basest of ways: "I have never heard any available reference made to grand truths of religion, or principles of morals . . . [M]inisters . . . spend all their time pretending to find express sanctions of slavery in the Bible; and putting words to this purpose into the mouths of public men who do not profess to remember the existence of the Bible in any other connexion."[8]

It is important to know that belief in white supremacy (and its rationale for enslaving and oppressing people with dark skin because they were "bad") did not originate in America. Some of the most respected early church fathers, including Origen, Jerome, and Augustine, who during the third and fourth centuries aligned more with the religion of empire than with the religion of creation, had already planted the idea that Black or dark skin was proof of inferiority. Christianity as a religion, however, did not as a rule attach Black or dark skin to a belief in innate inferiority at that time.

But as time went on, that changed. As early as the tenth century, Black Africans were enslaved in parts of Europe, as well as Asians, and white people began to express disgust for people with dark skin. The idea of Black inferiority germinated and grew. French sociologist Roger Bastide "argued that it was Christianity that first introduced the Black/white color code into Western thought. White skin is used to express the pure while Black expresses the diabolical."[9] The conflict between good and evil, notes Forrest Wood, was seen as "a conflict between Christ and Satan, the spiritual and the carnal," and ultimately a conflict between "white and Black." This meant that "monotheism was inherently dichotomous."[10]

By the nineteenth century, through a process called transmogrification, the image of the Christ had changed from being Semitic to Aryan (an ancient racial-ethnic designation made infamous by Nazi Germany), his dark hair evolving into "the color of sunshine" and his dark eyes "magically taking on the color of the sky from which he descended and to which he returned."[11] Having Black skin was seen as one of the worst of all curses; the lighter an American of African descent was, the better, a view held by both whites and Blacks. Christianity, by now a compromised byproduct of the ministry of the Christ, was seen to be the salvation for those poor souls who had Black skin. They were not to worry because almighty God had made the souls of Black people white. There was hope for them, even if it came after death.

In the midst of the effort to cement the idea of the baseness, evil, and depravity of Black people was the Bible. If Christianity was the primary vehicle by which the ideology of white supremacy was carried, the words of the Bible were the fuel. In the span of time leading up to the creation of our country's founding documents, belief in the Bible as the inerrant Word of God was the rule. This made it highly unlikely, therefore, that anyone would dare to challenge the false creed that the Bible said it was God's will that Black people be enslaved.

The evolving Christianity of the nineteenth century was not the Christianity of the Christ, says Wes Howard-Brook. In *Empire Baptized*, he says that people, more accurately, religious leaders of their time, created a Christianity that was nothing like the religion that Jesus had taught and preached.[12] In *Saving Paradise*, authors Rita Nakashima Brock and Rebecca Ann Parker said that in earlier times, "Christians sought to help life flourish in the face of imperial power, violence and death. Though persecuted, they refused to surrender their identity as members of the church and the empire executed them for it."[13] This transformation of the religion of Jesus, or the religion of creation, had been going on for some time, and though race had little to do with it, the accumulation of power and wealth was at the center. Instead of being a religion of peace, Christianity was becoming militant; it became, in the eleventh century, admirable to "die" for Christ. In 1095 Pope Urban II launched the First Crusade and considered it a holy obligation to do so, fighting people in order to "impose on them the acceptance of Jesus."[14]

That was not the religion taught by the Christ. The morph from a religion of love to a religion of violence and power had been going on for thousands of years, but that is important to know because by the time this struggle on the "truth" of the Bible and the Gospels erupted in the United States, there were already two religions, according to Howard-Brook, in which adherents in both camps depended and called upon "the same God . . . [which] pulled in opposite directions."[15] Writes Howard-Brook:

> Let's call them the "religion of creation" and the "religion of empire." That is, we can understand one of the Bible's religions to be grounded in the *experience of and ongoing relationship with the Creator God, leading* to a covenantal bond between that God and God's people for the blessing and abundance of *all* people and *all* creation. The other, while sometimes *claiming* to be grounded in that same God, is actually a human invention used to justify and legitimate attitudes and behaviors that provide blessing and abundance for *some* at the *expense of others.*[16]

Clearly, the two religions mentioned by Howard-Brook were growing in size and impact. For people of African descent, the story of the exodus became both their proof and their hope that God heard the cries of the downcast, and it was hope that just as God had heard the cries of the Israelites, so God was hearing their cries, too.

But for whites, the Bible was the justification for all that they were doing; moreover, it was their proof that what they were doing was the will of God. They believed that the Bible proved that God had sanctioned slavery in the Hebrew Scriptures and permitted it in the New Testament. The fact that Jesus was brown-skinned and was persecuted for challenging injustice was overlooked or perhaps ignored because Jesus never said anything about the wrongness of slavery. Jesus' silence allowed preachers both in the North and South to defend the rightness of slavery. Clerics correctly claimed that there was no New Testament Scripture that said bondage was wrong. Letters written by two preachers to each other—Rev. Richard Fuller, a Southerner, and Rev. Francis Wayland, a prominent Northern preacher—are typical of the kind of rhetoric that white preachers shared about God and slavery. One such letter claimed, "What God sanctioned in the Old Testament, and permitted to use in the New, cannot be sin."[17] In an 1851 report to the Presbyterian Synod of South Carolina, James Henley Thornwell, who was the president of South Carolina College, wrote, "Where the Scriptures are silent, [the church] must be silent, too. What the Scriptures have not made essential to a Christian profession, she does not undertake to make so. What the Scriptures have sanctioned, she does not condemn."[18]

What about the Great Commandment's teaching that people should love their neighbors as themselves, and the Golden Rule's pronouncement that humans should do to others what they would want done to them (Matthew 7:12, NIV)? Those Scriptures were manipulated in order to satisfy the need to position the Bible on the side of racial oppression. The Golden Rule did not apply the same way to African slaves as it did to white people; masters were obliged to give slaves what they deserved as slaves, not as human beings with basic human rights. To "do unto others" meant that people were to do what they believed was best for those others, and many whites renounced the idea that they were violating that rule because they believed they treated their enslaved property very well.

Anything outside of that constrained definition was not in compliance with the Golden Rule because, they said, "emancipation was contrary to the spirit of the Golden Rule."[19]

Pastors, preachers, and teachers, in the North and the South, worked the Bible to fit their needs and what they believed life should be like for people of African descent. They refused to concede that slavery was a sin, that is, a wrong that God despised. They admitted that slavery was "a great evil" but not necessarily a sin.[20] Wood writes that "the idea that slavery could be evil but not sinful was an essential feature of the conservative Christian's theology because, in answering the charge that an all-good, all-powerful God would never permit evil, suffering, and injustice to exist, it enabled him to fit wrongdoing into God's greater plan of ultimate good."[21]

In the nineteenth century, Black people heard the same lessons about who they were and why they were where they were. They heard the arguments about how the Bible ordained and sanctioned their lot in life, but by this time enough Black people were reading to be able to interpret biblical truths in their own way. William R. Jones, author of *Is God a White Racist?*, said that what Black people got during this time, and which many hold onto even to this day, was "mis-religion,"[22] that is, a religion which forced upon Black people the God that white people had created to fit their ideology. Jones also concluded that, for Black people, there was yet another division, this one between religious traditions. Black people, he said, worshiped in one of two religious traditions: Christian and non-Christian theism, and religious humanism.[23] Christianity as practiced in the United States was a religion of empire, true, but also a religion of oppression.

The "truth" of the two racial groups were colliding. Black people could not reconcile their notion of a good God with a religion that seemed to honor, defend, and protect white supremacy. Religion in America was strange to them and more a function of the state than a way to know God. The Church of England had legally become the official religion of colonial Virginia in 1619, and in 1624, another law made it mandatory for white Virginians to attend and support the Church of England, or Anglican church. The Anglicans distrusted the religions of both the newly arrived Africans and the Native Americans. This put Black people, who were deeply spiritual, in a very bad place in which their enslavement

..rced them to abandon their religions in favor of the racist tenets of Christianity, which they largely rejected. Both African Americans and Native Americans at first distrusted and ultimately rejected this white religious faith, and with good reason: the Anglican church invested economically in enslavement and bought into the notion of the inferiority of Black people. Neither Black people nor Native Americans could understand the god of white people.

Though laws existed that required enslaved Africans to become Christian, there was no law that would ever be strong enough to pull Africans away from their innate spiritual core. They endured the inhumane treatment they received at the hands of white Christians, who considered them to be heathen, and they recoiled at the lessons they were being taught because white Christians thought everyone—Black and white—should be Christian. The enslaved Africans were very spiritual, but they had their own religion; this Christianity was less concerned with a relationship with God than with the importance of being aligned with the religion of the state. That concept was anathema to the Africans. In 1704, a slave catechism was developed to be used by the Anglican church's missionary division, the Society for the Propagation of the Gospel, for the express purpose of "instructing slaves in the way of the Bible."[24] Cotton Mather, a prominent member of the Puritan establishment, published The Negro Christianized two years after the slave catechism was written. For the discerning reader, it was easy to see how Mather's book used God as a tool in the hands of the religion of empire to keep Black people in line with the desire and will of the state. A typical lesson in the book included specific ways enslaved Africans were to act in order to have God's favor:

> Question: If you serve Jesus Christ, what must you do?
> Answer: I must Love God and Pray to Him and Keep the Lords-Day. I must Love all Men and never Quarrel, nor be Drunk, nor be Unchaste, nor Steal, nor tell a Ly, nor be Discontent with my Condition.[25]

What the Africans were being instructed to do was to be a Christian in ways that white Christians seemed to feel they did not have to be. They certainly did not feel Jesus Christ meant for them to love all men, never quarrel, or be drunk; if one only accounted for the numerous times white men were unchaste as they slept with Black women, one could say they were not chaste, and stealing was never the sole misbehavior of enslaved Africans. The distinction between the two religions became more and more stark.

The Puritans believed they had been called to make America a Christian nation. Paul Griffin notes that when they migrated to New England, they did not consider that there might be non-white people in their midst, so when they encountered Native Americans as well as Africans, they were surprised, for they believed that they had been called to create a new country for white people. Even as they professed belief in God and in Jesus' message of love found in the Gospels, they realized that they had a major problem with Black people. They could not understand why they were even there. Richard Hakluyt, an English chronicler, "perceived Africans as a Black, beastly, mysterious, heathenish, libidinous, evil, lazy and smelly people who are strangely different to our superior white race."[26]

This type of disdain and disrespect for Black people only increased as the country moved closer to creating its founding documents, and all along the Bible was used to justify white supremacist beliefs. The white preachers and teachers were careful to cherry-pick chapters and verses in the Bible which protected their belief in white supremacy and convinced the Africans that their enslavement was endorsed by God. So intent were white slave owners to protect the institution of slavery and avoid giving any hint that God might be in favor of those who were enslaved that they taught the slaves with a redacted Bible that omitted much of the Old Testament references and stories about freedom.

This so-called Slave Bible was published in London in 1807 and was "used by some missionaries to convert and 'educate' enslaved Africans about Christianity."[27] It told about Joseph's enslavement but left out the portions of Moses' story where he led the Israelites to freedom. In addition to the deletion of the story of the exodus, verses which would have given hope to enslaved Africans were left out, including Exodus 21:16 (KJV): "And he that stealeth a man, and selleth him, or if he be found in his hand, he shall surely be put to death," and Galatians 3:28 (KJV): "There is neither Jew nor Greek, there is neither bond nor free, there is neither male nor female; for ye are all one in Christ Jesus"[28] was eliminated as well. In the normal Christian Bible there are sixty-six books, including both the Old and New Testaments, but the Slave Bible was redacted to include only parts of fourteen books, and the Book of Revelation was omitted. The notion of the Bible being sacred, that is, unable to be altered or changed, then, was destroyed as slave owners continually sought to make sure "the Bible" was on their side.

Thus, slavery was helped along and protected by organized religion, which used the Bible as its primary weapon. Few people wanted to oppose God, which is what they felt they would be doing if they challenged the way they were being taught. White people, many of whom owned slaves, wanted the Africans to understand that while Jesus granted salvation, not all people received the same kind of salvation. The Africans were taught that salvation for them meant being saved from Satan, not from slavery itself. The way whites taught the Bible supported their commitment to the empire's tool of slavery rather than to the God who created "everything that was made" as a comrade in enslaving other human beings. Their God, however, was not the God of people who craved freedom, dignity, and respect.

The Making of Two Religions

By the eighteenth century, the belief had been firmly established that Black people were aberrations in God's world. If they were not created by some other deity, before Adam and Eve, then whites certainly believed that Blacks were created by God to be enslaved. While Black people refused to believe that God had created them to be enslaved, many whites believed that God had created them solely to be enslaved. Both using the same Bible, the two races came to radically different conclusions. James Cone wrote in *Said I Wasn't Gonna Tell Nobody*, published after his death, that "white and Black theologians had made Christianity white, completely identified with European and white American culture."[29] Something had gone horribly wrong with Jesus' religion; Cone recalled a time early in his career when an editor, looking at publishing *Black Theology and Black Power*, said that "Christianity . . . had been corrupted by white supremacy."[30] Cone directly identified and called out the gist of the two Christianities practiced in this country when asked to give a meaning of the gospel. He was challenged by a white faculty member who asked him why he had written *Black Theology and Black Power*, and Cone responded:

> I wrote it because I had to . . . I had no other choice, as a theologian, but to write the truth of the gospel of Jesus for America. Jesus's gospel today is Black Power, that is, the proclamation of liberation of Black people from white supremacy "by any means necessary," to use the language of Malcolm X . . . The silence of white theology about slavery, segregation, and lynching spoke loudly about its inherent heresy.
>
> Any message that is not related to the liberation of the poor in society is not Christ's message . . . Any theology that is indifferent to the theme of God's liberation of the poor is not Christian theology. Because American theology has ignored the Black poor, and the poor generally, it is not Christian theology. Period.[31]

That process of making two religions, with two different standards of truth, had to continue to be developed and refined, because the religion of white people would never succumb to being in support of the basic decency of Black people and their right to equality.

Though nobody said it, monotheism was essentially discounted. There could not be just one God, some reasoned. They latched onto the theory of polygenesis, an idea which had been in existence since the Renaissance, a time when there also were conversations about the "great chain of being." A Philadelphia physician, Samuel George Morton, began in 1820 to study human and animal skulls and decided, based on the result of his research, that "various races had evolved from separate origins."[32]

The theory of the great chain of being held that "human races could be lined up from the most superior to the most inferior. The order, then, was God, white people, an arrangement of non-white people, with Blacks at the bottom."[33] The great chain included Europeans, Romans, and Greeks at the top of the chain, with Asians, American savages (sic), and Negroes at the bottom.[34] Charles White, who in 1799 published *An Account of the Regular Gradation in Man, and in Different Animals and Vegetables*, wrote, "In whatever respect the African differs from the European, the particularity brings him closer to the ape."[35] The science of the day was pre-empting the Word of God, as recorded in the Book of Genesis. The idea of there being multiple origins caught on; it was as though those who believed in the inferiority of Black people were relieved that they could let God off the hook.

The conversations and arguments revealed different ways that Ham's sin had been understood and taught. Josiah Nott, quoted earlier in this book, supported this view that Canaan, Ham's son, had been white, with his conclusion that "nonwhite peoples of the world had separate origins and that the Bible, therefore, applied only to Caucasians."[36]

Ibram Kendi notes that "ever since Europeans had laid eyes on Native Americans in 1492, a people unmentioned in the Bible, they had started questioning the Biblical creation story."[37] While some pro-slavery advocates breathed a sigh of relief because of the confusion over how Black people got here, others were furious that the monogenetic biblical account of Creation was being challenged. In spite of their protestations, however, the multiple origin theory assuaged the troubled souls of many.

What were the men who would become the founding fathers of America thinking and internalizing? They wrestled. The Revolutionary War had been fought in the name of freedom. Patrick Henry's "Give me liberty or give me death!" was a sentiment with which they agreed, yet many of them owned Black people and did not want to give them up. Some of them were religious, and some were Christian. All of them knew the Great Commandment, and they were uncomfortable thinking that their enslavement of other human beings was out of the will of God, yet they relied on select words in the Bible to comfort their guilt-ridden souls. How could they question the Word of God, some mused. After all, the Bible said in several places that slaves were to be obedient to their masters. Either they did not know or chose to ignore that the slavery talked about in the Bible was not the chattel slavery practiced in America, so they comforted themselves in the words found, for example, in Colossians 3:22-24 (Freedom Bible [CEV]):

> Slaves, you must always obey your earthly masters. Try to
> please them at all times, and not just when you think they are

watching. Honor the Lord and serve your masters with your whole heart. Do your work willingly, as though you were serving the Lord himself, and not just your earthly master. In fact, the Lord Christ is the one you are really serving and you know that he will reward you.

Dr. Benjamin Rush, one of the signers of the Constitution, who espoused anti-slavery sentiments also seemingly took great comfort in the biblical words, declaring that "slavery was a special means of salvation granted to Negroes by God."[38] He wrestled with the Black presence on earth, stating that people should not fret because color differences were only skin deep, but also explaining the Africans' darker skin was the result of their being "victims of leprosy," he said, apparently concluding that blackness was a medical problem.[39]

Therefore, it seems that the Bible was a fluid text, subject to a wide range of interpretations that served the interests of not all but instead a very few of its readers. As many scholars, scientists, and politicians wrangled over what this nation was, they realized that what it was not was a solely white nation, as many believed God intended it to be. At one and the same time, the Bible was both a help and a problem. It was the Word of God, but it was fraught with too many words that would lead non-white people (and women as well) to believe in their God-given right to be free and to have full American citizenship. The Bible was getting in the way of the smooth development of a white nation. African Americans, in the meantime, were caught in the crosshairs. They refused to accept the commonly held notion that they were a mistake, a "problem," as W. E. B. DuBois would later write about in *The Souls of Black Folk*. African American clerics bristled at the theology they were being fed. Many, like Nathaniel Paul, a Black Baptist preacher, wondered at the silence and passivity of God, and some, like AME Bishop Daniel Payne, wondered if God even existed. "If he did exist, is he just? If so, why does he suffer one race to oppress and enslave another?"[40] Where was God, and how could God allow one race to talk about and be willing to fight for their freedom while simultaneously depriving another of their right to be free? It was an unfixable contradiction in their eyes.

In 1772, Blacks listened closely to angry white colonists talk about their God-given right to be released from tyranny; they watched while these same whites formed what were called Committees of Correspondence "for serious discussion of their common means of defense against the oppressive acts of the British parliament."[41] Vincent Harding says that in the "pre-Revolutionary days of the 1700s, many Black men and women carefully appraised the rising struggle and searched for opportunities, advantages, cracks in the wall."[42] If the Bible would not direct their path to freedom, their own souls would do so. Harding said that in this pregnant time of the birthing of a free country, "Africans who were being held captive moved . . . in daily defections from the system," resulting in thousands of them relocating in Florida, Canada, and the Indian lands.[43]

The separation of Africans from the white God grew during the furor leading up to the Revolutionary War. They could see the contradiction between the behavior and the rhetoric of freedom. They heard white patriots talk about the equality of all men under God, and, knowing that they were not included in the classification of "all men," they began to share the same rhetoric and proclaim its relevance to their own situation. Though their oppressors did not know it, they were helping to form the foundation of the cry for freedom for the people they had so badly disrespected. Harding notes that in 1774, two years before the outbreak of the war, someone wrote, "a Grate Number of Blacks in Massachusetts petitioned that patriotic legislature, saying, 'We have in common with all other men a natural right to our freedom without Being depriv'd of them by our fellow men as we are a freeborn Pepel and have never forfeited this Blessing by any compact or agreement whatever.'"[44]

God and religion were important to the African Americans during this time, but more and more they were rejecting the God who led the churches which sanctioned their second-class citizenship and abhorrent treatment. That was not their God. During this time, a number of independent Black churches sprang up as Blacks searched for a God in whom they could trust. Because they could see the blatant hypocrisy of those, among them George Washington, who appeared to be ambivalent about Blacks, large numbers of Blacks defected to the British side during the Revolutionary War.

When the war was over and the founding fathers gathered to draw up the documents that would set America apart from all other nations, they brought to the table the toxicity of white supremacy and a Bible whose value was at best ambivalent because of the issue of race. Present-day Americans reject the notion that this country was founded in racism, but it was, and the Bible did little, if anything, to help the founders craft a document that would honor the religion of creation and the teachings of Jesus the Christ. In spite of their using the name of God, a cultural and civil religion took deep root in the new country, and the founders were poorly equipped to dig the poisonous root out to make room for a government "of the people, by the people, and for the people" that would garner the favor of almighty God. By this time, Blacks had already rejected the white God who was silent in the face of white supremacy and who seemingly was a partner with those who sought to make life miserable for those whose skin was Black.

The Power of Ideas

The war had been fought; the new nation had won its independence from England. This new land was setting itself up as the paragon of virtue, an exceptional nation as it pertained to the cause of democracy, and an authentic one as it pertained to Christianity. If one believed that to be a Christian, one had to follow the lessons of Jesus the Christ, something was clearly wrong, right from the beginning. The Great Commandment and the Golden Rule were being ignored. Instead of adhering to these foundational teachings of Jesus, so-called good Christians were enslaving people of African descent with little thought as to whether or not Jesus would approve of what they were doing.

The new America was about building itself and its power and using God along the way to cement its cultural and ideological beliefs. Even more than before the war, the church and the state would become bedfellows, with the state depending on the church to help advance its policies. For a while, before the new theology was cemented, white people had attempted to figure out who God really was. They had tampered with the Bible in ways that supported their beliefs while avoiding repercussions from God. But none of that ambivalence was obvious once the colonists declared that they were Christian. At this point, they mythologized the story of Jesus. They celebrated his birth and resurrection, but between Christmas and Easter their churches relied on ornate rituals and moral platitudes to express their allegiance to the Christ. A basic tenet of Jesus' teachings was that "the least of these" should be a priority in the lives of those who followed him. Matthew 25:31-46 said that inasmuch as followers took care or did not take care of the poor, the naked, the hungry, and the thirsty, they did or did not respect and honor God. The new nation, however, ignored that Scripture as well as many others. The disinherited remained disinherited, even as men gathered to draft America's document of independence. Slavery was still an integral part of what made America, America.

In spite of that reality, the words penned are still glorious: "We hold these truths to be self-evident, that all men are created equal." No other nation in the world had composed such astounding and powerful words, but they were void of truth even for those who penned them. America was incapable of living up to its own creed. White supremacy had already infected the soul of the country. Reinhold Niebuhr writes that "the Anglo-American colonists . . . saw their purpose as to make a new beginning in a corrupt world . . . They believed that they had been called out by God to create a new humanity. They believed . . . that this covenant with God marked America as a new Israel."[45]

The new country was proud—guilty of "spiritual pride," said Niebuhr. "Americans came to see themselves as set apart, their motives irreproachable, their actions not to be judged by standards applied to others."[46] America believed itself to be acting on God's behalf, but if that was the case, there already was a serious problem, for the God of America was a God who sanctioned and allowed horrendous oppression of other human beings. Worse, a good number of those who composed America's founding documents doubted the very humanity of the people their government, policies, and ideology oppressed. In the end, Americans were no light in the darkness; they were merely people who had had the good fortune to escape religious persecution but who, once free, proceeded to oppress others. Niebuhr noted that "all men are naturally inclined to obscure the morally ambiguous element in their political cause by investing it with religion. This is why religion is more frequently a source of confusion than of light in the political realm."[47]

It is probably safe to assert that of the fifty-six signers of the Declaration of Independence, most of them believed in and ascribed to the belief that America was morally and principally exceptional and superior to all other nations. Most also believed in God, and some claimed to be Christian. These men were descendants of the Puritans, those zealous souls who came to the new world believing that the church they established here was purer and less corrupt than any other church in the world. Niebuhr writes that there was a belief that "Jesus Christ had manifested his kingly office toward his churches more fully than ever yet the sons of men saw."[48]

The problem was that the idea of white supremacy had already taken root in the American psyche. Plato, who believed in the power of ideas and said that they are eternal reality, said they cannot be eradicated; they simply take new expression. Plato's philosophy had long been studied and internalized by students, and his theory of three different classes of people, each with a different function, was as much a part of American thinkers and politicians' psyches as was the doctrine of Ham to students of religion and theology. Plato taught that people are ruled by either the love of wisdom, the love of honor, or the love of money.[49] Those who were ruled by the love of wisdom were the people destined to rule, those who loved honor were to be involved in the military, and those who were driven by a love of money were to work the land as farmers and artisans. Rulers were said by Plato to have gold in their souls; members of the military, silver; and farmers and artisans, bronze. According to Plato, those with gold in their souls were to rule all others, and members of the lowest class were to be subservient to the highest class.[50]

Thus, the signers had learned their ideas about the rightness of racism from their lessons at school and from their pastors. They had internalized ideas that had become "eternal reality," making them captive to their hatred, fear, and greed—all integral components of the white supremacist mindset.[51] In spite of the glorious words of the Declaration of Independence, Americans had been defined and shaped by white supremacist beliefs, including those who wrote the precious and sacred document itself. Harding says that "the revolution for white liberty ended with Black slavery carefully protected in the basic document of the new, 'free' nation."[52] Blacks realized, Harding continued, "that they would have to look elsewhere for true revolutionary inspiration. The white American Revolution was not ours."[53]

Religious Leanings of the Founders

Of the fifty-six men who signed the Declaration of Independence, thirty-two were Episcopalian, thirteen were Congregationalist, twelve were Presbyterian, two were Quaker, two were Unitarian, and one was Catholic, George Carroll of Maryland.[54] This roll call is significant in that the signers' religious affiliations indicate that they were at least familiar with the Bible. Their worldview had been shaped by both religious and secular sources. They were familiar with and perhaps involved in the debates about the origin of Black people; they were certainly involved in the "rightness" of Black people to be enslaved, the Bible and their religious affiliations notwithstanding.

Americans declare and believe that this is a Christian nation. Some scholars have declared that the founders were religious nationalists, and others have claimed "not only that the Founders held orthodox beliefs but that some were born-again Chistians."[55] Because of their religious affiliations, it is safe to assume that they attended church, were baptized, and participated in the celebration of the sacraments and ordinances of their churches. They may even have attended Sunday school and heard lessons about the will and the way of Jesus the Christ.

But their immersion in Christianity did not dictate their ultimate religious beliefs. Many adhered to a school of religious thought popular in the eighteenth century called Deism. Deists "argued that human experience and rationality, rather than religious dogma and mystery, determine the validity of human beliefs."[56] They knew about the ideas of Thomas Paine, a Founding Father and author of *The Age of Reason*, who called Christianity a "fable." They knew that Paine believed that "the Almighty [had never] communicated anything to man by . . . speech . . . language . . . or vision."[57] David Holmes, author of an article entitled "The Founding Fathers, Deism, and Christianity," said Paine created or believed in a distant deity whom he called "Nature's God," a phrase, notes Holmes, which is also used in the Declaration of Independence.[58] Deism, Holmes said, "subverted orthodox Christianity."[59]

Holmes notes that many of the founding fathers, in spite of having been raised in Christian churches, ascribed to Deist thought; George Washington's allegiance to Deism was revealed by his refusal as an adult to take Holy Communion. Holmes also noted that there are critical linguistic clues that give an idea as to the religious leanings of the founding fathers: non-Christian Deists, such as Paine, refused to use Judeo-Christian terminology and described God with such expressions as "Providence," "the Creator," "the Ruler of Great Events," and "Nature's God." Founders who fall into the category of Christian Deists used deistic terms for God but sometimes added a Christian dimension, such as "Merciful Providence" or "Divine Goodness." Yet these founders did not move further into orthodoxy and employ the traditional language of Christian piety.[60]

It does not appear that what we today call traditional or orthodox Christianity was a major influence or that it had a major presence in the writing of this nation's founding documents. Deism, says Holmes, "influenced a majority of the Founders . . . the movement opposed barriers to moral improvement and to social justice: Deism . . . stood for rational inquiry, for skepticism about dogma and mystery, and for religious toleration. Many of its adherents advocated universal education, freedom of the press, and separation of church and state."[61]

Orthodox Christians were among the ranks of the founders, but they were in the minority. Holmes writes that "Samuel Adams, John Jay (who was the president of the American Bible Society), Elias Boudinot (who wrote a book on the imminent Second Coming of Jesus), and Patrick Henry (who distributed religious tracts while riding circuit as a lawyer) all believed in Evangelical Christianity."[62]

Given this breakdown of the religious beliefs of the founders, it is probably safe to assume that the Bible's words were not the drivers of the men who wrote the Constitution; the evangelical presence among them was important, but there were not enough evangelical Christians to drive the direction of the words in the Declaration of Independence, the Articles of Confederation, and the Constitution. The writers leaned more on the power of reason than on the power of God, yet they knew the Word of God. If they were able to dismiss God as a genuine entity, as did Thomas Paine, the documents that they would draft as the sacred text of the new country would reflect their ambivalence about God and the importance of God in daily life. That ambivalence would most certainly be evident in the hypocrisy of those who wrote about the importance of freedom for all people while they simultaneously denied that same freedom to Black people, Native Americans, women, and others who would eventually become a part of what they called the United States of America. At the beginning of their work to shape the Constitution lay America's greatest contradiction.

Epigraph

Karen Armstrong, *The Case for God* (New York: Alfred A. Knopf, 2009), xvii.

NOTES

1. Karen Armstrong, *The Case for God* (New York: Alfred A. Knopf, 2009), xvii.
2. Jemar Tisby, *The Color of Compromise* (Grand Rapids, MI: Zondervan Reflective, 2019), 39.
3. Tisby.
4. Forrest G. Wood, *The Arrogance of Faith* (New York: Alfred A. Knopf, 1990), 38.
5. Paul R. Griffin, *Seeds of Racism in the Soul of America* (Cleveland: Pilgrim Press, 1999), 18.
6. Griffin.
7. Wood, 38.
8. Wood, 43.
9. Wood, 51.
10. Wood.
11. Wood.
12. Wes Howard-Brook, *Empire Baptized: How the Church Embraced What Jesus Rejected* (Maryknoll, NY: Orbis, 2016), 27.
13. Rita Nakashima Brock and Rebecca Ann Parker, *Saving Paradise: How Christianity Traded Love of This World for Crucifixion and Empire* (Boston: Beacon Press, 2008), xvii.
14. Brock and Parker, xx.
15. Wes Howard-Brook, *"Come Out My People!": God's Call Out of Empire in the Bible and Beyond* (Maryknoll, NY: Orbis, 2010), 7.
16. Howard-Brook, *"Come Out My People!"*
17. Wood, 99.
18. Wood, 100–101.
19. Wood, 65.
20. Wood, 66.
21. Wood, 67.
22. William R. Jones, *Is God a White Racist? A Preamble to Black Theology* (Boston: Beacon Press, 1998), xi.
23. Jones.
24. Wood, 72.
25. Wood.
26. Griffin, 14.

27. Becky Little, "Why Bibles Given to Slaves Omitted Most of the Old Testament," History, December 11, 2018, updated April 3, 2019, https://history.com /news/slave-bible-redacted-old-testament. The title of the Bible was "Parts of the Bible Selected for the Use of Negro Slaves, in the British West-India Islands."

28. Little.

29. James Cone, *Said I Wasn't Gonna Tell Nobody* (New York: Orbis, 2018), 46.

30. Cone, 48.

31. Cone, 71.

32. Wood, 98.

33. Shah Aashna Hossain, "Scientific Racism in 'Enlightened Europe,'" January 16, 2008, Serendip Studio, https://serendipstudio.org/exchange/serendipupdate /scientific-racism-enlightened-europe. See also Lisa Wade, "Whites, Blacks, and Apes in the Great Chain of Being," July 12, 2012, Sociological Images, https://the societypages.org/socimages/2012/07/12/whites-blacks-apes-in-the-great-chain-of-being/.

34. Hossain.

35. Hossain.

36. Wood, 99.

37. Ibram X. Kendi, *Stamped from the Beginning: The Definitive History of Racist Ideas in America* (New York: Nation Books, 2016), 50–51.

38. Wood, 82.

39. Wood.

40. Cone, 42.

41. Vincent Harding, *There Is a River: The Black Struggle for Freedom in America* (Orlando: Harcourt Brace & Company, 1981), 41.

42. Harding.

43. Harding.

44. Herbert Aptheker, ed., *A Documentary History of the Negro People in the United States*, cited in Harding, 43.

45. Reinhold D. Niebuhr, *The Irony of American History* (Chicago: University of Chicago Press, 1952), x.

46. Niebuhr, xi.

47. Niebuhr, xii.

48. Niebuhr, 25.

49. C. D. C. Reeve, trans., *Plato Republic* (Indianapolis: Hackett, 2004), 25 (347a 5-10; b-5).

50. Reeve, 415a 1-5; 415e 6; 417b 9.

51. Harding, 45.

52. Harding.

53. Harding.

54. "Signers of the Declaration of Independence," U.S. Constitution, https: //www.usconstitution.net/declarsigndata.html.

55. David L. Holmes, "The Founding Fathers, Deism, and Christianity," *Encyclopedia Britannica*, https://www.britannica.com/topic/The-Founding-Fathers-Deism -and-Christianity-1272214.

56. Holmes.

57. Holmes.

58. Holmes.

59. Holmes.

60. Holmes.

61. Holmes.

62. Holmes.

4
All the Founders' Contradictions
Racist in Spite of God

Slavery is not a sin, a Moral evil,
For God never did, and never will, authorize men to
commit Sin.   —Rev. Dr. Richard Furman, 1828

The founding fathers came to the task of writing the Constitution of the United States with ideas about race that were sullied by more than a century of racist thought that had been brought here and propagated by the Puritans. Like the incident of smallpox-infested blankets that were given to erase Native Americans from this land that the Puritans would one day call their own,[1] the newcomers brought their racist-infected thinking that contaminated the possibility of "liberty and justice for all" before the words were ever written.

Our founders were wealthy, white, male landowners who benefitted from the pain of Black people in this country; they were members of Christian churches which for the most part supported the need for slavery and based that support on the words of the Bible. If the churches did not overtly support slavery and the racism that sanctioned it, their silence about it belied their complicity in its continuation as a part of American life.

A Biased Christianity

The churches suffered from a Christianity that was "infected," says Alan Davies in *Infected Christianity*. Davies opens his book with an observation offered by George L. Mosses, who wrote a history of European racism:

> Racism had sought an alliance with the main trends of the [nineteenth] century: nationalism, spiritualism, bourgeois morality, and the belief in science. But it also reached out to Christianity, in spite of its own claim to a monopoly over salvation . . . There were many pious Christians and good churchmen who consistently rejected racism, and others, such as the Quakers, who equally consistently helped the oppressed. But the record of most Protestant churches and of the Catholic Church was not one clearly opposed to the idea of racism.[2]

Davies identifies and isolates five modern "Christs" as evidence of the "racist contamination of Christianity since the rise of racism as a secular ideology in the West."[3] The five Christs are Germanic, Latin, Anglo-Saxon, Afrikaner, and Black.[4] Davies states that he considers racism to be "fundamentally incompatible" with Christianity, referring to Scriptures which proclaimed that God made everything that was made. He probes the question of how the Christ of America, the so-called Anglo-Saxon Christ, could ever have come to be since Jesus the Christ was not white and not European, but instead was Jewish. Davies reminds the reader that none of Jesus' disciples were white, either: "Neither Mary, the mother of Jesus, nor John, his beloved disciple, nor Simon, called Cephas, nor any of the Twelve Apostles was of Aryan descent."[5]

There is mention of people with Black or dark skin in the Hebrew Scriptures—a woman with dark skin affirms herself in spite of having Black skin: "I am Black, but comely, O ye daughters of Jerusalem, as the tents of Kedar, as the curtains of Solomon. Look not upon me, because I am Black, because the sun hath looked upon me: my mother's children were angry with me; they made me the keeper of the vineyards" (Song of Solomon 1:5-6, KJV). The beautiful woman apologizes for her color and tries to explain why she is so dark.

During the wilderness journey, the Hebrews were color-conscious; they considered white to be the color of purity and innocence, and Black, "which absorbs all colours and thus buries the light—to symbolize death, humiliation and mourning."[6] Davies's point is that ancient society was not color-blind, and the tendency to dehumanize people of color never lost its appeal or the belief in its authenticity. Davies further notes the notion, held by some Christians, that "not only had God placed on Ham's descendants the 'Black mark' of condemnation and servitude for their ancestor's sin, but God had actually done so for their own spiritual welfare."[7]

While philosophers like Thomas Paine and David Hume scorned the Bible and rejected it as myth, they nonetheless accepted their contemporaries' ideas about Black people and the belief in their inherent lack of worth. Hume wrote that in his opinion there were "four to five different kinds [of Black people] and all of them were naturally inferior to the whites."[8]

Davies writes that during the Enlightenment, the general white population, including philosophers like Hume and Paine, were flawed because the Age of Reason was flawed and because people of that time were not aware of their bias.[9] In their eyes, notwithstanding the accepted belief that God had made everything and everyone, whole races were deficient and "could be seen in much the same light as mentally deficient individuals."[10] The mere color of Black people marked them and caused people to judge and shun them at the same time. In explaining how Blacks even obtained a place on earth, some opined that there were several gods (polytheism, as opposed to monotheism), and others suggested that these aberrant individuals were created by some deity before the biblical account of creation. By the time the founders gathered to write the Constitution, their white supremacist ideas, affirmed by some interpretations of the Bible, were firmly in place.

With this white supremacist mindset firmly in place, there was no way the founding fathers were going to be able to construct a doctrine of egalitarianism, equality, and justice for all people. A Christianity that was infected with racism influenced their thinking, even if they were not consciously aware of it. In spite of some calling this nation Christian at its birth, it lacked the ingredients that would make that claim true. Whether they knew it or not, or acknowledged it if they did know, they were offspring of those who believed in the myth of white superiority, helped along by people like Samuel Morton, who was intent on proving the innate inferiority of Black people due to the shape and size of their skulls. Morton had decided that white people (also called Caucasian or Adamic) had the largest heads and therefore the largest brains, making them

the most intelligent of all human species. Black people, he concluded, had the smallest skulls; their intelligence was so low, he claimed,
that they were not worthy of emancipation. When Morton died in
1851, he was hailed as a hero and trailblazer in the study of the
Negro problem; he was remembered as "one of the brightest orna-
ments of our age and country . . . who had contributed most materially in giving to the Negro his true position as an inferior race."[11]

As Morton was being hailed, the "Aryan myth" was being codified and solidified as a marker of racial superiority, and it was said
to explain the "sacred origins of the human race."[12] Says Davies,
"The Aryan was really an Adamic figure; he was at once both 'the
primordial Ancestor' and the noble 'hero.' [He was the] exempla-
ry model that must be imitated in order to recover racial 'purity,'
physical strength, nobility [and] the heroic 'ethics' of the glorious
and creative beginnings . . . [he was] a healing symbol who could
restore the lost vitality and marvelous energies of youth."[13]

People in Europe and then in America were teaching that the
Aryan model was the representation of racial superiority. The reason the United States was such a great country, some posited, was
because it was created by Anglo-Saxons, who were Aryan, who represented the "highest kind of man on the evolutionary scale."[14] Proponents of the validity of the Aryan myth believed that the world
would one day be ruled by Anglo-Saxons and that they had been
chosen by God to do the same. Long before the eugenics movement
began in this country, clergy, philosophers, teachers, and politicians
believed that the undesirables, including the poor, should be "eliminated as nature's outcasts."[15]

However, those proponents of Christianity who also were adherents of the principle of white supremacy had a problem. Jesus
the Christ was not white; he was a Palestinian Jew. In spite of that
fact, white Christians made Jesus one of their own; that is, they cast
him as being a white man. Teachers of religion were able to "present whiteness as religiously neutral, normal and natural."[16]

Since white Americans believed themselves to be the new Israelites, the new chosen people, they believed God was leading
them in their subjugation of non-white people as a part of their
divine assignment to be "trustees of the world's progress."[17] God
had selected them—the Anglo-Saxon Christians—to create, shape,
form, and ultimately save America. That kind of thinking was born

during the colonial days but was perhaps best summarized in 1874 by Dwight Harris, a professor of systematic theology at Yale College, who claimed that "God has always acted by chosen peoples," and to the Anglo-Saxon, "more than to any other the world is now indebted for the propagation of Christian ideas and Christian civilization."[18] Preachers believed and taught that God had "chosen" the Anglo-Saxon to "conquer the world for Christ by dispossessing feeble races and assimilating others."[19]

But who was Jesus? How could white Christians resolve the divide between their belief in the superiority of white people and the fact that Jesus was not white? The Christ had to be altered. Jews, or Semites, were already hated by the time that the US Constitution was written. White Christians could not deify a savior who was a member of a hated group of people, part of the population of the "feeble" races that already had been identified. Although it was a given assumption among colonists in America that Jesus was white, (based on classical artistic representations throughout all of Western and most of Eastern Europe), Jesus' whiteness was formalized in the nineteenth century.

French philosopher Count Arthur de Gobineau was largely responsible for this formalizing of Jesus' re-creation to suit white supremacy. He firmly believed in the superiority of the Aryans, a group to which the American Anglo-Saxons belonged. Count de Gobineau and another Frenchman, Ernest Renan, who also was an ardent believer in the rightness of white superiority, were among the first French philosophers to make certain racist claims about Jews. They said that Jews, though white-skinned, had contaminated blood; therefore, they were not Aryan. The two Frenchmen also made clear their adherence to "Christian religious prejudice," which decried and denigrated everything Jewish, including the Talmud, which Renan said was "devoid of all morality."[20] According to Renan,

> the Talmud was a "typical product of the Semitic mind" while the "New Testament was in all likelihood the product of an Aryan mind." Here we see the formalized creation of a "white" Jesus. If Jesus was not exactly an Aryan, he was at least a Jew who, paradoxically, was exempt from the faults of his race. Renan held that Jesus' exact origins could not be determined, but while it was impossible to "seek to ascertain what blood

flowed in the veins of him who has contributed most to efface the distinction of blood in humanity," the inner rupture between Jesus and Judaism could not be doubted.[21]

Davies said that other French writers added to the work of Renan and de Gobineau. An Aryan Bible, which was to be used for a "universal Aryan religion superior to Christianity," was composed by a man named Louis Jacilliot, who also taught that the name Jesus was a derivative of Zeus and not a Greek form of the Hebrew-Aramaic name Yeshu'a. As the frenzy to immortalize the rightness of white supremacy continued, Jesus was said to be a socialist, as compared with a capitalist, a class to which the hated Semites, or Jews, belonged. Socialist Christians were described as being enthusiastic, chivalrous, and unselfish, while Semites were accused of being mercenary, covetous, and conspiratorial.[22] The French thus developed what Davies calls the Latin Christ, whose characteristics were considered in the creation of the Anglo-Saxon Christ, to whom the founding fathers adhered.

Americans also realized that Jesus was not an Anglo-Saxon, a race glorified in the new country, but like the French they did not let that stop them from developing a Christ in whom they could believe. The Americans had inherited the gift of spirituality, taught Josiah Strong; therefore, "they were the true Hebrews, as opposed to the post-Biblical Jews." Americans, as pre-biblical Hebrews, were "proto-Christians," but biblical Jews were "anti-Christian." To be a Christian and an Anglo-Saxon and an American was considered to represent the highest pinnacle of human existence. Christ, the Americans were taught, was an American, or at least a proto-American, a proto-Anglo-Saxon, and a proto-Christian.[23]

Later proponents of the superiority of white people would have agreed with and approved of Strong's conclusions. Madison Grant, author of *The Passing of the Great Race*, wrote that the preservation of the superiority of the white race, specifically, Nordic whites, was "not just a matter of racial pride or of racial prejudice; it is a matter of love of country."[24] He would have had to adopt the reimagined Christ, because in his view dark skin was a sign of inferiority. He wrote that it is "race, always race, that sets the limit" to human endeavor and accomplishment.[25] He said that the "great mass of mankind" is "not free and equal," nor did God intend them to be. In terms of democracy and what it should be, Grant's position was clear:

> In the democratic forms of government, the operation of universal suffrage tends toward the selection of the average man for public office rather than the man qualified by birth, education, and integrity. How this scheme of administration will ultimately work out remains to be seen, but from a racial point of view, it will inevitably increase the preponderance of the lower types and cause a corresponding loss of efficiency in the community as a whole. The tendency in a democracy is toward a standardization of type and a diminution of the influence of genius. A majority must of necessity be inferior to a picked minority.[26]

The Tension between Liberty and Oppression

America's racial fabric was being formed and perfected. Everyone—Black and white—could feel the disconnect and the contradiction between fighting for liberty from an oppressing country while engaging in the oppression of human beings in one's own country. The Indians had already been removed from their land by a process of "legal genocide," according to Vincent Harding.[27] Slave ships—with names including *Brotherhood, John the Baptist, Justice, Integrity, Jesus,* and *Gift of God*—arrived on America's shores with Africans, destined to be oppressed on the basis of their race, with the oppressors feeling confident that they were doing the work and the will of God, who apparently approved of their treatment. Christianity was seen as the tool by which the savages could be reined in, but not as the justification for freeing them from slavery. Harding says white Americans sought to "define them in North American terms according to Euro-American social, political, and economic needs."[28] As enslaved Africans fought for their freedom and dignity, whites began to label them as "vicious and villainous," dangerous and a threat to the peace and stability of society.

By the mid-1700s, Africans comprised nearly a third of the population of Virginia. They were needed for their labor, but they were feared because they hated slavery and fought to be free. Whites formed slave patrols and in effect began the phenomenon of state-sanctioned violence against Black people as they sought to keep

Blacks "in their place," which was, in the minds of white people, enslaved. The enslaved Africans dreamed of being free from whites just as much as the whites dreamed to be free from England. There was nothing that could quench the quest for freedom of enslaved Black people; they rebelled in both the North and the South and "were willing to live outside the nets of white law and order, especially when that system mandated their degradation."[29]

They found hope in the early 1770s, as they listened to white people talk about their commitment to being loosed from bondage to England. They listened to the language of the Deists and the devout Christians; they heard arguments about the natural rights of men and internalized those words to strengthen them for their journey toward freedom. They held God in the center of all they did, but it was a different God. It was not the Anglo-Saxon God of America or the Latin God of the French; it was the God of liberation that they had internalized from their own understanding of the Scriptures. Their God and the God of their captors could not have been more different. Their God was not a God who preferred one race over another but was rather a God who delivered the oppressed from their oppression.

It is interesting that the narrative of the exodus was used by both Blacks and whites. The Puritans referred to their escape from England over the Atlantic Ocean (their wilderness) into the new land (their Promised Land) as a sign that God was with them. Enslaved Africans believed their exodus started on the foreign land to which they had been brought. Their wilderness was slavery, and God was leading them to freedom on the land to which they had been brought. While the Puritans had reached their Promised Land and believed God had commissioned them to do whatever they needed to do in order to conquer it—including exterminating the Native Americans and using Blacks to build the economy—the God of Black people seemed perpetually in the process of setting them free.

There were glimpses of hope. During the First Continental Congress, whites had proclaimed that they would "neither import nor purchase any slave imported after the first day of December next, after which time we will wholly discontinue the slave trade and will neither be concerned in it ourselves nor will we hire our vessel nor sell our commodities or manufactures to those who are concerned in it."[30] Christianity and God notwithstanding, the Constitution drafted in 1787 "wrote both the institution and benefits of slavery into" it.[31] The voice of God in the ears and hearts of the founding fathers was either ignored or muffled; their belief in and adherence to white supremacy was their guiding force. Rather than make a way for enslaved Africans to realize their exodus from slavery to freedom, the Constitution, written by religious men, protected their status as slaves. Harding notes:

> The Constitution . . . guaranteed the right of slaveowners to track down Black fugitives across state lines and have them delivered back into captivity. It promised the use of federal armed forces in any struggle against insurrections . . . so firmly etched was the guarantee of Black bondage that only a grim and bloody war would expunge it from the laws. Thus, the revolution for white liberty ended with Black slavery carefully protected in the basic document of the new, "free" nation.[32]

In spite of the fight for freedom, America had "committed itself to the practice of racism and to the eventual related developments of capitalism."[33]

The words of the Bible, apparently having no impact on the whites who were shaping what America would become, were impotent in dismantling the hold of white supremacist thinking on their minds. Though whites who traveled to the new land had tasted and experienced what it felt like to sit on the shore of the "rivers of Babylon," estranged from hope and from religious freedom, they failed to see or care about the plight of enslaved Africans who were now sitting on these American shores. Neither the Great Commandment nor the fact that God despised injustice apparently fazed them. They seemingly did not know, had not read, or did not care about the words in Isaiah 10:1-2: "Ah, you who make iniquitous decrees, who write oppressive statutes, to turn aside the needy from justice and to rob the poor of my people of their right, that widows may be your spoil, and that you may make the orphans your prey!"

The words of a God fed up with the oppression of people did not shame those who believed in the rightness of slavery over the law and word of God. While they concentrated on being pious, their piety did not include treating enslaved Africans as true children of God who were as human as they. Had they not read:

When you come to appear before me,
    who asked them from your hand?
    Trample my courts no more;
bringing offerings is futile;
    incense is an abomination to me.
New moon and sabbath and calling of convocation—
    I cannot endure solemn assemblies with iniquity.
Your new moons and your appointed festivals
    my soul hates;
they have become a burden to me,
    I am weary of bearing them.
When you stretch out your hands,
    I will hide my eyes from you;
even though you make many prayers,
    I will not listen;
    your hands are full of blood.
Wash yourselves; make yourselves clean;
    remove the evil of your doings
    from before my eyes;
cease to do evil,
    learn to do good;
seek justice,
    rescue the oppressed
defend the orphan,
    plead for the widow. (Isaiah 1:12-17)

Blacks, disappointed in the hypocrisy between white Americans' words and actions, read the same words in the Bible and came away with an entirely different interpretation. The Anglo-Saxon God was not their God; that white people were not convicted of the folly of white supremacy was a disappointment but not a deterrent. They continued their wilderness journey. In 1787, the year the Constitution was being drafted, Absalom Jones and Richard Allen decided that they would no longer accept being discriminated against in church because of the color of their skin and walked out of St. George Methodist Episcopal Church after being yanked from their knees while praying with white worshipers. Clearly, they internalized the words of the Bible differently than whites. "Stand fast therefore in the liberty wherewith Christ hath made us free, and be not entangled again with the yoke of bondage" was for them permission and encouragement from God to claim their freedom and their dignity (Galatians 5:1, KJV). Jones and Allen decided to "launch out into the deep, and let down [their] nets" (Luke 5:4, KJV), as Jesus commanded in the Gospel, as they crept from the safety net of white Christian denominationalism into the wilderness of forming a new Black denomination.

The Same Words, Different Interpretations

Clearly, by the time the Constitution was put together, there was a definitive line between the God of Blacks and the God of whites, and the Bible of the two races as well. While both groups read the same words, they walked away with radically different interpretations, and they relied on different parts of the Bible for justification of their theology, as well. Jesus the Christ says nothing about slavery in the Gospels, a fact that pro-slavery advocates did not fail to miss. But Jesus did give the Golden Rule and did command people to love, respect, and forgive each other. Black preachers more often than white preachers (especially those who supported slavery) relied much on and taught the Christian mandates listed above. Richard Allen preached that "God himself was the first pleader of the cause of slaves," but he also preached that:

> God, who knows the hearts of all men, and the propensity of a slave to hate his oppressor, hath strictly forbidden it to his chosen people, "Thou shalt not abhor an Egyptian because thou wast a stranger in his land." The meek and humble Jesus, the great pattern of humanity, and every other virtue that can adorn and dignify men, hath commanded to love our enemies, to do good to them that hate and despitefully use us.[34]

Allen appeals to the discouraged souls of enslaved Africans, reminding them of the favor and love of God, and urging them to "[P]ut your trust in God, who sees your condition; and as a merciful father pitieth his children, so doth God pity them that love him; and as your hearts are inclined to serve God, you will feel an affectionate regard towards your masters and mistresses, so called, and the whole family in which you live."[35]

Allen says to his listeners that if they are bitter toward their owners, they will "transgress against God." Thus, we see an African American, once a slave himself, use the Scriptures to encourage forgiveness of those who have made their lives miserable and to concentrate on not offending God, who has shown them favor, in spite of their earthly condition.

Pro-slavery preachers, however, used the Scriptures in a way that encouraged the adoption of their culture and society. In 1820, an article in the *Richmond Enquirer* made a point of showing how the Bible—which many believed to be the actual voice of God—ordained slavery. In that article, the author said, "The volume of sacred writings, commonly called the bible, comprehending the old and new Testaments, contains the unerring decisions of the word of God."[36]

Other points in this same article that are considered true are (1) the admonition that there could be "no prescription against the authority of God," (2) "that God is infinitely just and wise in all decisions," and (3) that "if one or more decisions of the written word of God sanction the rectitude of any human acquisitions, for instance, the acquisition of a servant by inheritance or purchase, whoever believes that the written word of God is verity itself, must consequently believe in the absolute rectitude of slave-holding."[37]

In these proclamations of the rightness of the Word of God, there is strangely no mention of Jesus, though the writers and preachers of said sermons profess to be Christian. In an examination of the religious arguments used by pro-slavery preachers and advocates, Larry Morrison notes a story in which a reporter wrote that Leviticus 25:44-46, which says that people may acquire slaves from aliens "and they may be your property," was the indisputable Word of God, "written by the finger of the Almighty."[38] The only caveat was that the Israelites were not to enslave one of their own. That Levitical text reassured whites that their enslavement of Blacks was in line with the Bible because they were enslaving "aliens," that is, Africans, and not members of their own race. Preachers ignored Jesus' words because he had been silent about slavery. Said one writer in the eighteenth century, Jesus' "'general maxims of charity and benevolence' could not be regarded as 'proofs against slavery' because 'if the custom had been held in abhorrence by Christ and his disciples, they would, no doubt, have preached against it in direct terms.'"[39] Rev. Dr. Richard Furman wrote in 1828 that the

"Christian religion had nothing to do with slavery, except . . . that the total silence of its Divine Author upon the subject, and the positive injunction of obedience upon bondmen . . . seem to make the inference inevitable that he considered the institution as altogether a matter of political expediency."[40]

The issue with both the Bible and Constitution being ineffective in fighting racism was directly related to the split between the way Blacks and whites read the Bible and therefore interpreted the Constitution. Whites in favor of slavery leaned on the Bible—primarily on the Old Testament but on the New Testament as well—as proof of God's involvement in and approval of slavery. The Bible was the "inerrant" Word of God and could not be touched. The fact that some read the Bible in an entirely different way, including some of the same passages that Southern pro-slavery readers referred to, prompted some pro-slavery advocates to issue a stern criticism because they were convinced that Northerners were abandoning the Bible. In January of 1820, for example, Senator William Smith of South Carolina claimed that he would not be astonished to find out that Northerners were attempting a "new version of the Old and New Testaments," a "new model . . . to suit the policy of the times." They would "throw off such parts as were uncongenial to their interests, and leave the residue to God." Smith finished with a particular concern of his: "They had already given the Scriptures an implied construction, as different in its literal sense, as they had that of the Constitution of the United States."[41]

What is noticeable about the passages lifted from Richard Allen's sermon, as opposed to those of pro-slavery advocates, is that Allen leaned on the words of Jesus, thereby addressing and honoring what Morrison calls the "spirit of Christianity." Conversely, the pro-slavery advocates relied upon a hard read of Old and New Testament Scriptures, which represented the "authority of the Bible."[42]

Those who leaned more on the Gospel teachings of Jesus were criticized as being "misguided missionaries" and were accused of seeking "worldly glory." Morrison noted, again in the *Richmond Enquirer*, that "in spite of the Biblical sanctions, the 'zealots of humanity' had denounced slavery."[43] The "spirit of Christianity" meant nothing to those who espoused the "authority of Scripture." They wrote that humans were not allowed to "separate the positive laws of God from the Christian religion." The words of Jesus, that he had come not to destroy the law but to fulfill it (Matthew 5:17), were taken by pro-slavery advocates to mean that the law as given in the Hebrew Scriptures was the will of God; Jesus was sent to teach us how to fulfill it. Nothing of Jesus' ministry of reaching out to "the least of these" or of embracing the unloved, the forgotten, and the downtrodden appeared in their defense of the practice of slavery. When it came to the Golden Rule, some pro-slavery advocates said that the rule did not apply to slavery, but if it were to be, pro-slavery advocates maintained that it merely meant that the master should treat his slave like he would want to be treated if he were a slave; never mind if that dictate was broken throughout the slave-holding era and beyond.

The people who were about to write the Constitution were influenced and shaped by their culture. They heard the way the Bible was used to defend and to attack slavery, and they could see that there was no intersection of the two points of view, no place that could be used to bolster their work should they choose to humanize enslaved Africans and end slavery. Perhaps a lack of a firm spiritual and biblical foundation on which to base their work and their decisions explains why the same split on the issue of slavery was present among the writers and signers of the Constitution. It stands to reason, then, that the Constitution, the sacred document of the state, would be as flawed on this issue as was the Bible, the sacred document of the church.

Epigraph

Rev. Dr. Richard Furman, *Exposition of the View of the Baptists, Relative to the Coloured Population in the United States, in a Communication to the Governor of South-Carolina*, 2nd ed. (Charleston: Printed by A. E. Miller, 1838), http://history.fur man.edu/~benson/docs/rcd-fmn1.htm.

NOTES

1. Patrick J. Kiger, "Did Colonists Give Infected Blankets to Native Americans as Biological Warfare?", November 15, 2018, updated November 25, 2019, History, https://www.history.com/news/colonists-native-americans-smallpox-blankets.
2. Alan Davies, *Infected Christianity: A Study of Modern Racism* (Kingston and Montreal: McGill-Queens University Press, 1988), ix.

3. Davies.

4. Davies, ix–x.

5. Davies, xi.

6. Davies, 5.

7. Davies, 12.

8. Davies, 13.

9. Davies, 14.

10. Davies.

11. Davies, 15.

12. Davies, 21.

13. Davies, 22.

14. Edward Blum, Tracy Fessenden, Prema Kurien, and Judith Weisenfeld, "Forum: American Religion and Whiteness," Center for the Study of Religion and American Culture, https://www.academia.edu/8606670/Forum_American_Religion _and_Whiteness; *Religion and American Culture: A Journal of Interpretation* 19, no. 1 (Winter 2009): 1–35.

15. Forrest G. Wood, *The Arrogance of Faith* (New York: Alfred A. Knopf, 1990), 210–11.

16. Davies, 63.

17. Wood, 210.

18. Wood.

19. Wood.

20. Davies, 63.

21. Davies.

22. Davies.

23. Davies.

24. Madison Grant, *The Passing of the Great Race* (New York: Scribner & Sons, 1916), ix.

25. Grant, 25.

26. Grant, 23.

27. Vincent Harding, *There Is a River: The Black Struggle for Freedom in America* (Orlando: Harcourt Brace & Company, 1981), 25.

28. Harding, 29.

29. Harding, 39.

30. Harding, 45.

31. Harding, 46.

32. Harding.

33. Harding.

34. Frank Thomas and Martha Simmons, eds., *Preaching with Sacred Fire: An Anthology of African American Sermons, 1750 to the Present* (New York: W.W. Norton, 2010), 107–8.

35. Thomas and Simmons, 109.

36. Larry R. Morrison, "The Religious Defense of American Slavery Before 1830," https://www.kingscollege.net/gbrodie/The%20religious%20justification%20of%20 slavery%20before%201830.pdf, 16.

37. Morrison, 17.

38. Morrison, 19.

39. Morrison, 24.

40. Morrison.

41. Morrison, 25.

42. Morrison.

43. Morrison, 26.

5
Oil and Water
The Futile Effort to Make America Free and Fair

> *Can there be a nobler cause . . . than that which, whilst it proposed to rid our country of a useless and pernicious, if not dangerous part of its population, contemplates the spreading of the arts of civilized life, and the possible redemption from ignorance and barbarism of a benighted quarter of the globe!*
> —Henry Clay, at the 1817 inauguration
> of the American Colonization Society

In *Go Tell It on the Mountain*, James Baldwin said, "Not everything that is faced can be changed, but nothing can be changed until it is faced." There is a painful truth that we need to own and face: given the history of the development of white supremacist ideology, America was never the "land of the free and the home of the brave." Even as America fought for liberty from England, the tacit understanding was that the fight was for the liberty of white people. People of African descent were a "problem" to white people from the moment the two races interacted. Ibram Kendi quotes the words spewed by Mississippi Senator Jefferson Davis, who would one day become the president of the Confederacy. Davis, incensed that a bill was before the Congress that would fund education for Black people in Washington, DC, said, "This Government was not founded by negroes for negroes, but by white men for white men." Davis scolded those who had proposed the bill and said that it had come from a false notion of racial equality. The inequality of the races, he said, was "stamped from the beginning."[1]

Although there were some Christians—clergy and lay persons alike—who despised racism and fought against the use of the Bible to justify it, the fact is that the majority of whites in America believed in the rightness of white supremacy because it was what they had been taught. Pastors, preachers, and theologians in both the North and the South taught that "the Bible said" that Black people were inferior; they quoted Scripture to bolster and support their positions. Saying "the Bible said so" was equal to saying "God said so," and nobody was going to argue with that. Christianity allowed and supported the right of masters to rule over their slaves. Old and New Testament Scriptures were used, including those from the Pauline Epistles to the Ephesians, which said, "Slaves, obey your earthly masters with respect and fear, and with sincerity of heart, just as you would obey Christ" (Ephesians 6:5, NIV). Preachers in both the North and the South taught that enslaved Africans should obey the Bible, which said:

> Let every man abide in the same calling wherein he was called. Art thou called being a servant? care not for it: but if thou mayest be made free, use it rather. For he that is called in the Lord, being a servant, is the Lord's freeman: likewise, also he that is called, being free, is Christ's servant. Ye are bought with a price; be not ye the servants of men. Brethren, let every man, wherein he is called, therein abide with God. (1 Corinthians 7:20-24, KJV)

Scriptures such as these were interpreted to make the state of being enslaved a holy calling, an opportunity for people to get close to God. Enslaved Africans were thus encouraged to be content with their condition, knowing that in the afterlife, they would be rewarded. Scriptures used to justify the enslavement of Africans were those which would affirm their belief in the whiteness of God. It was a hard argument to fight, as nobody wanted to offend God.

White supremacist thought taught whites to believe in their superiority and taught Blacks to believe in their innate inferiority. Paul Griffin says that "racism had become a Christian article of faith."[2] In addition, as we have already established, whites in general believed that Black people not only were heathens but also had been created that way. In addition, the arguments around polygenesis made it clear that not all white Christians were sure or convinced that Blacks had even been created by the one God in whom they professed to follow and believe.

The belief in God being white never lessened; if anything, it gained traction over time. When twenty-first-century television talk show host Megyn Kelly proclaimed that Jesus was white (though after facing fierce criticism she later conceded that he might not be white), she was reciting what she had been taught. Responding to an article written by a woman who argued that Santa Claus was white versus Black, Kelly said: "You know, I've given her her due. Just because it makes you uncomfortable doesn't mean it has to change. Jesus was a white man, too. It's like we have, he's a historical figure, that's a verifiable fact, as is Santa. I just want kids to know that. How do you revise it in the middle of the legacy and change the story and change Santa from white to Black?"[3]

Over time, proponents had been planting and fertilizing the belief in a white God, separating Jesus from his Jewish ethnicity and making him white so as to support their beliefs. White supremacy was inverting the religion of creation, as Wes Howard-Brook said, and according to Paul Griffin, it was doing it by using "perverted biblical and theological ideas."[4] Those lessons were the lessons carried into the Constitutional Convention of 1787.

Creating America

America, having won the Revolutionary War in 1776, and having drafted the glorious Declaration of Independence afterward, was deep in the process of creating the myth of who it was and what it stood for: that America was greater and different than any other nation could claim to be. White Americans believed that their country had been expressly chosen by God to be the example of what a nation should be. The virtual extermination of Native Americans in the 1600s and the enslavement of Africans was of no consequence; those events took place because white Americans believed Native Americans to be heathens, and because their settlement in America and their actions to cleanse it of such heathens had been sanctioned by God, who wanted this new nation to be the "new Israel." Reinhold Niebuhr noted the pedestal on which America placed itself:

> We had renounced the evils of European feudalism. We had
> escaped from the evils of European religious bigotry. We had
> found broad spaces for the satisfaction of human desires
> in place of the crowded Europe. Whether, as in the case of
> the New England theocrats, our forefathers thought of our
> "experiment" as primarily the creation of a new and purer
> church, or, as in the case of Jefferson and his coterie, they
> thought primarily of a new political community, they believed in
> either case that we had been called out by God to create a new
> humanity. We were God's "American Israel."[5]

Americans seemingly glorified the idea of freedom but because of the presence of Black people, they were already on the path to creating the contradiction between their beliefs and their actions. In spite of pushing the idea that American soil was "purer than any church of Christendom,"[6] the fact of the matter was that white America's dislike of Black people had already contaminated the soil. The root of white supremacy had been planted in New England, where in the 1600s laws had been passed which greatly encroached upon the capacity of Black people to live free and dignified lives. In 1670, a law that was passed in Boston made it legal for the children of slaves to be sold into bondage. None of the laws in New England protected the marriages of enslaved Africans, and families were frequently separated, as they would be later when the slave culture grew in the South. In Massachusetts, a law passed in 1703 made it illegal for Black people—both enslaved and free—to be out after 9 p.m. Massachusetts law also forbade sex outside of marriage. If a Black man, slave or free, broke this law he could be flogged or sold or both, but interestingly, the same law was not enforced against white men who had sex with Black women, which was definitely outside of marriage.[7]

In the South, laws were made, as well, which helped solidify the divide between white and Black. In Virginia, in 1667, a law was passed that indicated that no Black person could be made free because he or she had become a Christian. The law said:

> [W]hereas some doubts have risen whether children that are
> slaves by birth, and by the charity and piety of their owners
> made partakers of the blessed sacrament of baptism, should by

virtue of their baptism be made free, it is enacted and declared by this Grand Assembly, and the authority thereof, that the conferring of baptism does not alter the condition of the person as to his bondage or freedom.[8]

Other slave laws that were passed in Virginia included the following:

- prohibited baptized free Blacks and Native Americans from purchasing Christian servants
- legalized wounding or killing an enslaved person who resisted arrest
- compensated slave owners if any of their slaves were killed while resisting capture
- restricted slave meetings at gatherings, including funerals[9]
- punished slaves with thirty lashes on the back if they lifted their hand against any Christian
- decreed that a mulatto child born to a white indentured servant be forced to serve thirty years as an indentured servant[10]

By 1692, enslaved persons were denied the right to a jury trial. In 1705, free men of color lost the right to hold public office, and in that same year, free and enslaved backs were denied the right to testify as witnesses in court cases.[11]

All of these freedom-theft laws flew in the face of America's perception of itself as being the paragon of what a free society looked like, yet the myth of freedom continued to grow. In 1750, ever closer to the Revolutionary War and the drafting of the founding documents, Ezra Stiles, the president of Yale, "preached a sermon on the United States elevated to glory and honor in which he defined the nation as 'God's American Israel.'"[12]

The belief that America had a divine call to divide and conquer new territory in the new world did not disappear as we got further and further away from the landing of the Puritans. Jon Meacham writes in *American Gospel* that God was always in the conversation about developing the new nation. He says that the "Founders were politicians and philosophers, sages and warriors, churchmen and doubters . . . they delved and dabbled in religion."[13] The talk about God, however, did not render a particularly godly nation, at least not from the hands and mouths of the founders. Meacham notes that many of the founders were profoundly influenced by Deism; some deists held that there was a single creator God, but other deists, among whom were some of the founders, were lukewarm regarding that belief. Instead, they believed in Jesus the Christ, and that "he was a great moral teacher—even the greatest in all history—but he was not the Son of God!"[14]

How ironic it was that the founders who framed the core beliefs of the new nation, which called itself Christian, did not believe in Jesus as a divine figure! That would mean that their words and their actions were not Christian in the sense of following the Jesus of the Holy Bible, but that they were at best religious, influenced by words that they found in the Bible that were not the words of Jesus. What they were forming in this country was the religion of empire at the expense of the religion of creation. Jesus was a known entity, but his teachings were not central to many of the founders' belief systems.

Therefore, it was not difficult for them to adopt and adhere to principles of imperialism. Just as the Puritans had believed that God sent them to the new world to conquer the territory on the Atlantic shore, as the country grew religious people similarly believed and were taught that it was God's will that they expand westward. "Manifest Destiny" held that the United States was "destined by God" to expand its dominion and "spread democracy and capitalism across the entire North American continent."[15]

As they moved westward, in the name of almighty God, who had sanctioned and blessed their work, white Americans continued their quest for power, brutalizing large segments of the Native American and Hispanic populations that had long lived in the western part of the nation. The whites did not need to worry, however, about chastisement from God because they believed they were doing the work of God. What was happening was a clear demarcation of two Jesus figures—the Jesus of history (religion of creation), and the Christ of Protestantism. In spite of the Bible verse that gave all power to the name of Jesus (Matthew 28:18), the founders chose instead to latch onto a much less personal Christ who could be used by and manipulated for the purposes of the state. The words below, found in the Book of Philippians, might have been considered a challenge to the purposes of those who were in control of America's destiny:

> Let this mind be in you, which was also in Christ Jesus: Who, being in the form of God thought it not robbery to be equal with God: But made himself of no reputation, and took upon him the form of a servant, and was made in the likeness of men: And being found in fashion as a man, he humbled himself, and became obedient unto death, even the death of the cross. Wherefore God also hath highly exalted him, and given him a name which is above every name: That at the name of Jesus every knee should bow, of things in heaven, and things in earth and things under the earth; And that every tongue should confess that Jesus Christ is Lord, to the glory of God the Father. (Philippians 2:5-11, KJV)[16]

While they did not want a king, neither did they want people to give too much power to a deity. The idea of God was ever-present, but it was a God who agreed with the new Americans' ideas. Using the name Christ was a good way to keep the idea of Christianity afloat, but in reality, the religion that Jesus taught was not considered to be practical. Meacham notes that the first fight that the founders had was over faith, as they gathered in 1774, for the inaugural session of the Continental Congress. One of the attendees made a motion that they open with prayer, and two of the signers of the Declaration of Independence and later, the Constitution—John Jay of New York and John Rutledge of South Carolina—objected. Meacham says that the reason was because, as John Adams noted, "we were so divided in religious sentiments . . . [that] we could not join in the same act of worship."[17]

Freedom of religion was important to the founders, who, again, gave God credit for their having escaped religious persecution in England. Remember, the Puritans rejoiced in their having made it to the new world, where they were free of the religious bigotry they had experienced in England. The Anglican church, however, which was the Church of England in America, was oppressive and domineering in the early days of the formation and development of the colonies. A law passed in Virginia in 1624 required white Virginians to attend the Anglican church because it was the established church of the state. Virginians also were required to pay taxes to support the Anglican church.

As time went on, the colonists balked that, by law, they had to attend church and they had to pay taxes to support the church. Having escaped religious bigotry in England, they were not going to acquiesce and fall into the same situation here. They wanted all religions to be tolerated, including those that were brought here from elsewhere and those that were established in the new world by white people.

The religions of Black people and Native Americans were another matter that was quite concerning for the white people who controlled them. The whites disdained traditional African religions, and they certainly did not approve of so many Africans being practicing Muslims. Martha Simmons and Frank A. Thomas note in *Preaching with Sacred Fire* that enslaved Africans practiced various faiths, including Islam. While admitting that there are no precise records of the personal information of Africans brought to this country, including their native religions, Simmons and Thomas say that "10 percent of slaves from the ports between Senegal and the Bight of Benin . . . were Muslims."[18] They estimate that "there may have been as many as forty thousand African Muslims in colonial and pre-Civil War America"; however, they never formed into a "sizeable American community that passed its traditions from one generation to another," the authors noted.[19]

Thus, in 1776, as the founders gathered to write the Declaration of Independence, they experienced a general angst among themselves over the issue of religion. It is important to note that even though this country claims to be a Christian nation neither Jesus nor the principles Jesus taught were a part of the founding process. Thomas Jefferson was assigned the task of writing the document, and, according to Meacham, Jefferson said that the

> "document was intended to be an expression of the American mind." The writing of it was regarded as "an act of synthesis of the sentiments of the day, whether expressed in conversation, in letters, printed essays or in the elementary books of public right, as Aristotle, Cicero, Locke, Sidney, &c." God was essential

in the declaration Jefferson put together in his rented parlor, but the God he wrote of was in no explicit way the God of Abraham, much less God the Father of the Holy Trinity.[20]

From the outset, then, this nation could not be called Christian, and its founding documents did not, apparently, depend upon the Bible for inspiration or direction. Meacham notes that the founders wrote of "divine providence" and referred to the "supreme judge of the world" but "were no more specific to the God of the Bible than 'Creator,' and 'Nature's God.'"[21] The founding religion, Meacham notes, was "based more on religion of reason than of revelation."[22] While religious language was deemed Christian in the days before the Revolutionary War, it was greatly neutralized following the war. The founders, says Meacham, were making another declaration: "that Americans respected the idea of God, understood the universe to be governed by moral and religious forces, and prayed for divine protection against the enemies of this world, but were not interested in establishing yet another earthly government with official ties to a state church."[23]

There would be no reference to a deity to whom "every knee should bend, . . . and every tongue should confess" (Philippians 2:10). In the process of drafting this nation's foundational documents, the words of the Bible, or more specifically, the words of Jesus as found in the Gospels, were rendered impotent, incidental, and unnecessary to those charged with writing them.

Calling on the Name of Jesus

If the white population of this nation was ignoring the words of Jesus as found in the Gospels, enslaved Africans were not. There was religion that was defined as a function of Reason, there was religion that seemed to be governed by the study and practice of principles found in the Pauline Epistles, and there was a "Jesus" religion, that is, Christianity in the classic sense of being wedded to the words of Jesus the Christ. For the enslaved Africans, something was clearly wrong. Though many could not read, the message that they were getting from slave masters and preachers alike did not fit with their notion of what a good God was. In the period of time leading up to the Civil War, enslaved Africans, says Albert Raboteau in *Slave*

Religion, were shaping and crafting their own God and their own religion, which was far different from that of their white teachers.

Raboteau says that in the long process of enslaved Africans accepting Christianity, "it is important to remember that it was a dual process. The slaves did not simply become Christians; they creatively fashioned a Christian tradition to fit their own peculiar experience of enslavement in America."[24] The words of the gospel were powerful, and white people knew it; Raboteau said that "the danger beneath arguments for slave conversion which many masters feared was the egalitarianism implicit in Christianity."[25] Enslaved Africans rejected what they called "Bible Christians." In spite of being told about the goodness of God, the God of the slave masters seemed uncaring, not only about the Africans' enslavement itself, but also about the cruelty rendered to enslaved Africans as a normal part of their captivity. While whites who were writing the Constitution shied away from the Bible, Raboteau said that "Negroes . . . almost worshiped the Bible."[26] The slaves, instead of calling on Christ, called on the name of Jesus. It seemed that they fully accepted the words in Philippians. It was Jesus who heard them, Jesus who protected them, and Jesus who would save them. The slave masters knew how their slaves felt and did all they could to supersede the religion of the enslaved Africans with the religion of white people, but they did not succeed. Raboteau said:

> [T]he uses to which slaveholders had put the Bible would lead some slaves to distinguish their own experiential Christianity from the Bible Christianity of their masters. Ex-slave members of a church in Virginia, were quite alarmed that those who were concerned for their souls' salvation should attempt to look for instruction or comfort from the Bible . . . they said their masters and their families were Bible Christians and they did not want to be like them.[27]

Though they would not verbalize it in this way, Black people were realizing that the Bible was being weaponized, used as a tool to perpetuate their oppression. They staunchly rejected that and latched onto the Jesus of the Gospels who "died that we might all be free." There was, in other words, a distinct break in the practice of religion in this country: the religion of white people, which had a God which supported the oppression and even the annihilation of different groups of people, and the religion of Black people, which fully accepted the message of liberation contained in the Gospels.

What Black people knew, because it was what they had been taught, was that God was white. The love of God, of the white God, did not extend to Black people. That God did not even insist that Black people were human. Even though many white people did not consider Black people to be human, they in fact owned their own humanity and cherished it. They believed in the Creation story as found in the Book of Genesis, and they believed that they had been created by God; therefore, they were good in God's eyes. Though they would not say it in the same way, James Baldwin said in 1962, "the Christian world has revealed itself as morally bankrupt and politically unstable."[28] He put into words what many Blacks leading up to the Civil War and beyond may have felt:

> The universe, which is not merely the stars and the moon and the planets, flowers, grass, and trees, but *other people*, has evolved no terms for your existence, has made no room for you, and if love will not swing wide the gates, no other power will or can. And if one despairs—and who has not—of human love, God's love alone is left. But God—is white. And if his love was so great, and if He loved all His children, why were we, the Blacks, cast down so far?[29]

Bible Christianity was not, in the eyes of many Black people, the Christianity of God. It was the religion of white people, used to justify their treatment of Blacks, a sentiment that Blacks soundly rejected. The God they studied and believed in had apparently abandoned white people, for they were bereft of the capacity to follow the Golden Rule and the Great Commandment. They, Black people, would be faithful to the words of Jesus, and in so doing, would assure their salvation after death and perhaps their liberty before death. Perhaps they believed, as Baldwin wrote years later, that "white people, who had robbed Black people of their liberty and who profited by this theft every hour that they lived, had no moral ground on which to stand."[30] It was their belief in the words of Jesus that kept them afloat in a world and a system designed to make them drown. They had nothing but their God, and they seemed to know instinctively that only by leaning on and practicing the commands of their Jesus would they be able to survive. God saw it all, and God would reward them if they followed Jesus and did what Jesus taught his followers to do.

Their weapon was the Gospel. They picked up and internalized messages of the importance of forgiving one's enemies. The words of the gospel of Jesus were like bitter medicine which, in spite of its taste, had the power to heal souls ravaged by oppression, so they would forgive their enemies: "Then came Peter to him, and said, Lord, how oft shall my brother sin against me, and I forgive him? till seven times? Jesus saith unto him, I say not unto thee, Until seven times: but, Until seventy times seven" (Matthew 18:21-22, KJV). Enslaved Africans internalized the lessons from Jesus' Sermon on the Mount to love their enemies and pray for those who despitefully used them (Matthew 5:43-47). The enslaved Africans learned that by following the words of Jesus, they could (and did) survive the brutality and cruelty of slavery and withstand and fight the message of white supremacy that they were inferior. They had nothing but their God and God's Son, Jesus, and they leaned on and used them both. The God of white people had nothing for them, and they knew it. The God of white people had little to no power to move white people to treat Black people as human beings first, and as American citizens second. Black people's God helped them to hold on and keep believing that the God who heard them would surely deliver them. And it was their God, their Jesus, who kept them alive.

An important factor to note was that there really was no image of Jesus for Blacks and whites to look at. The Puritans had no image of Jesus, either, for reconciling their notion of the rightness of white supremacy with what they assumed would have been the physical appearance of Jesus was problematic for them. Since there was no set image of Jesus for a long time, both Blacks and whites created their own image of him. For whites, he must have appeared as a white man, in spite of his Palestinian heritage and ethnicity. Edward Blum and Paul Harvey, in *The Color of Christ*, noted that "during the eighteenth and nineteenth centuries, Christ came alive in a physical presence . . . Before Jesus was known for being white in this America, he was venerated for being bloody red. . . . Jesus as a physical symbol was not to be found in the revolutionary republic."[31]

The "America of the founding era was anything but a Jesus nation," Blum and Harvey say, but "the white American Jesus first rose to power and prominence in the early 19th century."[32] What that says is that at the time the Constitution was drafted there already were two Gods. A conflict of interest ensued as white men who believed in slavery worked to write a document that would uphold their belief in a democratic republic. Already, Black people were the "white man's burden," as Rudyard Kipling would write in 1899:

> Take up the White Man's burden—
>   Send forth the best ye breed —
> Go send your sons to exile
>   To serve your captives' need.
> To wait in heavy harness
>   On fluttered folk and wild—
> Your new-caught, sullen peoples,
>   Half devil and half child.
>
> Take up the White Man's burden
>   In patience to abide
> To veil the threat of terror
>   And check the show of pride;
> By open speech and simple
>   An hundred times made plain
> To seek another's profit
>   And work another's gain. . . .
>
> Take up the White Man's burden—
>   And reap his old reward;
> The blame of those ye better
>   The hate of those ye guard—
> The cry of hosts ye humor
>   (Ah slowly) to the light
> "Why brought ye us from bondage
>   Our loved Egyptian night?" . . .

Take up the White Man's burden—
   Have done with childish days—
The lightly proffered laurel,
   The easy, ungrudged praise.
Comes now to search your manhood
   Through all the thankless years,
Cold-edged with dear-bought wisdom
   The judgment of your peers![33]

That non-white people would never be equal to white people was a foundational principle believed by most of the founders. The country that was "formed by white men for white men" was already a contradiction which would only become starker as the country grew.

Epigraph

Scott Malcomson, *One Drop of Blood: The American Misadventure of Race* (New York: Farrar, Steaus and Giroux, 2000), 189.

NOTES

1. Ibram X. Kendi, *Stamped from the Beginning: The Definitive History of Racist Ideas in America* (New York: Nation Books, 2016), 3.
2. Paul R. Griffin, *Seeds of Racism in the Soul of America* (Cleveland: Pilgrim Press, 1999), 35.
3. Hadas Gold, "Megyn Kelly: Jesus and Santa Were White," Politico, December 12, 2013, https://www.politico.com/blogs/media/2013/12/megyn-kelly-jesus-and-santa-were-white-179491.
4. Griffin, 35.
5. Reinhold D. Niebuhr, *The Irony of American History* (Chicago: University of Chicago Press, 1952), 25.
6. Niebuhr.
7. "Forgotten History: How the New England Colonists Embraced the Slave Trade," June 21, 2016, *Fresh Air*, National Public Radio, https://www.npr.org/2016/06/21/482986062/forgotten-history-how-the-new-england-colonists-embraced-the-slave-trade.
8. "Virginia Slave Laws," Digital History, http://www.digitalhistory.uh.edu/disp_textbook.cfm?smtID=3&psid=71.
9. "Slave Law in Colonial Virginia: A Timeline," https://www.shsu.edu/~jll004/vabeachcourse_spring09/bacons_rebellion/slavelawincolonialvirginiatimeline.pdf.
10. "Slave Law in Colonial Virginia."
11. "Slave Law in Colonial Virginia."
12. Niebuhr, 25.
13. Jon Meacham, *American Gospel: God, the Founding Fathers, and the Making of a Nation* (New York: Random House, 2007), 8.

14. Meacham.

15. History.com editors, "Manifest Destiny," April 5, 2010, updated November 15, 2019, History, https://www.history.com/topics/westward-expansion/manifest-destiny.

16. The King James Version of the Bible is the version from which the founders would have read.

17. Meacham, 72.

18. Frank Thomas and Martha Simmons, eds., *Preaching with Sacred Fire: An Anthology of African American Sermons, 1750 to the Present* (New York: W. W. Norton, 2010), 3–4.

19. Thomas and Simmons, 4.

20. Meacham, 72.

21. Meacham, 73.

22. Meacham, 74.

23. Meacham, 78.

24. Albert Raboteau, *Slave Religion: The "Invisible Institution" in the Antebellum South* (Oxford: Oxford University Press, 1978), 209.

25. Raboteau, 102.

26. Raboteau, 240.

27. Raboteau, 242–43.

28. James Baldwin, *The Fire Next Time* (New York: Vintage International, 1993), 51.

29. Baldwin, 30–31.

30. Baldwin, 30.

31. Edward J. Blum and Paul Harvey, *The Color of Christ* (Chapel Hill: University of North Carolina Press, 2012), 9.

32. Blum and Harvey.

33. Rudyard Kipling, an avowed racist, wrote this poem as the United States engaged in the military takeover of the Philippines. The poem illustrates the United States's commitment to imperialism, seen as a divine order.

6
God, the Founders, the Doctrine of Ham, and the Segregated Gospel

> *The cross and the lynching tree are separated by nearly 2000 years. One is the universal symbol of Christian faith; the other is the quintessential symbol of Black oppression in America.*   —James H. Cone

> *White separatism created Black separatism, and the solidifying of both coincided with the creation of our nation.*   —Scott Malcomson

Black people, or the presence of Black people in the evolving nation, their particular way of believing in God already posed a problem for the men who would write the penultimate doctrine of liberty and justice. Religion was a part of American life and would not be ignored or dismissed, but it was a religion that failed to deliver a fatal blow to the belief in and practice of white supremacy.

The fifty-six men who signed the Declaration of Independence, of whom forty-one owned slaves, and the fifty-five men who framed the Constitution, of whom thirty-nine owned slaves, were greatly conflicted. Some were conflicted because of their religion, but many more were conflicted because slave labor was the source of their wealth and their chief livelihood. These men believed in God, but they also believed that God had made Africans inferior to white people and had thereby sanctioned and appointed Africans to be slaves. At least two framers, Richard Bassett and John Dickinson, opposed slavery and supported abolition, but the majority of the signers of the Declaration and the framers of the Constitution freely enslaved human beings, even as they fought for their own freedom as individuals and for the freedom of the new nation.

America had three foundational documents: the Declaration of Independence, drafted in 1776; the Articles of Confederation, drafted in 1777; and the Constitution of the United States, drafted in 1787. Episcopalian men comprised the majority of the signers and framers for all three documents, but men of other Protestant denominations were represented, as well, including Baptists, Methodists, and Presbyterians. A few of the men were Roman Catholics and Quakers, but none of them were Jewish. Though these men said they believed in God and thus were religious, it seems that few of them were practicing Christians—those who referred to, leaned on, or referenced the words of Jesus the Christ in their work of forming the nation.

We have already established the belief that in order to be Christian, one has to not only profess a belief in the Christ but also take to heart the precepts and principles of the religion of creation, that is, to do what Jesus the Christ taught us to do. One can be religious and not be Christian, according to that viewpoint. Thomas Jefferson, Benjamin Franklin, and many of those who formed the founding documents believed in God, whom they called Providence more often than not and to whom they referred to in their work of establishing the nation. But there was no pervasive inclination among them to make America a distinctly Christian nation. Jon Meacham notes:

> The hunger of many later generations of evangelical believers to see the nation's founding as a Christian event from which we have fallen is understandable; the myth of sin and redemption is as old as Genesis and is the motive power of the story of Jesus' death and resurrection. The preponderance of historical evidence, however, suggests that the nation was not "Christian" but rather a place of people whose experience with religious violence and the burdens of established churches led them to view religious liberty as one of humankind's natural rights.[1]

Patrick Henry was one of the founding fathers who deeply believed in Jesus and may have wanted the Constitution to have more of a Christian edge, but he was the exception. The founding fathers wanted no part or even a hint of religious sectarian domination in government; religious tyranny in England was a major part of the reason they had fled England. Therefore, their concern was not in making the Jesus of Christianity the center of their work. Jefferson said, "It does me no injury for my neighbor to say there are twenty Gods or no God. It neither picks my pocket nor breaks my leg."[2] The notion of God was so marginalized during the framing of the Constitution that some objected, saying that America had a "godless" Constitution.[3] There was always God, but not necessarily Jesus for those who constructed America's foundational documents. Americans, including those who were writing and debating the Constitution, were frequently reminded of what God had done for them, how God had made a way for the oppressed from England (all of whom were white) to get to the new world, and how God had been on their side as they settled in and made a new life. But nobody went to the cross and recited the life of Jesus the Christ and what his birth, death, and resurrection had meant. Meacham says that "power, not God was at the center of the constitutional struggle . . . In the end, the Constitution failed to mention God nor did it invoke any synonym for a divine power or author."[4]

Because the founders did not want the new nation to be too religious, there was a genuine struggle between them and those who wanted God and religion to be more prominent. Religion was necessary, the founders believed, to help keep human beings in order. James Madison acknowledged that humans were weak and prone to behavior that was not necessarily just. "If men were angels," he said, "government would not be necessary,"[5] so religion was tolerated but not pushed, and no particular sect—including Christianity—was held up as the religion of the state. The founders pushed religious freedom, meaning that any and all religions in the new country would be tolerated and supported. The variety of religious sects in the nation would help prevent any one denomination from becoming dominant. The founders were defining and perfecting their idea of what American liberty and freedom were about.

While they made room for religious diversity, they made no mention and no room for racial diversity. The people who were members of the different sects in this country were white for the most part. Black people and Native Americans were present but not considered to be a part of the American whole. Disregarding non-whites, the founding fathers instead were working to create for whites "perfect equality and freedom among all religious denominations and societies."[6]

By 1788, the Constitution was ready to be ratified, and religious representatives were a part of the festive day. Benjamin Rush, one of the signers, said, "Pains were taken to connect ministers of the most dissimilar religious principles together, thereby to show the influence of a free government in promoting Christian charity."[7] White men of every religion, having been created "equal," were guaranteed "life, liberty, and the pursuit of happiness." Nowhere in this celebration of liberty were the fate and status of Black people mentioned. The founders were working to overcome and defeat religious prejudice and abuse of religious power. Rush noted, "The Jew joined the Christian; the Episcopalian the Presbyterian . . . and all walked arm in arm, exhibiting a proof of worldly affection, and testifying to their approbation of the new constitution."[8] It seems that the definition of pluralism for the founders revolved more around religion than around race, but the religion represented was not the religion of creation or of Jesus.

What the founders held as holy was the American mind and its capacity to reason. America, "God's American Israel," had been formed out of European chaos. Reinhold Niebuhr says the mindset of the founders was fairly consistent, summed up by Jefferson, who believed that the new nation was not formed from the inspiration of any biblical symbolism but by the "power of Nature's God,"[9] who wanted these men to make a new beginning in a corrupt world. God had allowed the new Americans to break with tyranny, and God was making a way for these new Americans to take advantage of the "wide economic opportunities that would prevent the emergence of those social vices which characterized the social life of an overcrowded Continent of Europe."[10] If enslaving Africans enabled the new white Americans to create a land of economic prosperity for the men who had been called to form this country, then so be it. And that sentiment would carry over into the way the American government would be formed and ultimately run. Slavery was, for a while, more a labor issue and not a race or a religious issue. As the Black population continued to increase, however (due to the influx of Africans brought over by white slave traders), the colonists made haste to create laws that would keep Black people under control. They believed that God would have no issue with that.

Slavery, Laws, and the Declaration

Long before the signers and framers of the Declaration of Independence and the United States Constitution, respectively, gathered to sign and write these documents, Americans in the thirteen colonies were writing race laws prohibiting Blacks from even expecting to have full rights and freedom. Scott Malcomson writes that "racial lawmaking and enforcement were born from the coincidence of skin color and slavery and were directed at controlling labor more than race relations."[11] Whites believed they had the right, and they knew they had the power, to keep Black and Native American people under their employ. In the late seventeenth century, laws were passed in Virginia that made it clear that Blacks could and should be hired "for profit," Christian or not. This was the character and shape of what Edmund Morgan called "the American paradox, the marriage of slavery and freedom."[12]

By the 1770s, lawmakers in colonies, attempting to keep their enslaved profit makers in tow, passed laws specifically designed to "govern Blacks," because of their "barbarous, wild, savage natures, and the disorders, rapines and inhumanity to which type are naturally prone and inclined."[13] Blacks began to be criminalized, and the dehumanization of them was more pronounced. While some whites chose to label Blacks' desire for freedom as indicative of their "brutal" nature, others, while calling them "stupid," recognized that they were, in fact, human and should be expected to revolt. Malcomson says "the attribution of negative qualities to Blacks grew in response to a white need to ignore the qualities of Blacks as humans—mainly because humans, everyone knew, would not accept a life of slavery. They could be expected to fight for their freedom."[14] The "liberty to amass wealth was the reason most people came to America."[15] The humanity or lack thereof of Black people was not the concern of those who used their labor to become wealthy.

Those who were coming to make and to sign America's sacred documents were spiritually inundated with the premises of white supremacy. Benjamin Franklin decried that America had too many

Black people: "Black slaves have already blacken'd half America," he said.[16] America, he said, should be "white and English."[17] Franklin believed that Pennsylvania could well become a "colony of aliens," which clearly bothered him, and he went on to state his belief that "the number of purely white people in the world is proportionately very small."[18] He questioned why the colony of Pennsylvania should be contaminated by the presence of Black people—"sons of Africa," he called them—when they had the opportunity to exclude all Blacks and "tawneys," a group which included Germans and people from Asia. It was this mindset that was present at the drafting of our sacred documents.

Franklin was not an orthodox Christian and seemed to have little regard for the experience of revelation supported by Christian belief. He was raised by devout Puritan parents who also were Calvinists. That meant that he was taught that God was sovereign, and that God, through his mercy, chose to offer salvation to human beings through the birth, death, and resurrection of Jesus, God's Son. He was taught that men and women were required to do good works while they were yet alive.

While Franklin never rejected the sovereignty of God, he rejected the teaching that Jesus was the Son of God and worthy of deification. He believed that Jesus was the greatest moral teacher the world had ever had, but that he was not God.[19] He believed that people needed to treat each other with honor and dignity, although it is not clear if he believed that requirement extended to white people and the way they treated Black or "tawney" people, so he was criticized for his lack of adherence to orthodox Christian teachings. Shortly before he died, he was asked about his beliefs, and he wrote:

> I believe in one God, Creator of the Universe. That he governs it by His Providence. That he ought to be worshipped. That the most acceptable Service we render to him, is doing Good to his other Children. That the Soul of Man is immortal, and will be treated with Justice in another Life respecting its Conduct in this. . . . As for Jesus of Nazareth, . . . I think the system of Morals and Religion as he left them to us, the best the World ever saw, . . . but I have . . . some Doubts as to his Divinity; though' it is a Question I do not dogmatism upon, having never

> studied it, and it is needless to busy myself with it now, where
> I expect soon an Opportunity of knowing the Truth with less
> Trouble.[20]

He died six weeks after writing this.

Earlier in his life, Franklin also had taken issue with the Lord's Prayer, and he rewrote it. His version, he believed, was "more suitable [for] readers:"[21]

> Heavenly Father, May all revere thee, And become thy dutiful
> Children and faithful Subjects. May thy Laws be obeyed on
> Earth as perfectly as they are in Heaven. Provide for us this Day
> as thou has hitherto daily done. Forgive us our Trespasses and
> enable us likewise to forgive those that offend us. Keep us out
> of Temptation and deliver us from Evil.[22]

Franklin called himself, and is called by others, a Christian. While he believed that God required humans to treat each other as they would like to be treated, there is little evidence that his religious beliefs were strong enough to pull him away from the fangs of white supremacy which were deeply embedded in the soul of America, even as the Constitution was drafted. George Washington, a slave owner, gave evidence of the founders' wrestling with their consciences when he wrote in 1774, "We must assert our rights, or submit to every imposition that can be heaped upon us, till custom and use shall make us tame and abject slaves, as the Blacks we rule over with such arbitrary sway."[23]

The founding fathers could not help but be deeply influenced by the American contradiction of fighting for liberation while enslaving human beings at the same time. Between 1777 and 1804, slavery was abolished from Pennsylvania northward, and abolition began to be argued throughout the colonies. Abolition societies sprang up "everywhere after the Revolutionary War except in the Carolinas and Georgia."[24] Founding fathers, including Franklin, John Adams, Washington, Jefferson, Henry, Madison, and Thomas Paine were all anti-slavery in principle, although some of them continued to own slaves in practice.[25]

John Adams and Benjamin Rush favored a gradual emancipation of all slaves, for they recognized the inconsistency of espousing freedom and equality while embracing slavery and the slave trade as a business. In England, Samuel Johnson, a writer and devout Anglican who did not support the formation of the new country apart from England, scoffed at the hypocrisy he saw developing: "How is it that we hear the loudest yelps for liberty from the drivers of Negroes?" he asked.[26] Adams, a future president who never owned slaves, called slavery "a foul contagion in the human character."[27] But even though he despised slavery, he remained silent when scorching words denouncing slavery were written into and then removed from the first preamble to the Constitution, largely because delegates from slaveholding states, including Georgia and South Carolina, threatened to leave the process if the troubling words were left in the text.

Remember, the colonists were proud of having escaped from the tyranny of the king of England; the first version of the preamble reflected that they fully blamed him for having "plundered our seas, ravaged our coasts, burnt our towns, . . . transporting large armies of foreign mercenaries to complete the works of death, desolation, and tyranny."[28] To that list of grievances, Jefferson added that "it was the Christian King of Great Britain who was responsible for the horrors of the slave trade."[29] Jefferson apparently feared that too much opposition to the slave trade would jeopardize the writing and acceptance of the Declaration of Independence, which he was not willing to do, even if he agreed that its presence in the new country was the fault of the king of England.

Neither Adams nor Jefferson signed the Constitution; Jefferson was representing his country in France, and Adams was doing the same in England. But they both knew that slavery was a snag that could not be denied, for there was no greater threat to the reality of a "more perfect union" than the presence of slavery. At the time the Constitution was signed, there were more than 700,000 enslaved Africans, who, notes David McCullough, had "no freedom whatsoever."[30] Slavery existed in every one of the thirteen colonies except for Massachusetts. The southern colonies drove the conversation and debate on slavery, including Maryland, Virginia, and the Carolinas, which collectively accounted for 500,000 of the 700,000 enslaved Africans.

Secularism, Religion, and Slavery

In spite of the founders' adherence to religion and at least the moral precepts taught by Jesus the Christ, the swirling debates were never about the human condition of the enslaved Africans. There was nothing, apparently, that Jesus' teachings could do to sway them; the goal was economic. Enslaved Africans were the necessary tools which helped men and colonies become wealthy. Some saw the seed of capitalism growing with great speed. James Warren, president of the Massachusetts Provincial Congress and a Paymaster General of the Continental Army during the Revolutionary War, was disgusted and disturbed by what he saw. Money was the center of the purpose of the new country, he decided. "Patriotism is ridiculed; integrity and ability are of little consequence."[31] Warren and others believed that the new country was imitating the journey of Rome, a nation which believed in and practiced imperialism. Slavery in the United States would assure that the nation would never be united because the quest for profit would always take precedence over respect for all human beings. Adams agreed. A moral shift had taken place in the country, obvious at the signing of its signature document. The sacredness of a country which vowed to respect the idea of all men being created equal was already compromised, even as the document was signed into perpetuity.

Thus, the country began its journey as a viable but deeply flawed nation. Its Declaration of Independence was signed in 1776, right after the Patriots of the new world defeated the Loyalists of Great Britain. They fought to get rid of their attachment to tyranny, and they won. Shortly thereafter, in 1781, the states of New Hampshire, Massachusetts Bay, Rhode Island, the Providence plantations, Connecticut, New York, New Jersey, Pennsylvania, Delaware, Maryland, Virginia, North Carolina, South Carolina, and Georgia created and signed the Articles of Confederation. It was that document that produced the name that would define the new nation forever after, the United States of America. Vesting the power of government in each individual state, the Articles of Confederation said nothing about slavery: "[E]ach state retains its sovereignty, freedom and independence, and every power, jurisdiction and right, which is not by this confederation expressly delegated to the United States, in Congress assembled,"[32] the document declared. Not until

1787 did delegates of twelve of the states meet in Philadelphia to draft what we now call the Constitution of the United States.

We already have established that the signers were conflicted when it came to agreeing upon who was worthy of American freedom. Even though Paine believed that the new nation "had the power to begin the world over again,"[33] the new beginning was already compromised, the notion of all men being equal severely tainted. Paine and others believed that God—their God—was pleased with the nation that they had created. They believed that their God believed some people to be unworthy of freedom and equality. Meacham says that at the time the Constitution was being created, this nation had no "codified" religious identity. This is an important point because the claim of many is that this nation was founded on Christian principles. At its founding, however, the United States had a relationship with a Muslim nation, Tripoli, and the two nations had forged a treaty recognizing and respecting that religion, which clearly was not Christian. In that treaty, Article II reads, "The government of the United States of America is not in any sense founded on the Christian Religion; as it has in itself no character of enmity against the laws, religion, or tranquility of Mussulmen."[34]

Meacham says that there was never a debate about the principle laid forth in the Treaty of Tripoli (1796), which clearly defined the new nation as "secular, not religious." It is telling that the passion of liberty centered more around new Americans having religious freedom, a way to practice any religion they wanted without interference from or influence by the government. With the Treaty of Tripoli, the new Americans had declared America to be a secular nation. Conflict between Christians and Muslims had existed for a long time, and the new nation clearly wanted none of that.

Even as they shied away from potential conflict with Muslim nations, as well as from any religious sect controlling the citizens through the government, the Americans continued to "use religion of partisan, political ends, to divide voters by painting the opposing candidate as immoral or unfaithful."[35] That was a reality in spite of the fact that nowhere in the Constitution does it say that there should be separation between church and state; that phrase came from a letter written by Thomas Jefferson to the Danbury Baptist Association in Connecticut that was fighting what its members perceived to be the encroachment of the church in their political affairs. In that letter, Jefferson wrote, "I contemplate with sovereign reverence that act of the whole American people which declared that *their* legislature should make no law respecting an establishment of religion, or prohibiting the free exercise thereof, thus building a wall of separation between Church and State."[36]

Religion was a presence; the signers and framers of the Declaration of Independence and the US Constitution alike were conscious of the presence of God, but Jesus the Christ was not so much a presence. The founders held God—or at least the Christian God as defined by the person and presence of Jesus—at bay. Historically, religion had long controlled the state or been intricately involved in the affairs of the state, but scholars, writers, and politicians could not see where the infusion of religion in the affairs of the state had improved the propensity of religious men to treat others equally, as children of God, nor had it created a solid and unshakable foundation of ethics. Religious people picked and chose those to whom they would show mercy or extend the offer of equality. Being aware of God, and even worshiping God, did not guarantee that they would treat other human beings with dignity. God did not force the religious to be concerned about others or care about their well-being. There were a few voices in the new republic that spoke against slavery and injustice meted out to Black people, but too few. The Constitution reflected the general ambiguity about race and slavery that existed in the eighteenth century but which had not begun there; the ambiguity, as we have seen, had begun long before the founders ever took pen to paper.

The Puritans quoted the Bible, and they talked about love as they landed in the new world, but their definition of love seemed to be diametrically opposed to the love described by Jesus. The words in their Bible, or their interpretation of it, were used to justify the genocide of Native Americans, just as their interpretation of the Bible had resulted in the escalation of white supremacy and what the spiritualist Howard Thurman called the "segregated Gospel." Whatever the Christian ethic was meant to be, as established by Jesus the Christ, it had been sorely compromised by the time the United States came into being. Thurman writes, "For a long time, the Christian Church has profoundly compromised with the demands of the Gospel of Jesus Christ, especially with respect to the meaning and practice of love."[37]

Neutralizing the Gospel

A major problem was the way Christianity was constructed around racist and sexist interpretations of the Bible. For hundreds of years, the Bible had been the sacred text of those who called themselves Christian. The name and the life of Jesus were certainly the foundation for the teaching and preaching of the gospel, but as time progressed, the actions of those who described themselves as Christian seemed to ignore the teaching of Jesus. Peter J. Gomes, in *The Scandalous Gospel of Jesus,* writes that "nowhere in the Gospels is there a claim that he came preaching the New Testament, or even Christianity."[38] People favored the Bible over the gospel, wrote Gomes.[39] Gomes further says that "if we look carefully at what constituted [Jesus'] preaching, we might be surprised to find out how much the Gospel is at odds with Christianity."[40] What seemingly happened, perhaps from the time of the Roman Empire and when religious writers like Origen and Tertullian and Athanasius were writing Christian doctrine, is that the teachings of Jesus were made secondary to the needs and teaching of the empire. That which may have been the weapon to neutralize racism—the gospel—was "lost" in the Bible, according to Gomes.[41]

The doctrine of Ham, which had conveniently provided the substance for the belief that Black people were inferior and were pegged by God to be perpetually enslaved, was never far from the consciousness of the people who thrived during this time. The white supremacist interpretation of the Bible came from whites' need to establish themselves as the favored of God, the new Israelites, and the new chosen people. No one would doubt their authority or what they shared as being truth if they pointed to almighty God and God's words, found in the Holy Bible, which were used to bring about conformity to certain social expectations. White people needed Jesus to be white, but existing images did not portray him as such. The Puritans avoided showing images of Jesus and actually destroyed them. His image as a brown man and not an Aryan model would have "challenged the authority of white supremacy" and compromised their capacity to explain how the Son of God would have been a Palestinian Jew.[42] As the image of Jesus began to emerge and become whiter over time, it was easier to push the story of the doctrine of Ham and the theory of Black inferiority. The Bible was neutralized and contaminated as a viable text for proving God's intention of "liberty and justice for all." And the gospel was equally neutralized because the arguments pushing white supremacy ran counter to the words of Jesus, the gospel.

That both the Hebrew Scriptures and the New Testament epistles talked about and seemed to justify slavery added fuel to the white supremacists' argument concerning their theology having been given to them by God. Leading up to the writing of the Constitution, the Puritans and Americans could not have a radical revolutionary like Jesus as the focus of people's religious sensibilities because Jesus was a troubling presence. He troubled the waters of injustice found in the Roman Empire, where he lived. Edward J. Blum and Paul Harvey write that "despite the public dominance of white Protestantism, the America of the founding era was anything but a Jesus nation."[43]

The words of Paul, a wealthy Roman citizen who became Christian, turned out to be the voice of and for white Protestants, for Paul urged slaves to be obedient to their masters, and this became a fundamental text for white Christian belief. The problem, however, was that the theology of Jesus was sidestepped and ignored. By the twentieth century, Jesus' image was more and more becoming that of a white man with Nordic features, including wavy hair and blue eyes. Such depictions made Americans feel justified in their cultural beliefs and practices. But long before the twentieth-century Jesus emerged, the founding fathers were treading the waters of white supremacy as they tried to create a document that would assure all of God's children would be free.

Neither the ignoring of Jesus and his words nor the disregarding of his theology from daily religious life as practiced by white Christians was discussed during the writing of the Constitution. If the founding fathers peripheralized God, they peripheralized Jesus even more. The church of Jesus was morphing from being a "church of virtuous minority" to a "church of an oppressive majority."[44] More than allegiance to religion, the founding fathers wanted Americans to pledge obeisance to the state, a principle supported by Paul. Historians chronicling the dawn of Christianity in the first century interpreted the new Christians' challenge to the state—the Roman government—as heroic. But America's founding fathers, on a quest to become a new nation, did not want their new government to be similarly challenged. Jesus' teachings challenged the precepts of both the religious and world systems of his day (and ours), but the founding fathers, who had deemed their native governments to be at fault, wanted no such defiance directed at the government they were establishing. The Bible helped religious leaders keep the people in line, honoring the government over any principles of Jesus that might have encouraged rebellion. Religious people, that is, people who belonged to a church and called themselves Christian, were expected to become enablers and supporters of the government, walking not ahead or behind it but alongside it. In so doing, the Bible, already compromised, lost whatever power it might have had to be an effective tool to fight racism.

Movement from Jesus to the State

It is important to state that at this point, whiteness mattered. The men who framed the Constitution believed in whiteness as much as they believed in the inferiority of Black people. By the time they were meeting to frame the Constitution, the beliefs that Black people were inherently lazy (though they worked in the hot sun from dawn to dusk), were stupid (though they learned to read and write mostly on their own in spite of the barriers put before them), and were highly sexed and dangerous (though Black women were consistently raped by white men) were more or less fixed. Black people had been dehumanized and criminalized, actions which helped many whites justify their treatment of their enslaved Africans and Black people in general.

Malcomson states that Jefferson, a key member of the team that wrote both the Declaration and the Constitution, "despised" Blacks and wanted as few immigrants as possible to come to the United States. He said that immigrants would bring "the principles of governments they leave. . . . These principles, with their language, they will transmit to their children. In proportion to their numbers, they will share with us in legislation. They will infuse into it their spirits, warp and bias its directions, and render it a heterogeneous, distracted mass."[45] Blacks being in the mix of American society as full-fledged human beings distorted the whiteness that Jefferson and others cherished so much.

Malcomson said there were three things which defined the United States as a nation, a definition which the presence of Blacks compromised:

> the best of Englishness . . . Americans' miraculous combining, alone in the universe, of this Englishness with natural right and reason . . . . [and] whiteness, but therein lies a difficulty: not all whites are American, . . . when considering European immigrants, those immigrants were not white . . . [b]ut when considering Blacks, the prospective replacements for slaves are identified as white, and only as white. In a real sense, the Europeans become white in America.[46]

"[I]f all Blacks were 'removed beyond the reach of mixture,' as Jefferson put it, white Americans might cease to be white. America could then become its higher self, the one for which men had so recently fought and died."[47]

By the time the men gathered to write our sacred Constitution, the problem, according to Malcomson, was not slavery; instead, it was "a white way of thinking from which they felt unable to extricate themselves or their country." Malcomson says they "desperately wanted to start over with a new set of principles, but they couldn't imagine starting over with a population of free Blacks."[48]

The Bible was no help to them in addressing their deep-seated idolization of whiteness and the way it made them think. The problem was not so much the Bible itself but was rather the way it had been used to support a specific ideology. If the religion of Jesus had been compromised, it was because those who read the Bible had felt free to ignore many of the words of Jesus. The Bible became a text to be used to form and protect Protestantism, which was called Christianity but which was a religion without much Jesus in it. Religion itself became truncated. American Protestantism moved away from Jesus and toward the state. Its goal was the accumulation and maintenance of power. With the highest sacred document rendered impotent in the face of white supremacist ideology, there was no way the Constitution was going to be anything more than a document tainted by white supremacy, written to protect white people, especially white men, at all cost.

Epigraphs

James H. Cone, *The Cross and the Lynching Tree* (Maryknoll, NY: Orbis, 2011), xiii.

Scott Malcomson, *One Drop of Blood: The American Misadventure of Race* (New York: Farrar Straus Giroux, 2000), 108.

NOTES

1. Jon Meacham, *American Gospel: God, the Founding Fathers, and the Making of a Nation* (New York: Random House, 2007), 84.
2. Meacham, 85.
3. Meacham, 87.
4. Meacham, 90.
5. Meacham, 94.
6. Meacham, 98.
7. Meacham, 99.
8. Meacham.
9. Reinhold D. Niebuhr, *The Irony of American History* (Chicago: University of Chicago Press, 1952), 25.
10. Niebuhr.
11. Scott Malcomson, *One Drop of Blood: The American Misadventure of Race* (New York: Farrar Straus Giroux, 2000), 172.
12. Malcomson, 173.
13. This was the language used in laws passed in South Carolina in the late 1700s. Also see Malcomson, 175.
14. Malcomson.
15. Malcomson, 176.
16. Malcomson, 177.
17. Malcomson.
18. Malcomson. Also see Leslie Patrick, "African American and Civil Rights in Pennsylvania," *Pennsylvania Heritage* (Spring 2010), http://www.phmc.state.pa.us /portal/communities/pa-heritage/african-americans-civil-rights-pennsylvania.html, 1.
19. Patrick.
20. Patrick.
21. "A New Version of the Lord's Prayer," Founders Online, https://founders .archives.gov/documents/Franklin/01-15-02-0170.
22. "A New Version of the Lord's Prayer."
23. Malcomson, 178.
24. Malcomson, 179.
25. "How Many of the Signers of the Declaration of Independence Owned Slaves?", http://www.mrheintz.com/how-many-signers-of-the-declaration-of-inde pendence-owned-slaves.html. Of the signers listed, only Thomas Paine and John Adams never owned slaves.
26. David McCullough, *John Adams* (New York: Simon & Schuster, 2001), 133.

27. McCullough, 134.

28. McCullough, 131.

29. McCullough.

30. McCullough, 398.

31. McCullough.

32. History.com editors, "Articles of Confederation," October 27, 2009, updated September 27, 2019, History, https://www.history.com/topics/early-us/articles-of-confederation.

33. Meacham, 103.

34. Meacham.

35. Meacham, 104.

36. Meacham, 105.

37. Howard Thurman, *The Luminous Darkness: A Personal Interpretation of the Anatomy of Segregation and the Ground of Hope* (reprint; Richmond: Friends United Press, 1980–1981), 3.

38. Peter Gomes, *The Scandalous Gospel of Jesus: What's So Good about the Good News?* (New York: HarperCollins, 2007), 11.

39. Gomes.

40. Gomes, 20.

41. Gomes.

42. Edward J. Blum and Paul Harvey, *The Color of Christ* (Chapel Hill: University of North Carolina Press, 2012), 8.

43. Blum and Harvey.

44. Gomes, 40.

45. Malcomson, 182.

46. Malcomson.

47. Malcomson, 183.

48. Malcomson, 184.

7
Slavery, Capitalism, and the American Way

Christianity and the "political creed of Americans" de-mand the removal of this "inconsistency from the land of liberty." —Benjamin Franklin

After the American Revolution—which seemed at the time to portend slavery's imminent demise—a meta-static transformation and growth of slavery's giant body had begun instead. —Edward E. Baptist

The problems that would plague America were never just about slavery but were always about the uncomfortable need this country had for these enslaved human beings who would build their economy. It was enslaved Africans who made America the capitalistic giant it eventually became.

In 1777, the year after the Revolutionary War was won and the Declaration of Independence signed, men gathered in York, Pennsylvania, to draft the Articles of Confederation, the first written constitution of the United States. It was in this document that the new nation, which consisted of thirteen states, was first called the United States of America, and the articles were signed by some men who had also signed the Declaration of Independence, including Benjamin Franklin. The Articles of Confederation made no mention of slavery, but the architects of the new country were uncomfortable, for the irony of their working to create a country which valued liberty even as they supported slavery was ever in their consciousnesses.

The nation was growing rapidly, with states having the power to run their own affairs somewhat independently from the federal government. That posed a problem for the federal government because it did not have the power to tax the states for the revenue to accommodate the needs of the new nation. The labor of Black people was driving the economy; at the time the Declaration of Independence was written, more than 500,000 Africans were enslaved. White Americans were wrestling with what to do with these creatures who were at once valuable for their labor but problematic because they were considered to be so inferior to white people. While white people in the North and the South wrestled, the nature and intensity of the struggle was more pronounced in the South, where slave labor was key for the sustenance and growth of the agrarian economy in which these enslaved individuals did what few white men would do—and they did it for free. What would happen if they were free? The concern was that they would compete with whites for jobs and "everything else"[1] That was not an acceptable option.

Even as the Articles of Confederation were being written and thought moved toward changing those articles into what would become the final version of the United States Constitution, there evolved the schizoid thinking in many white people who realized the economic worth of Black people but who did not like their presence in "their" country. Conversations about colonizing Africans back to Africa were widespread and popular. Scott Malcomson says that "the earliest proposal for colonizing Blacks had appeared in a Philadelphia paper, from the pen of an abolitionist, in 1768, but the real center of colonization sentiment was in Virginia, the cradle of both slavery and freedom."[2] Notes Malcomson: "In 1777, a proposed emancipation bill suggested that freed Blacks be sent to some other locales where they might become truly free and independent, and that the same number of white people be imported to take their place. One of the three signers of this bill was Thomas Jefferson."[3]

At the same time that the issue of getting rid of America's Blacks was on the minds of many who gathered to write the Constitution, so was the myth of the purity and innocence of the new nation. America was "exceptional, more moral than any other nation," many whites believed. They could see but could not figure out how to rectify the contradiction between what they were feeling and what they were doing, or wanted to do, and there was not enough commitment to principles of justice found in the Bible—specifically in the words of Jesus—to help them recognize or make them care about the ominous table they were setting for what would become America's legacy. Years later, Gunnar Myrdal would write that "there is a Negro problem" in the United States:

> To the great majority of white Americans, the Negro problem
> has distinctly negative connotations. It suggests something
> difficult to settle and equally difficult to leave alone. It is
> embarrassing. It makes for moral uneasiness. The very presence
> of the Negro in America, his fate in this country through slavery,
> Civil War and Reconstruction, his recent career and his present
> status, . . . in fact his entire biological, historical and social
> existence as a participant American represent to the ordinary
> white man in the North as well as in the South an anomaly in
> the very structure of American society.[4]

Myrdal wrote in the twentieth century what the Rev. Dr. William Barber has repeated in this century, that is, that the "American Negro problem is a problem in the heart of the American."[5] Myrdal said that the racist belief system of America is deeply ingrained and has been since the founding of the nation, and he called it the "American dilemma," which is

> the ever-raging conflict between, on the one hand, the
> valuations preserved on the general plane which we shall call
> the "American Creed," where the American thinks, talks and acts
> under the influence of high national and Christian precepts, and,
> on the other hand, the valuations on specific plans of individual
> and group living, where personal and local interests: economic,
> social, and sexual jealousies, considerations of community
> prestige and conformity, group prejudice against particular
> persons or types of people, and all sorts of miscellaneous wants,
> impulses and habits dominate his outlook.[6]

The American mind was at once forming and fighting against itself. While the goal was to be more moral and less tyrannical than any nation before it, the importance of whiteness, coupled with the need for the labor of the Blacks they so detested (yet depended upon to enable them to shape America into a new empire) made the American mind both morally weak and able to excuse tyrannical behavior. Certainly, economics was a major part of the reason that the founders gathered to draft the final version of the Constitution. Remember, slave labor had been key in pushing the South to economic soundness. As long as the agrarian South was the driver of American economic growth, the North was reluctant to acquiesce to the South's demand for slavery to be written into the Constitution. When the cotton gin was invented, however, it brought the North into the economic machine of American society, and neither the North nor the South seemed much concerned about ending slavery or with the lingering consequences of their having dehumanized Americans of African descent.

Instead, both the North and the South continued to use enslaved Africans to do the work that would make them and this country wealthy. It is not clear that they had even thought or strategized about what they would do, and how they would make their economy continue to grow, if they had succeeded in sending the Africans to Africa. The Africans could withstand the brutal heat and sun of the South as they worked the fields and would in time be considered to be disposable labor as they worked in the factories of the North. Their lives were not valued, but their labor was highly valued and needed.

In the Black church, which came about largely as a revolt against the dehumanization of Black people even in church, the voices and the spirit of Black people began to surface in new ways. They heard the conversation about being sent back to a continent many of them by this time had never known, and though some Blacks flirted with and liked the idea, many of them—perhaps the majority—did not. This was their land. They had literally poured blood, sweat, and tears into rich Southern soil. They had been robbed of their homes; they had suffered the pain of being separated from their families; they had learned how to cope in a country whose notion of God was foreign to them but where their notion of God saved them. They had borne the whip thrown about by white supremacy and survived. They had listened to the rhetoric of white Americans who fought for freedom and liberation from Great Britain and had internalized it as their own. They had ignored the voices of whites who denounced them when they sought to escape slavery. There was no man who was greater than God, and no purpose of God greater than for all whom God created to be free.

When Gabriel Prosser organized a slave revolt in 1800, he and the other slaves were unfazed by critical and frightened whites, such as the contributor to a Virginia newspaper who wrote, "Liberty and equality have brought this evil upon us. A doctrine which, however intelligible and admissible, in a land of freemen, is not only unintelligible and inadmissible, but dangerous and extremely wicked in this country, where every white man is a master and every Black man is a slave."[7] Because whites believed God sanctioned such thinking, and their God seemed to encourage them to find a way to rid America of Blacks by sending them back to Africa, Black people's God of the Hebrew Scriptures encouraged them to lean on God and desired the enslaved Africans to be free in America, not in Africa.

Many whites who may have been considered to be progressive in the area of race did not realize their deeply embedded racist thinking and attitudes. Rev. Robert Finley, a white preacher who in the 1800s considered himself to be a friend of Black people, thoroughly believed in the rightness of colonizing Black people. He believed that "it would benefit America by helping the country to be cleared of free Blacks and those freed slaves who were no longer needed or wanted."[8] He believed and proclaimed publicly that "having free Blacks in the neighborhood was unfavorable to our industry and morals, and might lead to 'intermixture.'"[9] While he believed that racial slavery was "the great violation of the laws of nature,"[10] he also believed that Africans and African Americans who had had the benefit of living in America could improve the lives of Africans who had never left the motherland and who thus had not been as blessed as Americanized Blacks. By 1820, the Constitution had been signed by its framers, including Thomas Jefferson, James Madison, James Monroe, and Samuel Adams.[11] These founding fathers were among other prominent people in American society who agreed that ridding the country of Blacks was a good idea as a principle of government, but they could not escape their ambiguity about how the enslavement of human beings could be right in the eyes of God and in the eyes of everyone who professed belief in God.

The white way of thinking was veering further and further away from any possibility of embracing the idea of freedom and equality for Black people. White people recoiled from and rejected even the idea that they might be considered to be racist. They thought, correctly, that their way of thinking did not reflect positively on them, but they had also been taught that slavery was the will of God. Blame for the situation was deflected. Jefferson, ever the wordsmith, worked to absolve whites of any guilt or discomfort about the way they thought when he said that "slavery and the presence of Blacks in America was not their fault but was, instead, due to the colonialist greed of the government of Great Britain." He said that white people, including slave owners, were "blameless" and that once the Blacks were removed from America, the nation could live up to its intended greatness.[12]

But slavery was good for building the American economy. While not wanting to use the words "slave" or "slavery" in the Constitution, it was clear that the framers approved of slavery for its economic value, so the document was written so that "the upper and lower South would get to expand slavery through both the Atlantic slave trade and the internal trade."[13] Also, "the Northeast would earn profits by transporting the commodities generated by slavery's growth."[14] Keeping slavery was a way to insure that there would be "a more perfect union," says Edward Baptist in *The Half Has Never Been Told*. Its expansion "helped unify the government and a stronger economy."[15]

That slavery was built into the Constitution for reasons not least of which was economic expedience caused Frederick Douglass later to condemn the Constitution and the United States as "a corrupted, wholly complicit slave society."[16] This was a country Douglass said he "could not love," and said, "I desire to see its overthrow as speedily as possible and its Constitution shivered in a thousand fragments."[17] Douglass saw the Constitution as a flawed document that was "at war with itself" and that was written from the perspective of pro-slavery men.[18] He was aware of the economic reasons for the nation wanting to hold onto slavery, but he decried the base moral and religious hypocrisy he saw in the document. He realized that the rights alluded to in the Declaration of Independence referred to the natural rights of human beings, and he realized that in the minds of those who wrote and supported that document, Blacks were not considered human. He based his outrage, he said, on "two great Scriptures: the Constitution and the

Bible," and demanded that "the nation's hypocrisy be exposed."[19] Douglass was not only seeing but also exposing the drastically different ways white and Black people of this nation thought and the critically different ways in which they believed in, related to, and called on God.

The Constitution and Protection of Economic Interests

In spite of 500,000 enslaved Africans (out of a total population of 2.5 million) working the fields and building the economy, by the time the framers met, the nation was experiencing economic struggles.[20] The United States was in debt, so part of the argument during the writing of the Constitution was how America's captives would be considered in the apportionment of tax revenue. While some framers argued that slavery should be abolished, others vehemently disagreed. The number of legislators in the House of Representatives was to be based on population, but what about the enslaved Africans? Should they be counted, too?

At the same time that the conversation about how to get rid of the enslaved souls by colonizing them was taking place outside of the convention, the conversation inside the sweltering room was whether and how to keep them for the sake of the economy. The South had the most to lose because its economy had been built on the backs and the labor of enslaved Africans. Therefore, the Southern representatives were not willing to even consider giving up their source of profit. Some of the framers believed slavery should be abolished, but it was clear after extended arguments that that was not going to be, so they figured out how to write slavery into the Constitution without ever using the word "slavery."

Another issue was slave trading, an additional cash cow for the South, which in the new, federally run government, would become an economic boon for the entire nation. While some argued that the slave trading business should stop, delegates from the states of Georgia, North Carolina, and South Carolina threatened to leave the convention if slave trading was discontinued. A compromise was reached when the framers said that slave trading should end, but not until 1800, and in Article 1, Section 2, Clause 3 of the Constitution, they inserted the three-fifths compromise:

> Representatives and direct Taxes shall be apportioned
> among the several States which may be included within this
> Union, according to their respective Numbers, which shall be
> determined by adding to the whole number of (free) Persons,
> including those bound to Service for a Term of Years and
> excluding Indians not taxed, three fifths of all other persons.

Slavery, probably more because of its economic importance than because of rabid racism of the framers, was always in the center of how this nation was formed. Though he owned plenty of slaves, Jefferson complained that "slavery turned whites into despots."[21] Oliver Edwards, one of the framers who would later become a chief justice of the United States Supreme Court, was clearly irritated by all of the attention given to the issue of freeing the slaves. He said, "Let the economic interests of white Americans dictate whether the Atlantic slave trade should be closed, . . . and as slaves multiply so fast in Virginia and Maryland that it is cheaper to raise them than import them, let us not intermeddle with internal forced migrations."[22]

There was no mention of the brutality and cruelty of the slave trade business because forming the nation was about money and the battle to extricate themselves from what they believed was the tyranny of British rule. The founders apparently did not think about the tyranny they were now creating in their new national home, which would only grow worse as time went on. Religious beliefs and principles had little to no place in these discussions, either. John Rutledge, another framer who also went on to become a chief justice of the nation's high court, dismissed the religious sniveling of a few as he declared, "Religion and humanity have nothing to do with this question . . . interest alone is the governing principles with nations."[23]

The framers also were aware that criticism about slavery was increasing, and they wanted to make sure their economic interests were protected by law, so they wrote into the Constitution a provision which guaranteed that enslaved Africans would be forever ensnared in the web of slave society. In Article 4, Section 2, Clause 3, they wrote:

No Person held to Service or Labour in one State, under the
Laws thereof, escaping into another, shall, in Consequence of
any Law or Regulation therein, be discharged from such Service
or Labour, but shall be delivered up on Claim of the Party to
whom such Service or Labour may be due.

The framers worked hard to make the new government a democratic republic, meaning that the power of the government resided
in the people and that the country would have an elected leader
rather than a monarch. It is fair to say that they were aware of
how other republics had faltered and failed, falling too often into
the hands of a dictator or despot, so they wanted to make sure that
the government they created would prevent that from ever happening in the United States. They cared about the rights of free white
men whom they deemed entitled to rule over enslaved Africans and
women, but this document of "we the people" was clearly tainted
by white supremacist ideology which spawned and supported both
racism and sexism.

The framers protected the national economic interests which
were the direct result of slave labor, but they also left the door open
for states to do what they wanted concerning slavery. In 1793,
Congress, empowered by the Constitution, passed the first Fugitive Slave Act, which authorized local governments to seize escaped
slaves and return them to their owners. Furthermore, a law was
enacted to impose a fine on anyone who helped the escapees in their
quest for freedom.

The 1793 law was not strong enough for Southern slave holders, however, so in 1850, the second or revised Fugitive Slave Act
was passed. Part of the Compromise of 1850, this law forced citizens to assist in the capture of runaways and denied enslaved Africans the right to a jury trial. It also increased the fine levied against
people who helped slaves escape and made it possible for them to
face prison time. The 1850 act empowered federal deputies to be
involved in the capture of runaways and paid them for returning
slaves to their owners. The Constitution opened the door for these
acts to be passed. Though both of them were repealed in 1864,
the pathway for their passage in the first place was created by the

framers who had made provisions in America's sacred document for the capture and return of enslaved Africans.

If America was about pluralism, the thoughts, ideas, struggles, and words of the framers made it clear that pluralism was about religious freedom, not racial freedom and dignity. Patrick Henry remarked that it was "little surprising that Christianity, whose chief excellence consists in softening the human heart, in cherishing & improving its finer feelings should encourage a practice so totally repugnant to the first impression of right & wrong."[24]

Some wondered, as Meacham recounts, how "so many avowedly religious people choose to live in a country that allowed slavery?"[25] Perhaps it was because the framers, who believed in Reason and in God as "Providence," were not inclined to believe in and embrace Jesus as the Son of God, a deity worthy of respect and worship. Some of the framers and observers of what was going on were angry and uneasy. Some Americans, says Meacham, "objected to the Godlessness of what the scholars Isaac Kramick and R. Laurence Moore called 'the Godless Constitution.'"[26] It is striking that while the framers believed that God governed the affairs of people and had led them to the point of new nationhood, they yet made no mention of God in the Constitution as they sought to justify the use of and brutality against human beings for economic growth. For the millions who would look to this document for direction, the founders included no moral voice to express how Jesus would view the heinous mindset called white supremacy.

Longing for a God Who Is Near

The die was cast for the growth of America's troubling, racist "white way of thinking." Many years later, essayist James Baldwin would express what could well have been the thoughts of many Blacks during the framing of the Constitution. The Anglo God had been carefully and dutifully established. Who could or would argue with that? The Anglo God had given the new Americans the canvas on which to print their sacred document, and there would be no changing it. Baldwin wrote of this fact of American life in 1962: "I had realized that the Bible had been written by white men. I knew that, according to many Christians, I was a descendant of Ham, who had been cursed and that I was therefore predestined to be a slave."[27]

The whiteness of the world, written into the Constitution and preached in white churches, was a source of pain, confusion, and for some Blacks a reason to reject the white God. The love of the white God was sullied by white supremacist thinking. Baldwin wrote of the despair felt when Black people realized that not even God was on their side, according to the way white people taught about God: "If one despairs—as who has not—of human love, God's love alone is left. But God—and I felt this even then, so long ago on that tremendous floor, unwillingly—is white. And if His love was so great, and if He loved all His children, why were we, the Blacks, cast down so far?"[28]

During the slavery days of America's formation, some Blacks, including Denmark Vesey and Gabriel Prosser, fought being subsumed by slavery and by the notion that their blackness made them capable only of being slaves. But other Blacks were subsumed and compromised in terms of their selfhood; they bought the lessons taught that the only way to be close to God was to follow the way of the Anglo God. Rev. Alexander Crummell, a Black man, was a great supporter of the idea of colonizing Black people, and he believed in the "moral advance of Christian civilization" that Black people needed to embrace and accept. He believed in the rightness of Christianity as taught by white people. He believed that Africans "had no past worthy speaking of, just vista upon vista of the deepest darkness." He said, "So far as Western Africa is concerned, there is no history. The long, long centuries of human existence, there, give us no intelligent disclosures."[29] He believed that Black people could be saved by and through the Anglo-Saxon race and said they should bear responsibility "for saving Africa."[30]

Crummell, no doubt, would have rejected the observations of Baldwin, who understood how the country's laws were affecting Black people, and how God was the supposed God of all. Baldwin's twentieth-century use of the word "Christian" is radically different from Crummell's use of it in the nineteenth century. For Crummell, Christianity had been defined by whites who demoted Jesus almost to the status of advisor. According to their definition, Providence, the word used by many whites to describe God, was the head of all that lived; God had caused and created slavery and ordained it; and God had decided that Black people were the least of all peoples created. The Christianity of which Baldwin writes, however, is one in which Jesus is central to all that is said or done.

Black people had been moving toward Jesus for a long time. For them, this transcendent God of which white people spoke was too far away to hear their cries or to be concerned about their situation. They did not need a faraway God; rather, they needed a God who could and would walk with them under the blazing sun, who would be with them while they endured the brutality of slavery; they needed a nearby God as they screamed in agony as their children or spouses were ripped out of their lives. Black people needed a God they could call by God's first name, a God who would be there and hear the cries of women being raped by white masters, a God who would give comfort as some jeopardized their lives in order to escape in search of freedom. The Anglo God would not do it; the Anglo God was much like the white people who tormented them. Black Christians were people who called on the name of Jesus and viewed their faith and lives through a Christological lens as opposed to a cultural and ideological lens posing as the theology of righteousness. Baldwin wrote:

> White Christians have . . . forgotten several elementary
> historical details. They have forgotten that the religion that is
> now identified with their virtue and their power—"God is on
> our side," . . . came out of a rocky piece of ground in what is
> now known as the Middle East before color was invented, and
> that in order for the Christian church to be established, Christ
> had to be put to death, by Rome, and that the real architect
> of the Christian church was not the disreputable sun-baked
> Hebrew who gave it his name but the mercilessly fanatical and
> self-righteous St. Paul. . . . When the white man came to Africa,
> the white man had the Bible and the African had the land, but
> now it is the white man who is being reluctantly and bloodily
> separated from the land and the African who is still attempting
> to digest, or vomit up the Bible. . . . The struggle . . . [involves]
> the historical role of Christianity in the realm of power—that
> is, politics—and in the realm of morals. In the realm of power,
> Christianity has operated with an unmitigated arrogance and

cruelty . . . since a religion ordinarily imposes on those who have discovered the true faith the spiritual duty of liberating the infidels.[31]

Baldwin makes the critical observation that the religion of the Anglo God was based on the words of Paul and not on the words and teaching of Jesus the Christ, and that displacement had its roots in the Roman Empire as people tried to define who Jesus was and what Jesus required. It was there, as well, that Christianity was made the religion of the state, which forever compromised its allegiance to practicing what Jesus taught.

Making Christianity the Religion of the State

The year was 325 CE, and people who had aligned themselves with the teachings of Jesus the Christ had been brutalized for two hundred years. It was time for something to change, for this religion to be codified and standardized. Bishops from all over the eastern half of the Roman Empire gathered at Nicea to figure out, once and for all, who Jesus was.

During his time on earth Jesus was a polarizing and political presence. He challenged both the religious establishment and the government, and officials of both systems hated him for it. As a Palestinian Jew who had been born on the wrong side of the tracks, Jesus knew oppression. He knew what it felt like to be marginalized and exploited because of one's status in society. The Roman Empire was just that, an empire intent on seizing more power and one whose rulers sought to shut down any and everyone who opposed them. Those who forged ahead in their criticism against the government knew that they faced the most extreme and brutal of punishments—crucifixion—the punishment of choice for the worst offenders, a group to which political activists belonged. Crucifixion tended to be reserved for "slaves, disgraced soldiers, Christians and foreigners."[32] It was an act of terror, done to send a message of warning to those who believed it was their duty to change the corruption in the government that was causing so many people to suffer economically, politically, and socially. The historian Tacitus observed that the protectors of the Roman government were cruel beyond words:

> [We] have sought in vain to escape [the Romans'] oppression by obedience and submissiveness. [They are the plunderers of the world. . . . If the enemy is rich, they are rapacious, if poor, they lust for dominion. Not East, not West has satiated them. . . . They rob, butcher, plunder and call it "empire," and where they make a desolation, they call it "peace."[33]

There was no peace, and empires before the Roman Empire had oppressed others, as well, including the Assyrians, Babylonians, and Persians. Jesus and those who followed him would have known the risk—and the horror—of crucifixion. It was a slow, painful death, meant to be that way. Sometimes the beams were hung along main thoroughfares so that people engaged in the duties of daily life could be reminded of what would happen to them if they dared challenge the power system. They would not have been able to escape from the shrieks of pain coming from the victims. The ultimate cause of death for victims was usually asphyxia, caused by the weight of the body being pulled by gravity onto the lungs of the victim, making it impossible to breathe. Sometimes, those who had died were left on the beams for a time so that people traveling those roads would be met with the smell of death. Jesus knew the kind of death to which he would be subjected.

Crucifixion remained the punishment of choice for those the government considered to be rabble rousers until the fourth century CE, when Constantine outlawed it. He had seen the suffering of those who called themselves Christian. Jesus had not made their decision to follow him easy; even the Lord's Prayer was filled with messages that would have enraged the emperor.[34]

The squabble and confusion about who Jesus really was began during his earthly ministry (Matthew 16:13-20) and intensified after his crucifixion. People were confused. They had lifted him up as the Son of God, but if he had been the Son of God, how is it that he could have been killed by mortal men, and in such a disgraceful way? Only the worst criminals were crucified. Early believers needed for Jesus to be above mere humanness. Even as depictions of him began to emerge, artists created him to be a royal figure (making him white came later). If he was the "King of the Jews," and if he was the Son of God, he needed to look the part, and he had to be strong, like a warrior or a soldier. The crucifixion threw them into a quandary.

Believers began to try to make sense out of their confusion, and Obery Hendricks says that they "resolved their struggle by concluding that Jesus was not a being of flesh and blood at all. They came to believe that the Jesus upon whom their faith was built was a spirit only."[35] Hendricks continues, "As for his bodily form, they argued that because Jesus was a spirit, his body was simply an illusion that *seemed* to have materiality, shape and form. And, they continued, if Jesus only *seemed* to have had a material body, then he could not have been crucified—because there would have been no body to crucify!"[36]

The denial of Jesus' physical body came to be known as Docetism and was just one of the sources of conflict about Jesus that extended well into modern history. While Docetism caused some to wonder about the veracity of the crucifixion and the subsequent resurrection of Jesus that assured the salvation of all who believed, the pungency of Jesus' life, message, death, and resurrection was diluted by the controversy. The whole purpose of Jesus' life—to challenge the kingdom of Caesar and to make known to people that the kingdom of God mattered most—became the object of discussion and debate, and finally the reason for him to be peripheralized. Jesus preached that we should seek to make the kingdom of God "on earth as it is in heaven." That was not the desire of the Roman Empire; in fact, it was seen as a direct challenge to the power of the empire.

Enter Constantine, who believed that intervention by Jesus the Christ had resulted in his own major military victory. Because of that, the emperor decided to embrace Christianity, which up to this point was still the religion of creation or the religion of Jesus. He was so elated because of his victory, and so sure that it was Jesus who had brought him to that victory, that he reversed an edict passed in 303 CE which had criminalized the practice of Christianity. He began to notice in a different way the fighting among Christians that was commonplace and decided that he would do something about it. To Constantine, Christianity was about military power, not the building of community for the common good. He displaced God and Jesus as the heads of Christianity and made himself the head of what was now becoming the state religion of

Rome. There would be no kingdom of God on earth, the words of the Lord's Prayer notwithstanding. Hendricks says, "When Constantine converted to the faith, he also converted the faith to Constantine."[37] He then hand-picked clergy who would most reflect his belief about God (and Jesus) and the role of religion in the state.

The bishops argued. Like some of those who wrote the Constitution, they wrestled about who Jesus was. The council had been convened partly because there had been so much disagreement about Jesus; Arianism was a heresy that said Jesus existed but that he was "only a creature and not a deity."[38] They finally decided that Jesus "was from the substance of the Father, God from God, Light from Light, Very God from Very God, begotten, not made, of the same substance with the Father."[39]

The arguments for and against the deity of Jesus had been made, but importantly, the conflict about Jesus' divinity had lasting effects which were carried down through history. Jesus was a presence, but he was not *the* presence that would compel people to embrace his message of every person being equal in the eyes of God and worthy of dignity. That part of Jesus was comfortably set aside, the complications, implications, and results of which we are still seeing and experiencing. The ambiguity about Jesus' divinity may have figured prominently in the ability of the founding fathers to ignore him as they constructed a government designed to build wealth on the backs of enslaved human beings, and protect that goal at all costs.

Religion as a Tool of the State

The American way as mapped out by the framers at the Constitutional Convention was an extension of Constantine, who made religion a tool of the state and expected it to help in the building of the state. Constantine had been touched by his encounter with Jesus, but then he seemingly worked to put Jesus in his rightful place, which was behind the needs, purposes, and demands of the state. Similarly, the framers felt that nothing should impede the development of the new country because they were convinced that God had put them in place and ordained their methods of making the nation, including the annihilation of the Native American population and the enslavement of people of African descent. They had been called to make the new world "God's American Israel." As long as they stayed the course that they believed in their hearts that God had charted, America would be as it was called to be. White men would make America what it should be, a free nation for white people, and God was on their side.

To this day, it is the height of insult in this country to say that anything or anyone is racist, but the fact of the matter is that white supremacy, racism, and slavery are in the DNA of America's Constitution. In spite of the preamble's magnificent words, promising that the new country would "establish justice, insure domestic tranquility, provide for the common defence, and promote the general welfare," it remains true that "we the people" was a disingenuous phrase from the beginning because, as we have stated, that category was never intended to include Black people. The Constitution was flawed from the beginning. There would be no universal, no ubiquitous equality of people in this country. Even though the framers recognized the paradox of establishing a free country while enslaving an entire group of people, and some did not want their names associated with slavery though they were inclined to protect the institution because of its economic value, especially in the South they moved forward to create the paradoxical document. In an article which appears on the website for the James Madison Montpelier Center, the authors write that the founders "compromised their morals" in putting together the Constitution—bowing to slaveholders "in the name of economics."[40] They were careful not to write the words or include the words "slavery" and "slave" in the final document; John Quincy Adams called this a "careful omission, fig leaves under which the parts of the body politic are decently concealed."[41]

In spite of that omission, there were three clauses concerning slavery that did make it into the final document. The three-fifths clause, quoted above, made it possible for slaveholding states to count their slaves to boost their population numbers, which meant that states with large numbers of enslaved persons "ended up with more power in both Congress and on the US Supreme Court—thereby undercutting the power of the anti-slavery states."[42] Contrary to what most of us have been taught, the South did not particularly want the three-fifths designation for enslaved persons; instead, they wanted them to be counted fully to give the South more power in

Congress. However, a full count did not mean that the slaves would be granted full citizenship or the right to vote.

The second problematic clause in the Constitution is found in Article 1, Section 9, Clause 1, which reads:

> The Migration or Importation of such Persons as any of the States now existing shall think proper to admit, shall not be prohibited by the Congress prior to the Year one thousand eight hundred and eight, but a Tax or duty may be imposed on such Importation, not exceeding ten dollars for each Person.

This measure permitted the states to have twenty years of freedom to import Africans for the purpose of enslaving them; The states wanted that permission before the international slave trade was abolished. This so-called importation clause allowed a maximum $10 tax on each enslaved African, although it was never collected because some of the framers objected. They believed that imposing this tax would "acknowledge slaves as property," which they disliked; others "saw the tax as anti-slavery because it could be construed as penalizing importation."[43]

As discussed earlier, the fugitive slave clause, found in Article 4, Section 2, Clause 3, posed yet another weakness in the document. Because it obligates law enforcement to pursue fugitive slaves, it "implicates and involves the federal government and its officers in the active protection of people as property."[44]

Thus, from its inception, the Constitution protected the institution of slavery because the founders were deeply invested in building the economy of the country. Enslaved Black people were necessary. People knew it and felt the contradiction, but the institution of slavery was too much a part of what and who America was to correct the contradiction and end slavery. This contradiction was forever front and center in the evaluation and contemplation of American values. What were they, really? When Baptist minister Frances Bellamy was assigned the task of writing the Pledge of Allegiance in 1892, he wrestled with what his country stood for. The Civil War had come and gone, and Black people, though technically freed by the Emancipation Proclamation, were still not fully free. The fire and fury of dismantling Reconstruction was alive and responsible for helping to burn Blacks' hopes of becoming fully free in this country. Bellamy, it seems, wanted the words of the Constitution to be true, so he wrote, "I pledge allegiance to my flag—and to the Republic for which it stands—one Nation, indivisible with liberty and justice for all."[45] Because Bellamy was aware of the contradictions in the nation, his words seemed to indicate the longing he and others had for the Constitution to live up to its words. (The words "under God" were not added until 1954, by President Dwight Eisenhower.)

After the Civil War, the so-called Reconstruction Amendments—the Thirteenth, Fourteenth, and Fifteenth—were added. The Thirteenth Amendment officially abolished slavery in all states, "except as a punishment for crime whereof the party shall have been duly convicted." Because of the determination of Southern whites to maintain their source of cheap labor, Black people were arrested for trivial offenses, thereby making them criminals and eligible to be re-enslaved by individuals and corporations. The convict leasing program, which provided prisoner labor to private parties, such as plantation owners and corporations, was a scourge to the notion of freedom for Black people. The Thirteenth Amendment replaced the fugitive slave clause, which no longer served a purpose due to the abolition of slavery. However, many whites continued to be sympathetic to the belief in the rightness of Black servitude, and they continued to harass Black people.

The Fourteenth Amendment guaranteed the same rights to all male citizens and counted every citizen as a single individual. All persons born in the United States were citizens, this amendment held, and no state was allowed to "deprive any person of life, liberty, or property without due process of law"; nor was any state allowed to "deny to any person within its jurisdiction the equal protection of the laws." This amendment was regularly violated and ignored, however, since Black people were deprived due process and equal protection in both Northern and Southern states.

Finally, the Fifteenth Amendment, which was passed in February of 1870, made it illegal to deny any citizen the right to vote. Specifically, this amendment said, "The right of citizens of the United States to vote shall not be denied or abridged by the United States or by any state on account of race, color, or previous condition of servitude." This amendment, however, was violated and ignored by the states and by the federal government. The Voting Rights Act of

1965 had to be passed in order to give Black people the right to vote because the Fifteenth Amendment had been so blatantly ignored. It failed, say some constitutional scholars, because it "didn't provide any protection for voters."[46] Blacks were regularly and violently denied the right to vote, and many lost their lives while fighting to vote.

Because the Constitution was flawed from the beginning, and too ready to protect the rights and wishes of slave holders, it proved to be an ineffective document to end racism. The rhetoric was glorious, but the white supremacist foundation was too strong to be overcome by adding amendments. The Constitution was a document written to protect white people, particularly wealthy, white, male, Protestant property owners. At the cost of dignity and equality for Black people, the Constitution was written with the resolve to make sure the tools to make America a wealthy nation were protected and preserved.

Epigraphs

Ibram X. Kendi, *Stamped from the Beginning: The Definitive History of Racist Ideas in America* (New York: Nation Books, 2016), 121.

Edward E. Baptist, *The Half Has Never Been Told: Slavery and the Making of American Capitalism* (New York: Basic Books, 2014), xxvi.

NOTES

1. Scott Malcomson, *One Drop of Blood: The American Misadventure of Race* (New York: Farrar Straus Giroux, 2000), 180.
2. Malcomson.
3. Malcomson, 181.
4. Gunnar Myrdal, *An American Dilemma*, vol. 1: *The Negro Problem and Modern Democracy* (London and New York: Routledge, Taylor and Francis Group, 2017), xxvii.
5. Myrdal.
6. Myrdal, xxix.
7. Malcomson, 187.
8. Malcomson, 189.
9. Malcomson
10. Malcomson.
11. Malcomson, 190.
12. Malcomson, 190–91.

13. Edward E. Baptist, *The Half Has Never Been Told: Slavery and the Making of American Capitalism* (New York: Basic Books, 2014), 11.

14. Baptist.

15. Baptist.

16. David W. Blight, *Frederick Douglass, Prophet of Freedom* (New York: Simon & Schuster, 2018), 176.

17. Blight.

18. Blight, 215.

19. Blight, 233.

20. Baptist, 4.

21. Baptist, 6.

22. Baptist, 10.

23. Baptist.

24. Jon Meacham, *American Gospel: God, the Founding Fathers, and the Making of a Nation* (New York: Random House, 2007), 105.

25. Meacham.

26. Meacham, 87.

27. James Baldwin, *The Fire Next Time* (New York: Vintage International, 1993), 36.

28. Baldwin, 31.

29. Malcomson, 200.

30. Malcomson, 201.

31. Baldwin, 44–45.

32. See F. P. Retief and L. Cilliers, "The History and Pathology of Crucifixion," PubMed, https://pubmed.ncbi.nlm.nih.gov/14750495/; "How the Romans Used Crucifixion–Including Jesus's–as a Political Weapon," April 4, 2015, Newsweek [special edition], http://www.newsweek.com/how-romans-used-crucifixion-including-jesus-political-weapon-318934; also, various articles are available at the National Library of Medicine, https://pubmed.ncbi.nlm.nih.gov/?term=crucufixion.

33. Obery Hendricks, *The Politics of Jesus: Rediscovering the True Revolutionary Nature of Jesus' Teachings and How They Have Been Corrupted* (New York: Doubleday, Three Leaves Press, 2006), 31.

34. See Hendricks's analysis of the Lord's Prayer as a revolutionary, anti-government prayer in "Messiah and Tactician: The Political Strategies of Jesus," chap. 4.

35. Hendricks, 75.

36. Hendricks.

37. Hendricks, 89.

38. "Is Jesus God? Asked the Council of Nicea," https://www.christianity.com/church/church-history/timeline/1-300/is-jesus-god-11629651.html, 4.

39. "Is Jesus God?", 5.

40. "Slavery, the Constitution, and a Lasting Legacy," James Madison Montpelier, https://www.montpelier.org/learn/slavery-constitution-lasting-legacy.

41. "Slavery."

42. "Slavery."

43. "Slavery."

44. "Slavery."

45. Jeffrey Owen Jones, "The Man Who Wrote the Pledge of Allegiance," Smithsonian, November 2003, https://smithsonianmag.com/history/the-man-who-wrote-the-pledge-of-allegiance-93.

46. See Eric Foner, "The Right to Vote: The Fifteenth Amendment," chap. 3, *The Second Founding: How the Civil War and Reconstruction Remade the Constitution* (New York: W. W. Norton, 2019).

EXCURSUS

It was always about money.

The Christian Bible warns people that the love of money is the root of all evil (1 Timothy 6:10), but those words were never able to stop people from seeking money over mercy, profit over the well-being of human beings, especially and including African Americans. The fight for independence from England was just one part of the journey toward becoming a new nation. A second and enduring part of that journey was the creation of an economic system which would produce enough money for the new nation to thrive and thus have the resources necessary to increase its growth and potential for growth.

Capitalism did not originate in the United States. It was during the fourteenth century that an economic system that existed in Portugal and Spain, dubbed "mercantilism," began to spread throughout Europe.[1] Thomas K. McCraw writes that "in the early years, Americans' ravenous appetite for land was born of European deprivation confronting New World opportunity."[2] He continues:

> From the colonial period through the early national years, and on into the nineteenth century, everything seemed to be up for grabs in the new country. Vast, apparently unlimited tracts of land were given away by the government or sold at irresistibly low prices. To get the best land, neither the first colonists nor the pioneers pressing across the frontier had much compunction about dispossessing Native Americans or each other. Sometimes they resorted to outright murder. The movement west constituted a great epic, but in its details was not a pretty story.[3]

McCraw notes that "a handful of corporations existed at the nation's official birth in 1776,"[4] and said that capitalism "became integral to the American economy only in the middle nineteenth century but it was actually present at the creation [of this nation] 250 years earlier."[5] He continues, "In 1607, the settlers at Jamestown arrived under the auspices of the Virginia Company of

London. Puritans founded Boston in 1630 under the auspices of another English corporation, the Massachusetts Bay Company."[6]

William Penn and others who had fled from England because they were persecuted for their religious beliefs got a grant in 1681 upon arriving in the New World and "proceeded to develop their colony on both religious and commercial principles."[7] The Royal African Company was responsible for bringing large numbers of Africans to the Americas, and many white Americans participated in this business of trafficking people. McCraw writes that "the total number of Africans transported to the New World was about 10 million."[8] They were, by that time, the tools that the nation would use and exploit in order to move America toward becoming an empire, the most wealthy and most powerful nation in the modern world.

Religious and Economic Lines

The American way was thus becoming sharply defined along both religious and economic lines. While many to most of the Pilgrims and then the Puritans had little regard for the first group of non-whites to be dehumanized—the Native Americans—Christian Priber, a German immigrant, "understood the Indians as possessing a full humanity."[9] His beliefs were threatening to those who believed Native Americans should be eliminated in order for the new nation to get its footing. He said he had "come among the Cherokees only to preserve their liberties,"[10] but his desire to humanize Native Americans resulted in his eventual imprisonment. Scott Malcomson says two notions distinguished Priber's thought from that of the Revolutionary generation:

> These concern private property and race. The idea of private property contained a set of assumptions: that one could own land, objects, labor, and the money which measured their value; that these things were in some way transferable from one owner to another without changing their nature; that, in philosophical terms, property was "naturally" private; and that the simply taking of property, notably by the state, was a crime.[11]

The American way was being sharply defined along racial lines; Malcomson writes that "the Declaration of Independence characterized Native Americans as 'merciless Indian savages, whose known rule of welfare is an undistinguishable destruction of all ages, sexes, and conditions.'"[12]

Non-white persons in the New World, because of the symbiotic relationship between government and religion, had no chance of winning the argument against their being human and thus worthy of dignified treatment. Slavery, said many, "was at best a custom,"[13] and customs had no rights. Protestants, says Malcomson, "quickly came to rebel against constraints on expression, assembly, political representation, and, in the end property."[14] That these beliefs were expressed by Protestants, and that their voices were so prominent in the sixteenth century, long before the Constitution was drafted, helps explain the shape and the soul of America. The church helped form the bedrock of America's beliefs and seemed supportive of using human bodies in order to increase profits.

The Slave Trade

The legal Atlantic slave trade to the United States ended in 1807, but that did not stop the continuation of illegal slave trading. The idea of white supremacy, brought to the shores of this country from England, only grew as a dominant belief system of the United States. It seems that before there was ever a Civil War, war between the races was brewing, on racial grounds but also on economic grounds. White people in the North and the South had come to believe in the inferiority of Black people and that science had proven that "people of African descent were intellectually inferior and congenitally prone to criminal behavior."[15] In spite of the belief of some that slavery was a "flawed economic system that was inherently less efficient than the free-labor capitalism developing in the North," slavery persisted.[16]

Chattel slavery in this country was, ironically, writ into the new Constitution, institutionalizing it after the Revolutionary War, the war ostensibly fought for freedom. Freedom from England's oppression seemed to give Americans building this new country the freedom to oppress others. Edward Baptist writes that "America's modernization was about entrepreneurs, creativity, invention, markets, movement and change."[17] American leaders did not believe that slavery, however, was about any of those things; therefore they concluded, says Baptist, that "modern America and slavery had nothing to do with each other."[18]

But even as they spouted that belief, enslaved Africans were being made to walk in chains toward the South to be sold. A former slave, Lorenzo Ivy, shared with Baptist, "They sold slaves everywhere. I've seen droves of Negroes brought here on foot going South to be sold. Each one of them had an old tow sack on his back, with everything he's got in it. Over the hills they came in lines reaching as far as the eye can see. They walked in double lines chained together by twos. They walk 'em here to the railroad and shipped 'em south like cattle."[19]

Baptist notes that "only about 5,000 enslaved people were made to walk the hundreds of miles down old Indian-trading trails from Maryland to Georgia and South Carolina during the 1780s . . . but they were the trickle that predicted the flood."[20] He writes, "As tobacco prices plummeted in the 1780s, the prices of long-staple, or 'Sea Island' cotton rose. Then, in the early 1790s, Carolina and Georgia enslavers started to use a new machine called the 'cotton gin' . . . suddenly, enslavers knew what to plant in the Georgia-Carolina interior . . . To be sold [to slavers in Georgia] 'was the worst form of punishment.'"[21]

Enslaved people might have held hope in the law. They knew how the government was forming, how idealistic men were making a country, they said, where all people would be free. But their hope was ill-founded. In 1787, "the Constitutional Convention had allowed the [slave] trade to go on. In the twenty years since, citizens of the new nation had dragged 100,000 more people from the African coast."[22]

The enslaved African men and women were clearly valuable, too valuable to be let go. Even when in the 1780s some believed that the Middle Passage was too inhuman, even for those who consistently dehumanized Africans, the business of trafficking Africans continued. Some worried about the greed of planters that they saw emerging and increasing, but most Americans involved in making the country an economic giant seemed not to care. Virginia slaveholder George Mason was proud that his state had banned the slave trade business, and he made people angry when he made statements about the wrongness of slavery. His diatribes against slavery in-furiated those who were staunch supporters of it, and they spoke against him: "South Carolina's Charles C. Pinckney [said,] 'Virginia will gain by stopping the importations. Her slaves will rise in value and she has more than she wants.' Pinkney then defended slavery in the abstract. 'If slavery be wrong,' he said, 'it is justified by the example of all the world . . . In all ages, one-half of mankind have been slaves.'"[23]

Oliver Ellsworth, who would go on to become a justice of the United States Supreme Court, had never owned a slave, but he said that he "could not judge the effects of slavery on character."[24] He continued, "Let the economic interest of white Americans dictate whether the Atlantic slave trade should be closed. And, as slaves also multiply so fast in Virginia and Maryland that it is cheaper to raise them than import them, let us not intermeddle with internal forced migrations, either . . . religion and humanity have nothing to do with this question."[25]

"Interest," says Baptist, "was the governing principle shaping the Constitution."[26] People were willing, however, to put up with and support the forced movement and enslavement of Black peo-ple. Baptist writes, "There were many Americans, even white ones, whose interests were not served . . . Allowing slavery to continue and even expand meant political unity . . . Slavery's expansion soon yielded a more unified government and a stronger economy based on new nationwide capital markets . . . white Americans found in it the basis for a more perfect union."[27]

A Capitalist System

The American way was to create wealth through the system of capi-talism. It was intentional that the wealth, and therefore the gover-nance, of the country would be controlled by a few men. It is a fact that the founding fathers never intended to create what is called a direct democracy, where all people have a say in how government is run. James Madison believed that masses of people included in determining the direction of any democracy would lead to factions and tyranny.[28] The Constitution thus created the rules not for a direct democracy but rather for a representative republic where a "few enlightened men would make decisions for the many for the public good."[29] The system they envisioned and designed made inequity between classes and ultimately races a given. The writers of the Constitution saw no issue with the system they were devising, and the adherents of the Bible apparently did not either. Neither document took the time to envision what kinds of issues this system of government would create in the future.

After the Civil War, the weaknesses of the Bible and the Constitution to address the problems that came with economic and racial discrimination became stark. Baptist writes that "slavery and its expansion had built enduring patterns of poverty and exploitation."[30] The majority of Black and white Southerners were poor; poverty-stricken whites were no better off than were enslaved people who now found themselves free. Baptist says that many white farmers were so poor that they could not pay their taxes and debts and ended up losing their land and became sharecroppers themselves.[31] Freedom for Black people meant that they were no longer obligated to make and keep white people wealthy or at least economically comfortable.

Poor whites suffered, but so did wealthy whites who had made their wealth on Black labor. The Constitution had "built a union on slavery and embedded its expansion . . . in the fabric of the American political economy."[32] Slavery had made the nation large and wealthy; with it gone, both those qualities were felt to be in jeopardy.

Those who had been wealthy were going to let the situation stay as it was. Wealth produces the development of greed; the more wealth one has, the more one wants, and one is willing to do almost anything to protect and grow it. Corporations by this time had taken on a life of their own; years later, Mitt Romney, running for president in 2011, shocked the sensibilities of many when he said that corporations are people.[33] Ironically, it was the Fourteenth Amendment, one of the Reconstruction Amendments forged to increase the rights of freed African Americans, that was and is referred to in support of that claim. The amendment has been used to "exponentially expand the protection of all Americans and has been at the center of many controversial US Supreme Court cases, including *Roe v. Wade* and *Brown v. Board of Education*.

Sarah Pruitt said that "an 1886 headnote forever shifted the meaning of the 14th Amendment."[34] In that year, in *Santa Clara*

County v. Southern Pacific Rail Road, the court decided to grant corporations the same rights that are afforded to human beings. The case was brought because the state had "improperly assessed taxes to the railroad company,"[35] In the decision, Justice Morrison Waite said, "The Court does not wish to hear argument on the question whether the provision in the Fourteenth Amendment to the Constitution which forbids a state to deny to any person within its jurisdiction the equal protection of the laws applies to these corporations. We are all of the opinion that it does."[36] Since that case, many corporations have sued for the same rights granted to individuals. In 2010, *Citizens United v. Federal Election Commission* won its case, giving corporations sweeping rights that have implications to this day. Even though Justice John Paul Stevens wrote in *Citizens* case that "corporations are not themselves members of 'We the People' by whom and for whom our Constitution was established," it made no difference. The strength of capitalism in this country has only grown since the seed was planted even before there was a Constitution.

A New Form of Slavery

It was the love of money that drove angry whites to take extraordinary steps to keep some kind of servitude in operation after the Civil War, and perhaps it was the South's loss of the Civil War, accompanied by the Constitution's dedication to building a wealthy nation, that contributed to the re-enslavement of Black people. Greed, accompanied by anger and shame at having lost the war and a resentment of lost powers, fed into the system called contract leasing.

It is the deafening silence of the church during this time that is so deeply troubling. Douglas Blackmon, in *Slavery by Another Name*, opens that book by describing how one Black man, Green Cotttenham, was arrested and charged with "vagrancy" in 1908. Vagrancy was defined as "the offense of a person not being able to prove at a given moment that he or she was employed."[37] Cottenham spent three days behind bars, and when he was finally brought to trial, he was sentenced to thirty days of hard labor. Because he was unable to pay fees required of all prisoners, his sentence was extended to a year of hard labor.[38] Blackmon's description of Cottenham's experience is as troubling as it is riveting:

A few hours later, the company plunged Cottenhamin to the darkness of a mine called Slope No. 12—one shaft in a vast subterranean labyrinth on the edge of Birmingham known as the Pratt Mines. There, he was chained inside a long wooden barrack at night and required to spend nearly every waking hour digging and loading coal. His required daily "task" was to remove eight tons of coal from the mine. Cottenham was subject to the whip for failure to dig the requisite amount, at the risk of physical torture for disobedience, and vulnerable to the sexual predations of other miners—many of whom had already passed years or decades in their own chthonian confinement.[39]

Although they knew the system was against them, Black people fought for their share of profits to be made. Too often, however, they were robbed of honest wages for the work that they did and were lynched for daring to stand up for their rights. Anthony P. Crawford was one such victim. He was a successful entrepreneur and farmer who lived in Abbeville, South Carolina. Owned by Ben and Rebecca Crawford, "he walked 14 miles roundtrip to and from school every day," according to his great-great-granddaughter, the late Dr. Doria Johnson.[40] In 1916, Crawford confronted a white vendor for underpaying him for his cotton seed. The confrontation stimulated resentment and rage from the white residents of the town, and a white mob estimated to be anywhere from two hundred to four hundred people attacked him.

Johnson says that "his ordeal lasted all day. His body was beaten and dragged through town to show other Negroes what would happen to them if they got 'insolent.' Finally, he was taken to the county fair grounds and strung up to a tree and riddled with bullets . . . His family was ordered to vacate their land, wind up business, and get out of town."[41]

Violence against Blacks by angry whites because of money disputes and resentment was commonplace. In 1917, in East St. Louis an attack on Black people by a mob of whites erupted after 470 African American workers were hired to replace white workers who had gone on strike again the Aluminum Ore Company.[42] A rumor about an armed Black man attempting to rob a white woman began, and all hell broke loose. The description of the violence is graphic:

> As a result . . . white mobs formed and rampaged through downtown, beating all African Americans who were found. The mobs also stopped trolleys and streetcars, pulling Black passengers out and beating them on the streets and sidewalks.
>
> On July 2, 1917, the violence resumed. Men, women, and children were beaten and shot to death. Around six o'clock that evening, white mobs began to set fire to the homes of Black residents. Residents had to choose between burning alive in their homes, or run out of the burning houses, only to be met by gunfire. In other parts of the city, white mobs began to lynch African Americans against the backdrop of burning buildings. As darkness came and the National Guard returned, the violence began to wane but did not come to a complete stop.[43]

To assuage feelings of anger and shame, and to make a way to assure that profit making for the wealthy continued for as little money as possible, Black people, especially Black men, were terrorized and brutalized by the government. The corporations had more rights than did they, and neither the Constitution nor the Bible had much to say about it. It was because of the pure hellishness of Black life, with no protection from the Constitution or law enforcement, and little support from the preaching of the Bible, that Black worship became the experience and institution that saved the capacity of Black people to hold on and to hope.

Expressions of Grief and Joy

In the late 1970s, Hazel Bryant, the sister of the Rev. John Richard Bryant, now a bishop but at that time pastor of Bethel AME Church in Baltimore, Maryland, said in an interview, "Sunday is about 'grief release.'" To be honest, it was not apparent to me at that time what she meant, but as time has passed and I have learned so much about the failed hopes and dreams, the lack of protection from the government and from the Bible, it makes sense. "In the shouting, the singing, the crying," Ms. Bryant said, "Black people can let go of the pain, the mourning, the aching, and the sense of rage they we all carry. It is really about releasing our internalized grief."[44]

In *Been in the Storm So Long,* Leon Litwack writes of how the spirited worship of Black people was troubling to whites and some Blacks, who obviously had no understanding of the deep need to grieve, and then to praise God in spite of their pain. Henry McNeil Turner, a Black man, visited a worship service on Roanoke Island and "thought the Black parishioners worshipped 'under a lower class of ideas' and entertained crude conceptions of God."[45] The perception of this kind of worship as being "ignorant" caused some to avoid the services, their aversion characterized by one Black woman who said, "I won't go to the colored churches, for I'm only disgusted with bad grammar and worse pronunciation, and their horrible absurdities."[46]

The expressions of deep joy or deep sadness were necessary, but the services offended the sensibilities of some who believed that Black people's "greatest need is *orderly Churches* under the care of educated men."[47] Some white missionaries and preachers characterized Black worship as "simple and childlike": "They believe simply in the love of Christ, and they refer of Him and talk to Him with a familiarity that is absolutely startling. They pray as though they thought Christ himself was standing in the very room."[48]

For Blacks seeking spirit and soul relief and release, however, the disapproval of their worship indicated a lack of understanding of what they endured on a daily basis on the part of those who criticized them. They would and could sing, "It's me, it's me, it's me, O Lord! Standing in the need of prayer!" Black people, enslaved or finally free, were recipients of soul whippings that left lasting scars. They knew they were being used to build the Southern, and later, the entire American economy. They knew they were being cheated of money they earned by working long, hard hours. They lived in fear of being beaten or lynched, or even being run out of town because some whites did not like them. Litwack said that even in missionary work, the mark of capitalism was still there: "Although the emissaries of both races in the South stressed the importance of former slaves returning to work and proving their capacity for *free* labor, the suspicion grew that some white missionaries stood to profit materially from such counsel."[49] The reminder of the need and demand for and of Black people to work for whites to build the economy was never far from the surface. Litwack notes the observations of Rev. A. Waddell:

> Some of our white ministerial friends do more in the way of procuring farms, and keeping our poor race in ignorance, than any thing else. They are more concerned about the *cotton bag* than they are about *souls*. They pretend, when they are North, that they would come down here and do any thing for our race in the way of enlightening them; but, instead of this, when they see the cotton bag, they forget all about Christ and Him crucified, and the saving of souls.[50]

The Promises of God

That the Bible is correct in noting that the love of money is the root of all evil says much about the truth of that observation. If that sacred text, which was written over thousands of years, in many languages and by many people, could make that observation, there must not be a way around it. To this day, African Americans are still struggling to be counted as being entitled to the rights of American citizens as outlined in the Constitution, and they struggle today with a Christian interpretation of the Bible which seems anathema to the teachings of the Christ. In 1860, Frederick Douglass observed, "It will be a great work accomplished when this Government is divorced from the active support of the inhuman slave system."[51] Douglass was well aware of how wretched the capitalistic system was for Black people; he called it "an expensive and wasteful 'system of labor'" because it created an "aristocratic class who despise labor."[52] Douglass believed that the system "led to a broader contempt for all others who work for an honest living because a small Southern oligarchy had become masters of the United States."[53]

The slavery needed by capitalism has not gone away. Although slavery as a legal institution was abolished, slavery as an illegal institution has persisted. Black, brown, and poor people, Black and white, are being underpaid and overworked, living in abject poverty even as corporate presidents are becoming more and more wealthy. Immigrants, documented and undocumented, are continuing the work done by the underclass that has always been done as

they work fields and inside of meat processing plants, many without benefits. The voices of those oppressed largely because of the
impotence of both the Bible and the US Constitution in ending racism might be summed up by the words found in Jeremiah 31:15-17:

> Thus says the LORD:
> A voice is heard in Ramah,
>   lamentation and bitter weeping.
> Rachel is weeping for her children;
>   she refuses to be comforted for her children,
>   because they are no more.
> Thus says the LORD:
> Keep your voice from weeping,
>   and your eyes from tears;
> for there is a reward for your work,
>   says the LORD:
>   they shall come back from the land of the enemy;
> there is hope for your future,
>   says the LORD:
>   your children shall come back to their own country.

The American way notwithstanding, the promises of God are
what have kept Black people on their feet. No matter what the system has done to them in the past, as they release the grief that has
come with being oppressed, denied liberty as defined in the Constitution, and subjected to cruelty and dishonor based on skin color,
they have been—we have been—equipped for the interminable
journey on which we have been set.

NOTES

1. Solidarity Federation, section of the International Workers Association, http://
www.solfed.org.uk/a-s-history/unit-1-the-origins-of-capitalism.

2. Thomas K. McCraw, "It Came in the First Ships: Capitalism in America," October 12, 1999, Working Knowledge, Harvard Business School, https://hbswk.hbs.
edu/item/it-came-in-the-first-ships-capitalism-in-america.

3. McCraw, 2.

4. McCraw.

5. McCraw.

6. McCraw.

7. McCraw.

8. McCraw.

9. Scott Malcomson, *One Drop of Blood: The American Misadventure of Race* (New York: Farrar Straus Giroux, 2000), 45.

10. Malcomson, 44.

11. Malcomson, 45.

12. Malcomson, 46.

13. Malcomson, 47.

14. Malcomson.

15. Edward E. Baptist, *The Half Has Never Been Told: Slavery and the Making of American Capitalism* (New York: Basic Books, 2014), xiv.

16. Baptist, xviii.

17. Baptist, xxii.

18. Baptist.

19. Baptist. The church was complicit in the work of dehumanizing people of African descent so that they would become the tools used to build America's economy. Baptist notes that some preachers began to punish ministers who preached against slavery (16).

20. Baptist, 18.

21. Baptist. Enslaved Africans were made to walk an average of twenty miles a day, shoeless, two by two, with chains around their necks and their feet. Guarded by white slavers on horses, their total mileage to some destinations often totaled more than five hundred miles. They were dirty and smelly, not allowed to wash until they got to the slave markets where they would be displayed and sold. Baptist writes, "Men of the chain couldn't act as individuals; nor could they act as a collective, except by moving forward in one direction . . . people were angry, depressed, despairing, sick of each other's smell and the noises they made . . . At night, lying too close, raw wrists and sore feet aching, men in chains or women in ropes, argued, pushed and tried to enforce their wills . . . None of that matters to the Georgia-man as long as the chain kept moving" (25).

22. Baptist, 40.

23. Baptist, 10.

24. Baptist.

25. Baptist.

26. Baptist, 11.

27. Baptist.

28. Jeffrey Rosen, "America Is Living James Madison's Nightmare," The Atlantic, https://www.theatlantic.com/magazine/archive/2018/10/james-madison-mob-rule/568351.

29. Rosen.

30. Baptist, 411.

31. Baptist.

32. Baptist, 412.

33. "'Corporations Are People'—What Did Romney Really Mean?", August 13, 2012, Washington Post, https://washingtonpost.com/politics/mitt-romney-says-corporations-are-people/2011/08.

34. Sarah Pruitt, "How the Fourteenth Amendment Made Corporations into 'People,'" June 15, 2018, updated October 15, 2018, History, https://www.history.com/news/14th-amendment-corporate-personhood-made-corporations-into-people.

35. Pruitt, 3.

36. Pruitt.

37. Douglas A. Blackmon, *Slavery by Another Name: The Re-Enslavement of Black Americans from the Civil War to World War II* (New York: Anchor Books, 2008), 1.

38. Blackmon.

39. Blackmon, 2.

40. "Anthony Crawford—Father, Husband, Landowner, Farmer," told by Doria Johnson (2011), Amerika's Black Holocaust Museum, https://abhmuseum.org/anthony-crawford/, 1.

41. "Anthony Crawford."

42. Tabitha Wang, "East St. Louis Race Riot, 1917," June 1, 2008, BlackPast, https://www.blackpast.org/african-american-history/east-st-louis-race-riot-1917, 2.

43. Wang, 3.

44. Susan K. Williams Smith, personal interview with Hazel Bryant, 1978, New York.

45. Leon F. Litwack, *Been in the Storm So Long: The Aftermath of Slavery* (New York: Vintage, 1980), 459.

46. Litwack, 458.

47. Litwack, 459.

48. Litwack.

49. Litwack, 463.

50. Litwack.

51. David Blight, *Frederick Douglass: Prophet of Freedom* (New York: Simon & Schuster, 2018), 323.

52. Blight.

53. Blight.

8
The Church, Impotent

*I had been in the pulpit too long and I had seen too
many monstrous things. . . . I really mean that there
was no love in the church. It was a mask for hatred
and self-hatred and despair. The transfiguring power
of the Holy Ghost ended when the service ended, and
salvation stopped at the church door.* —James Baldwin

Years after the Constitution was written, ratified, and made over
by the insertion of the 13th, 14th, and 15th Amendments—Reconstruction Amendments, racism was still an unlanced boil in America, largely because the Protestant church, defined and shaped largely
by the Presbyterians, the Methodists, and the Baptists, had failed
to stamp it out. In a word, when it came to racism, the church was
impotent. It had developed and used a theology that for all intents
and purposes sanctioned not only racism but other forms of discrimination as well. It wasn't Christianity that the church practiced;
it was religion, a construct made by men who had a vested interest
in protecting their way of life and their prejudices. Their religion
was based on gaining and keeping power, as we have already noted.
Yes, their religion referred to Jesus as they did missionary work in
countries they deemed to be savage and in need of being converted
to the faith, but in their religious instruction was the belief that some
people were better than others and that was God's will.

The enslaved Africans realized it early and developed their
own religion, but the church as passed down was the white church,
which taught white beliefs. Yes, the Bible contained words that led
white theologians to believe and to teach that said human beings
were to have dominion over all that which God had made, but
Wes Howard-Brook makes the point that they were not to have

dominion over each other.[1] The church had been militarized, and so had been God. In the Hebrew Scriptures, God was portrayed as one who yearned for his people to be in community; Yahweh chastised those who would not and did not take care of the poor, the oppressed, the widows, and the downtrodden. But in the prophetic texts, God was also thought of as being a "warrior who would defeat the foes of Israel and slaughter the unrighteous."[2] Say Rita Nakashima Brock and Rebecca Ann Parker:

> While they proclaimed peace, they often imagined God as a warrior who would defeat the foes of Israel and slaughter the unrighteous. They sometimes hoped for the restoration of the monarchy built on justice . . . Such sentiments about restoration lent themselves to a nostalgic view of the conquest and colonization of Canaan and the establishment of Israel. That kingdom had established itself like other empires was no more virtuous than those empires, and ended in civil war.[3]

The perceptions of God that were created and survived created confusion, and if the conception about and understanding of God caused confusion, it would be impossible for the church to be an uncompromising whole. Was God loving and all-inclusive, or was God a soldier, always on the hunt for more power, often at the expense of the people he had created? Was God a God of peace or of violence? The church had no unified answer—not then, and not now.

The manufactured God—that of the Protestant church—presented an uncomfortable image and presence in the minds and hearts of the oppressed. Presumably, there was one God, but how could anyone who was not white and privileged believe in and trust that God? How did one walk around, as an African American, believing that he or she was forever cursed because of being a descendant of Ham? How did a Black person hold his or her head up knowing that many thought that the Bible said they were destined to be nothing but a slave? Most people did not know, or perhaps did not think about, that the Bible had been written by white men with a vested interest in keeping their power intact, and so they had no way of knowing or believing or even thinking that the way they were thinking was skewed, tilted to favor a certain race and a certain social class. James Baldwin was one of many who felt the contradiction that many Black people felt as they called on the name of Jesus; he said, "I felt that I was committing a crime in talking about the gentle Jesus, in telling them to reconcile themselves to their misery on earth in order to gain the crown of eternal life."[4] He continued:

> Were only Negroes to gain this crown? Was Heaven, then, to be merely another ghetto? Perhaps I might have been able to reconcile myself even to this if I had been able to believe that there was any loving-kindness to be found in the haven I represented. But I had been in the pulpit too long and I had seen too many monstrous things . . . I really mean that there was no love in the church. It was a mask for hatred and self-hatred and despair.[5]

If the church was impotent to fight racism, if its Bible had been ineffective in helping it fight racism, the evidence of that reality was encapsulated in Baldwin's words. And the spirits of the framers of the Constitution were surely saturated with the toxicity that exuded from white supremacist beliefs.

Religion Rather Than Christianity

By the time the Constitution was ratified on June 21, 1788, when New Hampshire became the required ninth state to ratify it, the mark of America as a nation whose foundation was based in white supremacist ideology and beliefs was set. Ibram Kendi notes that two years after the Constitution was ratified, the United States Congress passed the first Naturalization Act, which "limited citizenship to 'free white persons' of "good character."[6] The slave trade had been protected by the Constitution, as well as the ownership of slaves itself. Vincent Harding writes that "the revolution for white liberty ended with Black slavery carefully protected in the basic document of the new, 'free' nation."[7]

The white revolution was a stinging disappointment for enslaved Africans who desperately wanted to be free. Harding notes that the revolutionary leader of San Domingo said sadly, "Our God, who is good to us, orders us to avenge our wrongs. He will direct our arms and us. Throw away [the cross], the symbol of the

God of the whites who has so often caused us to weep, and listen to the voice of liberty, which speaks in the heart of us all."[8]

There were already two Gods—one in whom white people believed and one who appealed to Black people. Both Black and white people believed that their God was leading them—whites to enslave Blacks and to believe in their inferiority, and Blacks to fight for their freedom, regardless of the cost. Nat Turner and David Walker were two voices from the Black side of the struggle; Harding says they "had come speaking words of judgment, proclaiming news received from the living God, messages which white America found unbearable."[9] "Both men," Harding says, "presented profound challenges to American definitions of their white-owned God, questioned the white commitment to the nation's espoused religion, flatly declared that the American people did not know the ways of their own Lord."[10]

Under the guidance of their God, white people sought to destroy the spirits of Black people in order to manipulate them into accepting their enslavement, training them to be unconditionally submissive.[11] Blacks began to believe that the white God allowed the cruelty of whites toward enslaved Africans, as told by this man who was enslaved in Alabama:

> Some of them runned away, anyhow. My brother, Harrison, was one, and they set the n— dogs on him like fox hounds run a fox today. They didn't run him down 'till 'bout night, but finally they catched him, and the hunters fetched him to the do and say, "Mary Ann, here Harrison." Then they turned the dogs loose on him again, and such a screaming you never heard. He was all bloody and Mammy was a-hollering, "Save him, Lord, save my child and don't let them dogs eat him up." Mr. Lawler said, "The Lord ain't got nothing to do with this here," and it sure look like he didn't, cause them dogs nigh 'bout chewed Harrison up.[12]

Good, God-fearing white men seemed not to understand the Great Commandment, or perhaps they believed it was alright to ignore it. Their God inundated their understanding of justice, as when a judge in New Orleans ruled that a young Black man, who had grown tired of being abused by his owner, stabbed and killed him. The young man ran for his life but was captured and put on trial. His attorney argued that the young man had been provoked, but the court ruled that "the Law cannot recognize the violence of the master as a legitimate cause of provocation."[13] The young Black man was hanged.

God and church notwithstanding, Black people were not honored or protected anywhere. Slavery had been outlawed in the North by 1830, but white people were plagued by "self-righteous white racism, rapacious economic greed, and deep-seated, irrational fear of blackness."[14] Blacks were expected to "stay in their place," and the ever-present conversation about why Blacks even needed to be in the United States continued. The antebellum North preceded the South in constructing "barriers to Black equality and freedom"[15] that we have come to know as Jim Crow. In Massachusetts, for example, Congregationalists discriminated against northern free Blacks:

> Attempts to reduce the Black populations in New England cities and towns included targeting people of color for "warning out" as undesirables under the legal settlement laws; taxing their presence; advocating their wholesale transportation to African under the aegis of the American Colonization Society. In 1788, the Massachusetts legislature passed a vagrancy law that required the expulsion of all African Americans who were not citizens of the state. Over the next several years, 158 free persons of color were "warned out" of the state. In addition, Boston became the hub of a vicious campaign using "broadsides" to ridicule the physical characteristics, social behavior and institutions of Black persons. Mobs led violent attacks against communities of color in Boston and other Northern cities during the 1820s.[16]

The church in the North and the South was not doing a good job of spreading a message of egalitarianism or agape love, principles which Jesus espoused. Obery Hendricks says that the message of Jesus was to "treat the needs of the people as holy."[17] As enslaved Africans learned the Gospels, that dictum meant all people, but that was not the mindset of religious whites who believed in the rightness of slavery. As previously mentioned it seemed that religious whites were less committed to the gospel of Jesus and more aligned with the words of Paul and with parts of the Hebrew Scriptures which they contended supported their beliefs about the inferiority of Black people and the divine sanction of slavery. The Bible, and consequently, the church highlighted the difference between Christianity and religion. There were very religious people who read the Bible, went to church regularly, and yet believed in Jim Crow. They could resonate with the words of Paul, a privileged Roman citizen, and not so much with the words of Jesus the Christ. Paul makes reference to the Christ, but he had a far different life than did the oppressed to whom Jesus directed his ministry. Paul could always fall back on his Roman citizenship if his testimony for the Christ became too threatening to the state and thus threatening to his life (Acts 22:25). Paul's perspective was different from that of the oppressed because his life was different, and white Christians who believed in God did not identify with the oppressed. Says Hendricks, "Peasants in Jewish Palestine were typically vulnerable to raids by bandits and to arbitrary seizure of their property and produce by Roman soldiers, and women were often violated by them. Peasants were also subject to the pressure of multiple annual taxes that could amount to more than one-third of what in the vast majority of cases was no more than subsistence production to begin with."[18]

Paul revealed the mindset of the elite, those who honor the government and pledge allegiance to the government (Romans 13:1-7), a movement which had begun long before Jesus lived. We have already seen how Constantine appropriated Christianity to become the religion of the state. It was under Constantine that "the official canonical collection we call the New Testament functioned similarly to that of the Persian-era gathering of the book of Moses into a single unit," according to Wes Howard-Brook.[19] Any variation of those written words was labeled "heresy."[20] The religion of Jesus was moving further and further away from Jesus and was taking the Bible with it. Later, Charlemagne "demanded loyalty oaths" and instituted laws that made it a crime to break them. Brock and Parker note that "historian Roger Collins identifies Charlemagne's law codes as the origin of European notions of pure ethnic identities, defined as inescapable, essential traits."[21]

The church and the empire, then, had been at odds for centuries before the founding of the United States. Howard-Brook says the church of empire looked nothing like the church that Jesus had envisioned, and Hendricks argued that the chasm between what God wanted and what the empire sought were so radically different that Jesus advocated challenging the government. In the Lord's Prayer, says Hendricks, Jesus advises people to put God and the will of God before government, and because of this, Hendricks says, the Lord's Prayer is a revolutionary prayer. It directs people to do whatever they must to make God's kingdom rule on earth "as it is in heaven," a direct challenge to being willing to obey the government of the state at all costs.[22]

Part of the reason Paul's message seemed to support government over the will of God expressed by Jesus is because Paul believed in the second coming and that Jesus would be back soon. Everyone, then, needed to focus on their soon-coming eternal future and not be concerned with finite matters, such as the law of the land. When Jesus returned, he would reward those who had been obedient to the government, but this obedience—painful and unjust though it was—would not be required for long. As Jesus' immediate return seemed less and less certain, however, the message of Paul never changed, his words becoming a second gospel to burgeon and flourish, which was more comfortable for the oppressors than for the oppressed.

It was Paul, notes Hendricks, who changed the message of social, economic, and political justice for all to a message of personal piety, which exists to this day. Having a personal relationship with Jesus allowed many to exclude concern for the oppressed among them. This nation and its churches called themselves Christian but in reality they were religious, standing on, referring to, and respecting those words of Paul that emphasized personal piety. The religion of Paul was called Christianity, and it was a force within this country by the time it in fact became a country, but the religion of Paul, and its church, did not mandate that its followers seek liberty, justice, and equality for all. The Constitution recognized and mentioned God, but that God "was in no explicit way the God of Abraham, much less God the Father of the Holy Trinity,"[23] according to Meacham.

These two churches—the church of Jesus and the church of Paul, the church of community and the church of empire—existed alongside each other for thousands of years and did not intersect in the area of agreeing that God intended for all people to be equal.

The religion of Paul seemed to be a direct antecedent of the Christianity of both Constantine and Charlemagne, advising people to honor the state and its leaders, and that belief is a central belief of conservative Christianity to this day. The two Christianities have different foundational Scriptures. The religion of Jesus is grounded in the Gospels—Matthew, Mark, Luke, and John, and many of the core beliefs of Jesus are found in the Sermon on the Mount (Matthew 5–7 and Luke 6:17-49). The religion of Paul, by contrast, seems to be grounded in Romans 13:1-7:

> Let every person be subject to the governing authorities; for there is no authority except from God, and those authorities that exist have been instituted by God. Therefore whoever resists authority resists what God has appointed, and those who resist will incur judgment. For rulers are not a terror to good conduct, but to bad. Do you wish to have no fear of the authority? Then do what is good, and you will receive its approval; for it is God's servant for your good. But if you do what is wrong, you should be afraid, for the authority does not bear the sword in vain! It is the servant of God to execute wrath on the wrongdoer. Therefore one must be subject, not only because of wrath but also because of conscience. For the same reason you also pay taxes, for the authorities are God's servants, busy with this very thing. Pay to all what is due them—taxes to whom taxes are due, revenue to whom revenue is due, respect to whom respect is due, honor to whom honor is due.[24]

While Paul knew and loved Jesus the Christ, his religion, his gospel, is vastly different from the Good News of Jesus, where love and dignity were taught to be attainable by all God's children.

The Story of the Exodus

Interestingly, both whites and Blacks, with their different Gods, looked upon the story of the exodus as the word of God for them. In 1630, the Puritans referred to the story of the exodus as they landed on the shores of the new world. According to a documentary shown on PBS, the Puritans, unlike the Pilgrims who landed in America in 1619, did not break with the Church of England but wanted to reform it. Nonetheless, they cited religious persecution as one of their reasons for leaving England, and saw their sojourn across the Atlantic as a re-enactment of the exodus found in the Hebrew Scriptures. They believed they had been freed by God from their oppression and had entered into a sacred covenant with God.[25]

Enslaved Blacks welcomed the Civil War as the first step toward their exodus from their oppression. Black men and women were convinced that God was providing "a way out of the darkness of slavery and degradation."[26] Though the South, and not the North, initiated the war, the enslaved souls did not care; they were ready and willing to fight for the Union in quest of their ultimate freedom. They believed that God was forcing white people, especially white slave owners, to defend their rights.[27] Harding writes, "Men and women chose to believe that some mysterious movement of the Divine was among them, forcing a recalcitrant white America, against its will and desire, to fight for the rights of Black men. It was a strange theodicy, but it reigned in Black America."[28]

While Blacks were seeing the war as evidence of their exodus from the wilderness of slavery to freedom, whites were viewing it as evidence that the North had strayed from the faith. The North's opposition to slavery (such as it was) was viewed as secularism and as being in conflict with Christians in the South. Southerners felt that the Northerners had strayed from the teachings of the Bible, especially the words uttered by Paul and the Book of Romans that they had interpreted as being pro-slavery. Since it was God who ordained slavery, the North was out of line, they believed. Southerners also believed that God would rain justice on the North when the South won the conflict. When the Union won, however, the South was devastated. Just as slaves had wondered where God was when they were being beaten and abused by their owners, so whites wondered where God was as the South fell to defeat. How could God, who they believed had ordained slavery and racism, have let them lose? Over time, many in the South considered the Civil War a holy war, as did enslaved Blacks. For Southern whites, however, the holy war was fought because of Northern extremists "who failed to recognize the authority of the Bible or the Constitution,"[29] both of which the Southerners believed sanctioned slavery.

Many churches in the South advocated for slavery and counseled in favor of it. Some pastors voiced separating from Northern churches in their denominations that were anti-slavery. In 1845, "white Virginians joined with other Baptists in Augusta, Georgia, to found the Southern Baptist Convention, and with Methodists in Louisville, to help organize the Methodist Episcopal Church, South (MECS)."[30] Believing that God was on their side, it was not uncommon for Southern pastors to bless the weapons that the Confederate soldiers used. Jefferson Davis, who would become the president of the Confederacy, "directly encouraged ministers to support the cause by declaring ten different fast days during the war."[31] Some pastors preached that the war was chastisement for Southerners not having been grateful enough for the prosperity of the Southern economy, but they also preached that Southerners should still see themselves as God's chosen people. Kensey Stewart, an Episcopalian priest from Virginia, refused to pray for Abraham Lincoln in 1862.[32] The white churches were acting the way they believed their God ordained them to act. Freedom for Black people was not an issue for them; nor, in their view, was it an issue for God.

Preaching Obedience and Enslavement

Black people continued to hope that God would come through on their side. Their hope lay in their belief that the Civil War was their way to freedom. Abraham Lincoln was seen as needing prayer and direction; they asked God's blessings on the president, trusting him to "do what is just and right to all men."[33]

But Lincoln, a religious man in his own way, was conflicted. If we define white supremacy as the belief in the superiority of white people, Lincoln espoused what we today would call white supremacist rhetoric. In fact, it is said that he was blaming the Civil War on Black people when he opined that the presence of Blacks in America "was the cause of the present war."[34] In his 1858 debates with presidential candidate Stephen A. Douglas, Lincoln said:

> I am not, nor ever have been, in favor of bringing about in any way the social and political equality of the white and Black races. . . . I am not, nor ever have been, in favor of making voters or jurors of negroes, nor of qualifying them to hold office, nor to intermarry with white people; and I will say in addition to this that there is a physical difference between the white and Black

races which I believe will for ever forbid the two races living
together on terms of social and political equality. And insomuch
as they cannot so live, while they do remain together there
must be the position of superior and inferior and I as much
as any other man am in favor of having the superior position
assigned to the white race.[35]

The beloved president, whom America has deified as one of the
nation's greatest because he freed the slaves, was no friend of Black
people. He believed in the Constitution, and he understood the protections of slavery that were written into the document. He did not
like slave trafficking, which he worked to abolish, but he believed
in the innate superiority of white people, especially when white and
Black people lived on the same soil. Since he would rather that they
didn't live together, he was in favor of colonization. He believed
that the best way to get rid of enslaved Africans was to pay the
owners to give them up. In what was called compensated emancipation, he pushed for the removal of Africans from America in a way
which would ameliorate, and cater to, white slave owners.

The late historian Benjamin Quarles wrote that Lincoln "felt
that as long as slavery existed, . . . their citizens [Virginians] would
have much latent sympathy for the Confederacy, thus giving hope
to the Richmond government."[36] Lincoln needed to do a test run to
see how his plan would work, so he chose Delaware as the guinea
pig because it had few enslaved Africans and was a border state. If
the plan worked there, it might work in other crucial border states.
He drafted two bills, each granting "$719,000 to the state of Dela-
ware out of the national treasury," which amounted to $400 for
each enslaved African. One bill would terminate in 1867, and the
other in 1893.[37] But the plan went nowhere because Delaware was
opposed to emancipation "with or without compensation."[38]

The District of Columbia passed a bill to emancipate its enslaved Africans, and two months later it "placed at Lincoln's disposal half a million dollars to carry out the Act of Congress for
the emancipation of the slaves in the District of Columbia and to
colonize those to be made free by the probable passage of a confiscation bill."[39] The House Committee on Colonization "reported
that the highest interests of the white race—Anglo-Saxon, Celt, or

Scandinavian—made it imperative that the United States be occu-
pied by no one else."[40]

While the extent of Lincoln's involvement and investment in
the work of colonizing Black people is too extensive for the scope
of this book, it is important to note that Black people were not
in favor of colonization. In "An Appeal from the Colored Men
of Philadelphia to the President of the United States," a group of
prominent African Americans addressed their disapproval of what
the president was supporting. They wrote:

> We can find nothing in the religion of our Lord and Master,
> teaching us that color is the standard by which He judges his
> creatures, either in this life nor the life which is to come. He
> created us and endowed us with the faculties of the man,
> giving us a part of the earth as a habitation, and its products
> for our sustenance. He also made it sufficient in compass and
> fruitfulness to provide for the wants of us all, and has nowhere
> taught us to devour each other, that even life itself might be
> sustained. . . . While colonization, in many of its features might
> be advantageous to our race, yet were all of us to be sent out
> of the country, the population of the United States would be
> reduced nearly one-sixth part. It is doubtful whether the people
> seriously desire a depletion of this kind, however much they
> may wish to separate from us.[41]

The messages of egalitarianism and of Jesus that God desired
justice for all formed the foundation of belief for enslaved Africans.
However, these messages caused slave owners much consternation
and a tendency to steer away from the gospel of Jesus and toward
other parts of the Bible which supported their world and cultural
viewpoints. Prior to 1820, many Baptists in both the North and
the South were anti-slavery, but as the worth of slave labor became apparent in the Southern agrarian economy, more and more
religious people changed their minds. Their pastors preached that
slavery was biblical and that abolitionism was a sin. Regarding
slavery, some believed that "as a question of morals, it's been us
and God, . . . as a question of political economy, it is with us alone,
as free and independent states."[42]

Whites grew worried about the power of Black preaching, so much so that in some Southern states it was illegal for enslaved Africans to gather for church. Edward Baptist writes that an "Alabama newspaper warned of shrewd, cunning slave preachers."[43] He says that whites, on the heels of some slave revolts, believed that Black preachers, "feigning communication from God,"[44] would be able to inspire enslaved Africans to work to escape slavery. African American Christianity was a lightning rod for the slaves' belief that God desired their freedom, as opposed to white Protestant Christianity, which was a stabilizer for racial discrimination and bondage.

Religious white people were being taught that God was on their side, a message that African Americans were neither taught nor one that they believed about their God. Whites detested the presence of Black people in "their" country. Thomas Marshall, the son of John Marshall, who was the chief justice of the US Supreme Court from 1801 to 1835, bemoaned the very existence of Black people in America. He believed that slavery was "ruinous to whites," and that if Blacks remained in America, or specifically in his home state of Virginia, that "the whole country [of Virginia] will be inundated by a Black wave . . . with a few white faces here and there floating on the surface."[45]

While white preachers sought to free their white members' consciences by assuring them that God was on their side, they also worked toward cementing this belief in the minds of Black people—that God was on the side of their oppressors. The preachers developed and perfected their theology, gleaning much from the apostle Paul and reminding the slaves that the Bible said that they should obey their masters. They also taught that God had allowed and even ordained white people to enslave people of color. In other words, the message was, "Don't be angry at us. This is all the will of God."

In 1822, Rev. Richard Furman, president of the Baptist State Convention, gave an address entitled "Exposition Relative to the Coloured Population in the United States." In that address, he said it was lawful to hold slaves and that the entire subject would be considered "in a moral and religious point of view."[46] He desired to give his thoughts on the lawfulness of owning slaves, ". . . because they consider their duty to God, the peace of the State, the satisfaction of scrupulous consciences, and the welfare of the slaves themselves, as intimately connected with a right view of the subject."[47] Sentiments against holding slaves, Furman argued, are "not just," for "the right of holding slaves is clearly established by the Holy Scriptures, both by precept and example."[48]

As far as abiding by the Golden Rule, upon which so many Africans hung their hope, Furman laid out his understanding: "The Christian golden rule, of doing to others, as we would they should to do us, has been urged as an unanswerable argument against holding slaves. But surely this rule is never to be urged against that order of things, which the Divine government has established; nor do our desires become a standard to us, under this rule, unless they have a due regard to justice, propriety and the general good."[49]

Striking in Furman's address is the absence of any mention of Jesus, a stark contrast to the way enslaved Africans embraced Christianity, for the word "Christian" is used devoid of Jesus' name. If holding slaves were evil, Furman argued, the apostles themselves would have said it. Instead, he claimed,

> [These men] who were ready to lay down their lives for the cause of their God, would [not] have tolerated it . . . surely where the both master and servant were Christian, as in the case before us, they would have enforced the law of Christ, and required, that the master should liberate his slave in the first instance. But, instead of this, they let the relationship remain untouched, as being lawful and right, and insist on the relative duties.[50]

Furman concludes this rather lengthy address by saying, "the holding of slaves is justifiable by the doctrine and example contained in the Holy Writ; and is, therefore, consistent with Christian uprightness, both in sentiment and conduct."[51]

The Constitution had left a door open for the continued buying, selling, and utilizing of slave labor. By the mid-1820s, white supremacy, sanctioned by the Constitution, also was sanctioned by the Southern church, led by the Baptists. In 1860, the South's slave owners and those opposed to slavery split at the Democratic National Convention, with slave owners leaving the premises stating, "Slavery is our king; Slavery is our truth; Slavery is our Divine Right."[52] Christianity was taking on the identity of white supremacist ideology, using God as its anchor and justification. In Virginia, slaveholder George Fitzhugh said that he was "quite as intent on abolishing Free Society" as Northerners were on "abolishing slavery." When the war broke out, Fitzhugh framed the conflict as a war "between Christians and infidels."[53]

The glorious words of the Declaration of Independence about all men being equal were being contextualized, and clarification of what "we the people" meant was in full force. Those who were committed to the rightness of slavery believed in it more than they did the sanctity of the Union. Alexander Stephens, the first vice president of the Confederacy, refuted the words which said all men were equal. They were not, he said, adding that the Confederacy was founded on truth: "Our new government is founded upon exactly the opposite idea; its foundations are laid, its cornerstone rests, upon the great truth that the negro is not equal to the white man; that slavery—subordination to the superior race—is his natural and normal condition. This, our new government, is the first, in the history of the world, based upon this great physical, philosophical, and moral truth."[54]

The religion of white people—openly in the South but more clandestinely in the North—was being established as a different religion than the one taught by Jesus and embraced by enslaved Africans and their offspring for centuries to come. White religion was bold in its arrogance and surety that God was on their side. Ebenezer Warren, who was the pastor of First Baptist Church of Christ in Macon, Georgia, preached:

> Slavery forms a vital element of the Divine Revelation to man. Its institution, regulation, and perpetuity constitute a part of many of the books of the Bible. . . . The public mind needs enlightening from the sacred teachings of inspiration on this subject. . . . We of the South have been passive, hoping the storm would subside. . . . Our passiveness has been our sin. We have not come to the vindication of God and of truth, as duty demanded. . . . It is necessary for ministers of the gospel . . . to teach slavery from the pulpit, as it was taught by the holy men of old, who spake as moved by the holy Spirit. . . . Both Christianity and Slavery are from heaven; both are blessings to humanity; both are to be perpetuated to the end of time. . . .

> Because Slavery is right; and because the condition of the slaves
> affords them all those privileges which would prove substantial
> blessings to them; and, too, because their Maker has decreed
> their bondage, and has given them, as a race, capacities and
> aspirations suited alone to this condition of life.[55]

Helped along by the existence of slavery, the whitening of God was all but complete in this country by the mid-1820s. There had been a tendency in this country for some time to "identify the roots of American democracy with pre-Norman England and therefore with the Saxon origins of the English language itself."[56] White people, it seems, were obsessed with their whiteness. In 1882, Herbert Spencer told Americans that "the eventual mixture of the allied varieties of the Aryan race forming the US population would produce a finer type of man than has hitherto existed."[57] Americans believed completely that "the negro race" was inferior to the Anglo-Saxon, and that Blacks were doomed. "[N]othing can save the inferior race but a ready and pliant assimilation," according to Josiah Strong.[58] He wrote:

> What if it should be God's plan to people the world with better
> and finer material? To this result no war of extermination is
> needful; the contest is not one of arms but of vitality and
> civilization. Whether the extinction of inferior races before the
> advancing Anglo-Saxon seems to the reader sad or otherwise, it
> certainly appears probable . . . Thus, while on this continent God
> is training the Anglo-Saxon race for its mission, a complemental
> work has been in progress in the great world beyond. God has
> two hands. Not only is he preparing in our civilization the "die"
> with which to stamp the nations, but, by what Southey called
> the "timing of Providence," he is preparing mankind to receive
> our impress.[59]

The answer to a question, "Is God a white racist?" posed decades later by William R. Jones, seemed to be yes, not by God's doing but by the doing of a group of people who decided that they were superior to all other peoples. In his book by the same title as his piercing question, Jones recalls the question of W. E. B. Du Bois, "What meaneth Black suffering?" Jones wrote, "To talk about the *saving* work of God is to presuppose a conclusion about the *benev-olence* of God; it is to assert the essential goodness of God in spite of the prior 'evil' that makes his 'saving' work necessary. In sum, salvation is meaningless without the prior affirmation of God's be-nevolence toward man."[60]

Black people struggled. Who was this God? Their suffering insulted and did violence to the total salvation history of Chris-tian faith, which includes the creation, the fall of humanity, the incarnation and resurrection of Jesus, and the second coming of Jesus.[61] The God of white people is a problem; that God allows the suffering of Black people. Does that mean God ordains it? White supremacist theology would say yes. Jones says that the liberation theologian has to explain things which are not explicable. He must provide an explanation which "perceives [Black] suffering as nega-tive. He must show that God condones oppression, which Blacks do not believe is God's will or sanctioned by nature. He must, in sum, de-sanctify the suffering in question or else the oppressed will not regard their suffering as oppressive and will not be motivated to attack it."[62]

The idea of there being such a thing as "divine racism," as Jones posits, is troubling, but the white God that we have all been presented with is a problem. Alan Davies says, in describing the "Anglo-Saxon Christ," that "to be a Christian and an Anglo-Saxon and an American was . . . (for Josiah Strong) to stand on the very mountaintop of privilege,"[63] For Strong, the conclusion was that Christ was an American as well. This notion of the superiority of Anglo-Saxons was accepted even by some of the proponents of the social gospel, including Horace Bushnell, Washington Glad-den, and Walter Rauschenbusch.[64] Rauschenbusch was "explicit about his belief in the Aryan myth, and was known to speak of the superiority of white people (Anglo-Saxons) in both the political and religious arenas."[65] It goes without saying that after the Civil War, Anglo-Saxon beliefs reinforced the white church's opposition to the freedom gained by Black people through the Emancipation Proclamation.

White supremacy spread like the deadly Ebola virus, and the coronavirus most recently, killing the capacity of those infected to see or even consider that their way of thinking might be antithetical to the will of God expressed through Jesus. The biggest part of the problem was not the presence of the spiritual, social, and political virus itself, but the refusal to admit the illness and to seek a way to combat it and finally kill it. To this day, no widespread desire or energy has been devoted to extricating this deadly virus from the soul of America's religious and political landscape.

Epigraph

James Baldwin, *The Fire Next Time* (New York: Vintage International, 1993), 39–40.

NOTES

1. Wes Howard-Brook, *"Come Out My People!": God's Call Out of Empire in the Bible and Beyond* (New York: Orbis, 2010), 21.
2. Rita Nakashima Brock and Rebecca Ann Parker, *Saving Paradise: How Christianity Traded Love of This World for Crucifixion and Empire* (Boston: Beacon Press, 2008), 20–21.
3. Brock and Parker.
4. James Baldwin, *The Fire Next Time* (New York: Vintage International, 1993), 39.
5. Baldwin.
6. Ibram X. Kendi, *Stamped from the Beginning: The Definitive History of Racist Ideas in America* (New York: Nation Books, 2016), 121.
7. Vincent Harding, *There Is a River: The Black Struggle for Freedom in America* (Orlando: Harcourt Brace & Company, 1981), 46.
8. Harding, 47.
9. Harding, 101.
10. Harding, 101–102.
11. Harding, 105–106.
12. Brian Lyman, "'Where Was the Lord?' On Jefferson Davis' Birthday, Nine Slave Testimonies," *Montgomery Advertiser*, June 3, 2019, https://www.montgomeryadvertiser.com/in-depth/news/2019/06/03/alabama-state-holiday-jefferson-davis-birthday-where-lord-9-slave-testimonies/3740398002/, 9. A subheading on the article reads, "The voices of five men and four women, once held in human bondage, interviewed in Alabama in 1937."
13. Harding, 112.
14. Harding, 117.
15. Harding.
16. First Church in Cambridge, Congregational, United Church of Christ, Cambridge, Massachusetts, "Owning Our History: First Church and Race, 1636–1873," https://firstchurchcambridge.org/first-church-in-the-world/owning-our-history-first-church-and-race-1636-1873.
17. Obery Hendricks, *The Politics of Jesus: Rediscovering the True Revolutionary Nature of Jesus' Teachings and How They Have Been Corrupted* (New York: Doubleday, Three Leaves Press, 2006), 101.
18. Hendricks, 82.
19. Howard-Brook, 283.

20. Howard-Brook.

21. Brock and Parker, 231.

22. Hendricks, 101.

23. Jon Meacham, *American Gospel: God, the Founding Fathers, and the Making of a Nation* (New York: Random House, 2007), 72.

24. This Scripture is often quoted by those on the Religious Right. Former US Attorney General Jeff Sessions used this Scripture as the biblical justification for President Trump's policy of separating migrant children from their parents in 2017.

25. "People and Ideas: The Puritans," PBS, https://www.pbs.org/wgbh/pages/frontline/godinamerica/people/puritans.html.

26. Harding, 221.

27. Harding, 222.

28. Harding.

29. Charles F. Irons, "Religion During the Civil War," Encyclopedia Virginia, https://encyclopediavirginia.org/religion-during_the_civil_war#start_.

30. Irons, 2.

31. Irons, 4.

32. Irons, 5.

33. Benjamin Quarles, *Lincoln and the Negro* (New York: Oxford University Press, 1962), 106.

34. Quarles, 118.

35. Harding, 214.

36. Quarles, 101.

37. Quarles, 102.

38. Quarles.

39. Quarles, 109.

40. Quarles, 110.

41. "An Appeal from the Colored Men of Philadelphia to the President of the United States," https://static1.squarespace.com/static/590be125ff7c502a07752a5b/t/5eb4b69a05feaf0320dcf4a3/1588901531735/Gibbs%2C+Jr.%2C+Jonathan+Clarkson%2C+An+Appeal+from+the+Colored+Men+of+Philadelphia+to+the+President.pdf.

42. Adam Lee, "The Proslavery History of the Southern Baptists," Daylight Atheism, June 21, 2017, 5, https://www.patheos.com/blogs/daylightatheism/2017/06/pro-slavery-history-southern-baptists/.

43. Edward E. Baptist, *The Half Has Never Been Told: Slavery and the Making of American Capitalism* (New York: Basic Books, 2014), 210.

44. Baptist.

45. Baptist, 209.

46. "Richard Furman's Exposition," Furman University, http://history.furman.edu/~benson.docs/rcd-fmnl.htm.

47. Furman, 4.

48. Furman.

49. Furman, 5.

50. Furman.

51. Furman, 9.

52. Bruce Gourley, "Yes, the Civil War Was about Slavery," February 8, 2107, Baptists and the Civil War: In Their Own Words, http://civilwarbaptists.com/featured/slavery/, 3.

53. Gourley.

54. Gourley, 4.

55. Gourley.

56. Alan Davies, *Infected Christianity: A Study of Modern Racism* (Kingston and Montreal: McGill-Queens University Press, 1988), 78.

57. Davies.

58. Davies, 82.

59. Davies.

60. William R. Jones, *Is God a White Racist? A Preamble to Black Theology* (Boston: Beacon Press, 1998), xxv.

61. Jones, xxvi.

62. Jones, xxv–xxvi.

63. Davies, 83.

64. Davies.

65. Davies.

9
Not One Nation, Not One God

I know that . . . colored men, men of my complex-
ion . . . cannot expect . . . any mercy from the laws,
from the constitution, or from the courts of the coun-
try. . . . I stand here to say that if, for doing what I
did, . . . I am to go in jail six months and pay a fine
of a thousand dollars, according to the Fugitive Slave
Law, . . . I . . . say that I will do all I can for any man
thus seized and held, though the inevitable penalty . . .
hangs over me.
　　　　—Charles Langston, an abolitionist, as he faced
　　　　　　sentencing for helping an enslaved man

Both Christianity and slavery are from heaven; both are
blessings to humanity; both are to be perpetuated to the
end of time. 　　　　　　—A white Baptist in Georgia

As the spiritual, moral, and religious infection called white supremacy began to ooze from this nation's foundation, it infected
more and more people. Whites' belief in their superiority grew and
became entrenched all over the country, not just in the South, and
resulted in far too many Black people buying into the idea of their
innate inferiority.

The religion of Paul, which for this book is being equated with
the religion of empire, had been marinating for hundreds of years.
The interpretation of the Bible had been deeply influenced by those
who believed in a God who had ordained racism. There were whites
who believed in God's "benevolent paternalism" but also believed
that they were unable to move from their belief in Anglo-Saxon superiority. Horace Bushnell, an influential Congregationalist minister

who lived in the nineteenth century, voiced what may have been the sentiment of many white people: "Nothing can save the inferior race but a ready and pliant assimilation."[1] In order for there to be peace on this earth, Bushnell believed, the relationship between the oppressed and oppressor had to be maintained.

That belief about who God was and what God expected seemed to characterize the followers of the religion of Paul. Much later, Walter Rauschenbusch, a white Baptist minister born in the mid-nineteenth century, wrote, "Those who adopt the white man's religion come under the white man's influence. Christianity is the religion of the dominant race."[2]

While the framers may not have written words to that effect into the Constitution, it is unlikely that they were not deeply influenced by that belief system. They were in the world and of the world. The country they were envisioning and forming was not a nation where non-white people, particularly at this time people of African descent, would have a secure place. How could they, when men who had read and studied the Bible would make declarations on the rightness of slavery? Some of them despised and denigrated even the concept of democracy. The Rev. Robert Dabney, a nineteenth-century Presbyterian minister, who said that it was white people who were the victims in the slavocracy and were being forced to "pay taxes to pretended education to the brats of Black paupers,"[3] further said that a democracy was little more than a "mobocracy" and "argued that opposing slavery was tantamount to rejecting Christianity."[4]

What was Dabney's Christianity? Clearly, there was something going on. Christian nationalism, or the religion of Paul, was evolving. A "real" American was a white Protestant, one who did not believe that God required all men to be considered as equal. That was not the religion of enslaved Africans, and that God was not the God to whom enslaved Africans could or did relate.

Losing Hope in the Federal Government

Even though many Blacks believed the Civil War represented the hand of God intervening in the stubborn persistence of white supremacist ideas and practices, they also were losing hope in the federal government, which they had for some time considered their ultimate way out of oppression. Little by little, Black people were beginning to believe the rhetoric voiced by so many white people that it was impossible for Blacks and whites to live in America together. As Blacks grew restless and weary of fighting the system of white supremacy which was keeping them enslaved in the South and despised and discriminated against all over the country, whites, too, were growing more and more fearful that the disenchanted Black people would rise up against them. Toussaint L'Ouverture had waged a successful slave revolt in Haiti, which made whites very afraid that such a successful war against them could happen on the mainland. By 1831, leading up to the Civil War, at least three slave revolts occurred that were severe enough to feed the growing insecurity of white people. The revolts were led by Gabriel Prosser (1800) and Nat Turner (1831) in Virginia, and by Denmark Vesey (1822) in South Carolina.

In spite of a Constitution and a Bible that did not protect them but instead sanctioned slavery within their sacred pages, Blacks still strove for freedom and respect. Often to no avail, Black men plotted and planned ways to get from underneath the knee of economic oppression brought about by the white supremacist system. Complaints about being underpaid went unheeded and many times resulted in the arrest and/or hanging of those who dared to challenge the system. The threat of arrest or death, however, could not kill the slaves' thirst for freedom and equity. In 1856, in Dover, Tennessee, an estimated 150 Black men tried to rescue other Black men who had been arrested for their part in planning an unsuccessful attack on iron mills where they worked but from which they were not being equitably or fairly paid. The rescue squad was stopped by a larger group of armed, white men. Vincent Harding writes that "nineteen Black participants were hanged. Thereafter, . . . many Black heads were chopped off and as a warning to others, were placed on poles, creating new signposts in the heart of Tennessee."[5]

The message to Black people to stay in their place and not challenge the system which was cutting off their lifeblood is not unlike the messaging that the Romans used through the act of crucifixion. Nothing much had changed, it seemed, in the methodology of oppressors to keep those whom they oppressed under the thumb of the government. Some of the enslaved Blacks were able to escape from the South, but they returned and tried to bring others out of their suffering. There are countless stories of such men, including John Mason, a fugitive, who after escaping managed to help rescue more than two thousand Black people in the 1850s. At one point he was captured and ripped apart by dogs but managed to escape again.[6] The tenacity and the determination of enslaved people never waned, in spite of the white interpretation of the Bible and the Constitution, both of which were infected with white supremacist thought.

If neither the Constitution nor the Bible protected Black people, neither did the courts, as evidenced by the 1857 Dred Scott decision. Instead of affirming justice for all, and Blacks in particular, the decision revealed that the Supreme Court of the United States also was marred by white supremacist ideology. Dred Scott, a former slave who moved to Missouri from Alabama, decided to seek justice in the courts and sue for his freedom. Missouri was a free state and a free territory, thanks to the Missouri Compromise of 1820. Though his case languished in the system for more than ten years, it is reasonable to understand that he thought there was hope when it finally made its way through the lower courts all the way to the US Supreme Court. In spite of all he had been through and seen, Scott held onto the hope that he finally would see justice.

But he was sorely disappointed. Chief Justice of the Supreme Court Roger Taney ruled against him. In the first ruling, Taney declared that Congress had acted unconstitutionally when it passed the Missouri Compromise. He asked and answered his own question: "Can a negro, whose ancestors were imported into this country, and sold as slaves, become a member of the political community formed and brought into existence by the Constitution of the United States, and as such become entitled to all the rights, privileges and immunities guaranteed by that instrument to the citizen?"[7]

No, said Taney, who went on to explain that "the Founding Fathers had never intended African people to be a part of 'We the people . . .'" He ruled that "neither Dred Scott nor any other person of African descent had any citizenship rights which were binding on white American society."[8] There were no rights of a Black man that a white man was bound to respect, said Taney, and his court ruled that the Missouri Compromise was unconstitutional because the Congress had "no authority to deprive white citizens of their right to enjoy Black property north of the Missouri line."[9]

Given this lack of support from the federal government and its branches, Black people looked for release from a bondage which had resulted in their spirits being shredded and their families broken up. They had lived and worked in spite of carrying unspeakable emotional and physical pain that resulted from being beaten and raped, from having their families ripped apart, and from the sense of hopelessness that there was no one in this country into which they had been brought who cared about them and their well-being. John Brown, the noted, feared, and hated abolitionist, proposed that there should be a separate state with complete sovereignty just for Black people within the Union. (Ironically, this was the same line of thinking adopted by Confederates a few years later.) He proposed "an independent community . . . established within and under the United States but without . . . state sovereignty, similar to the Cherokee nation of Indians or the Mormons."[10]

Brown and some others drew up a constitution with forty-eight articles, using the US Constitution as a model. Nothing in their constitution or rhetoric indicated that Blacks wanted to overthrow the American government; they wanted to live within the United States as human beings and not as objects. They even wanted their flag to be the American flag! Some in Brown's camp balked, but Brown was insistent: "The old flag is good enough for me. . . . Under it, freedom was won from the tyrants of the old world, for white men. Now, I intend it to do duty for Black men."[11]

The slave revolts were another way of addressing the overwhelming presence of injustice, but for the most part they failed. Nat Turner was ultimately murdered by a company of the United States Marines when his slave revolt failed. Black people noted that men fighting for the freedom of Black people had "died under the laws of the Constitution."[12] As the country moved ever closer to war, members of both parties made it clear that "freedom of Black men, north or south, had no place in their priorities."[13] The Constitution was failing Black people, and the white people's God was silent.

Abraham Lincoln must have internalized the reality of something having gone dreadfully wrong. How could two different groups of people identify God so differently and expect entirely different input from their God? Toward the end of the Civil War, many Southerners could not understand why their God, who they believed was on their side, had let them lose. Lincoln pondered that quandary as he wrote these words in his second inaugural address:

> One-eighth of the whole population were colored slaves, not distributed generally over the Union, but localized in the Southern part of it. These slaves constituted a peculiar and powerful interest. All knew that this interest was, somehow, the cause of the war. North and South . . . both read the same Bible and pray to the same God; and each invokes His aid against the other. It may seem strange that any men should dare to ask a just God's assistance in wringing their bread from the sweat of other men's faces; but let us judge not that we be judged. The prayers of both could not be answered; that of neither has been answered fully. The Almighty has his own purposes.[14]

Lincoln was trying to understand the mind of God, who could at once have raised Jesus from the dead but who also, according to the Bible, let Job suffer horribly. Who was this God? And what was this Bible that contained words that both the oppressor and the oppressed used? For pro-slavery people, there was the doctrine of Ham, and for abolitionists, Exodus 21:16, which says, "Whoever kidnaps a person, whether that person has been sold or is still held in possession, shall be put to death." Hence, the Bible of American Christianity did little to eliminate the institution of slavery or the suffering it caused. Frederick Douglass remembered that it was after his master "found the Lord" that he became even more vile and violent, a fact which disappointed Douglass. "Christianity neither made him to be humane to his slaves, nor to emancipate them. If it had any effect on his character, it made him more cruel and hateful in all his ways; for I believe him to have been a much worse man after his conversion."[15]

Conformity to the State

Clearly, something was amiss in the understanding and practice of Christianity. Christianity to many whites in power was really civil religion; Jon Meacham says that there was no separation between church and state as Thomas Jefferson had advocated in the letter to the Danbury Baptists in 1801. As stated before, the Baptists in the state of Virginia were like most people who had emigrated from England to the new world. They did not want the type of intrusion by religion into the affairs of the state that they had experienced in England, so there was no ostensible sectarian involvement in the United States government. "The separation argument," said Meacham, "was largely a cover for politicians to play to the Protestant majority, but the Protestant majority did not seem willing to undo the work of the Founders."[16] Isaac Cornelison said, "America was without a church but not without a religion,"[17] which seemed fine to most, but it was strange and problematic for some that America identified as a Christian nation. The US Supreme Court said in 1892, "[W]e find everywhere a clear recognition of the same truth: . . . this is a Christian nation."[18] But if being Christian means one follows the teachings of the Christ, then America clearly wasn't a Christian nation. The founders, not mentioning the need to follow Jesus as being a requirement to be labeled Christian, nonetheless took the position that this was not a Christian nation. Andrew Seidel, in *The Founding Myth*, explains that the belief that America was founded on Christian principles was erroneous from the beginning. We have already referred to the Treaty of Tripoli, establishing a friendship between the United States and Tripoli and ratified unanimously by the United States Senate in 1796, which said explicitly that the "United States is not a Christian nation."[19] Seidel says that the commonly heard proclamation that this country was founded on Judeo-Christian values is categorically false; he quotes a 1992 *Newsweek* article which stated that "the idea of a single Judeo-Christian tradition is a made-in-America myth. Judaism is Judaism because it rejects Christianity, and Christianity is Christianity because it rejects Judaism."[20]

The founders were clear. John Adams wrote, "The government of the United States is not, in any sense, founded on the Christian religion."[21] And Thomas Paine, one of the signers of the Declaration of Independence, wrote, "Mingling religion with politics should be disavowed and reprobated by every inhabitant of America."[22]

The pro-slavery, white supremacist camp of biblical belief and interpretation was always said to have come from a literal reading of the Scriptures, and those who saw things differently than did they were said to be practicing open-ended interpretation which many considered heretical. The white supremacist faction referred to the epistles, as mentioned before, specifically those verses which admonished slaves to obey their masters (Colossians 3:22; Ephesians 6:5; 1 Peter 2:18-20). They also referred to Paul's letter to Philemon, where he sends a slave, Onesimus, back to his master. Paul writes (Philemon 8-16):

> For this reason, though I am bold enough in Christ to command you to do your duty, yet I would rather appeal to you on the basis of love—and I, Paul, do this as an old man, and now also as a prisoner of Christ Jesus. I am appealing to you for my child, Onesimus, whose father I have become during my imprisonment. Formerly he was useless to you, but now he is indeed useful both to you and to me. I am sending him, that is, my own heart, back to you. I wanted to keep him with me, so that he might be of service to me in your place during my imprisonment for the gospel; but I preferred to do nothing without your consent, in order that your good deed might be voluntary and not something forced. Perhaps this is the reason he was separated from you for a while, so that you might have him back forever, no longer as a slave but more than a slave, a beloved brother—especially to me but how much more to you, both in the flesh and in the Lord.

Onesimus was a slave living in the Roman Empire who had emancipated himself and become attached to Paul. Though Onesimus faced grave danger because escaped slaves could be severely punished, he loved God and Paul's message about Jesus and was willing to risk his life to assist Paul in spreading the gospel. However, the law required that a runaway slave be returned to his owner, so Paul had to send Onesimus back to Philemon. Because Philemon also was a Christian, Paul believed that his appeal to him to receive Onesimus as a Christian brother would be heeded. The story does not include those details, however.

Slave holders and preachers read and studied this story and concluded that they could do no less; returning escaped slaves to their masters was the will of God. One preacher said in 1823 that "all the sophistry in the world cannot get rid of this decisive example. Christianity robs no man of his rights, and Onesimus was the property of his master, under the laws of his country, which must be obeyed, if not contrary to the laws of God."[23]

In "The Religious Defense of American Slavery Before 1830," author Larry R. Morrison notes that "the proslavery appeal was always to the authority of the Bible and never to the spirit of Christianity."[24] The Bible and the gospel are two different entities, though the gospel is part of the Bible. The Bible has often been and continues to be used to support the status quo. It is a political document clothed in a theological covering. By contrast, the gospel of Jesus Christ is something entirely different. First, it clearly identifies Jesus as the Son of God; in the Gospels Jesus is as close to God as anyone can get. And the message that Jesus taught was anything but status quo. Jesus challenged not only the government but also the church leaders. In that sense, Jesus' gospel is counter-culture. The late Peter Gomes said that "the Gospel can easily be lost in the Bible."[25] He added that the "Bible is at odds with conventional Christianity."[26] The Bible as interpreted by the religion of empire urges conformity with the state, while the words of Jesus, contained in the Gospels, urge rejection of the state in the areas where it neglects the well-being of "the least of these" (Matthew 25). Gomes says, as we have already suggested, that "we make the Bible conform to our beliefs."[27] The Bible has been used as a convenient tool to preserve power. The words of Jesus are considered to be too incendiary and threatening to the cause of the state. The words of the gospel gave hope to the hopeless, while many other words of the Bible were used to deepen and justify that same hopelessness.

The name of almighty God was almost always used as slave holders chose selected passages in the Bible to justify their actions. In 1845, an Episcopal bishop, the Right. Rev. William Meade, addressed enslaved Africans, saying, "Almighty God hath been pleased to make you slaves here, and to give you nothing but labour and poverty in this world, which you are obliged to submit to, as it is His will that it should be so. Your bodies, you know, are not your own; they are at the disposal of those you belong to."[28]

Clergymen and statesmen who held the Bible dear used that book to justify their cultural inclinations. Some argued vociferously that Jefferson was wrong to have said "all men are created equal," because in their minds, that was not the case. The God of the Bible was different from the God of the Gospels. General James Ham-mond, who was governor of South Carolina in 1845, wrote to Rev. Thomas Clarkson, a British abolitionist in what are known as "Let-ters to Clarkson":

> I firmly believe that American slavery is not only not a sin, but especially commanded by God himself through Moses, and approved by Christ through His Apostles, . . . I endorse without reserve the much-abused sentiment of Governor McDuffie that "slavery is the corner-stone of our Republican edifice," while I repudiate as ridiculously absurd that much-lauded but nowhere credited dogma of Mr. Jefferson that "all men are born equal," . . . Slavery is truly the corner-stone and foundation of every well-designed and durable Republican edifice.[29]

That line of reasoning would not have been that of those who need-ed the hope of the so-called Good News, which is what the gospel is said to be. The gospel was unsettling to those who were attempting to make the case for the rightness of slavery because people would rather be confirmed than confronted in their religious walk. The Bible was used to protect the self-interests of the state and the rac-ism of the masses; to confront people from the pulpit would have been disastrous to the state's goal to cement and increase its power. However, the gospel, spoken by one who was a member of the op-pressed masses himself, was intended to give hope to those who otherwise had no hope. The good news for the downtrodden was bad news for those in power and wished to remain so. Thus, the gospel was made subordinate to the Bible, resulting in the Christi-anity of Christ being pushed further and further into oblivion.

The Effects of Reconstruction

The Civil War was fought, followed by the era of Reconstruction. Although some refused to say that the war was fought over slavery, slavery was in fact the driver of the conflict. While many soldiers from the North were eager to fight to save the Union and claimed to be anti-slavery, that did not mean they were pro-Black. When Lin-coln submitted the Emancipation Proclamation, whole regiments of some Northern troops deserted because they did not want to fight for the freedom of Black people. The white soldiers were afraid that if African Americans were set free, they would migrate to the North after the war and take jobs from whites.

In all, more than 185,000 Black people fought in the Civil War. Believing that the war had been sent by God to help rid the United States of slavery and insure their freedom, they were more than willing to join the fight, in spite of being paid less than white soldiers, not having uniforms that fit, and often being assigned to menial jobs. None of that mattered. They believed they were fighting for their freedom. State militias had not allowed Africans and African Americans to join their ranks, and up to this point, the United States Army had never accepted Black soldiers. As the president worried and strategized on how to save the Union, he decided to free "all persons held as slaves within any states in rebellion against the United States." They would be, said the Emancipation Proclamation, "forever free."[30]

Once the war was over, Reconstruction began, and the three Reconstruction Amendments were added to the United States Constitution. The Thirteenth Amendment abolished slavery and all of its formal aspects. The Fourteenth Amendment guaranteed to all basic citizenship rights and protections, and the Fifteenth Amendment gave all male citizens the right to vote. It seemed that the struggle for dignity and freedom that Blacks fought for had come to an end, and for about a decade, the three Reconstruction Amendments protected them.

But that protection would come to an end. There was no law and no respect for any God that was strong enough to kill the white supremacist thinking of many whites in the North and the South. It is important to continue interjecting that white people from the North, though presumably very religious, were not friends of Black people. General William Tecumseh Sherman, a celebrated Union soldier, for example, was said to deplore Black people, including Black soldiers. He "opposed their employment as soldiers, drove them from his camp even when they were starving, and manifested toward them an almost criminal dislike," noted Doris Kearns Goodwin.[31] The war's end meant that not only Southern but also Northern soldiers had to figure out what to do with freed Black men who had fought for their freedom and for the saving of the Union. Sherman issued Special Field Order No. 15, which allocated plots of land to the freed African and African American soldiers, and the Freedman's Bureau was put in place to deal with "America's problem."[32] The passage of the Reconstruction Amendments seemed to be exactly what this nation needed to deal with its systemic white supremacy and racism, and while they helped mitigate a bad situation, in the end, their power was largely neutralized by white supremacist policies and practices.

While the Thirteenth Amendment abolished or outlawed slavery (except if a person had been convicted of a crime), the Fourteenth Amendment was conceived in such a way as to define what made one an American citizen and give the federal government the power to protect the rights of all American citizens, white or otherwise. At its heart were good intentions, and any discriminatory state laws could be overturned by the federal government. However, the intrusion of the federal government in state affairs riled Southerners, already sulking because they had lost the war. The Confederacy officially ended when the war was over in 1865, so its eleven states were technically still a part of the Union against which they had fought. However, they resented the Union and what they perceived to be interference from the federal government. Because they still wanted to govern themselves, the Southerners were offended by the increased federal power, represented by the Reconstruction Amendments, which fueled their resentment toward the federal government.

The Fourteenth Amendment, in declaring that all persons born in the United States were in fact Americans, served to encourage Blacks while it bothered rebel Southerners. The South still wanted to be separated from the Union. One lawmaker said he would be "perfectly willing to waive national representation entirely for ten years if the North would agree to let the Southern states try the experiment of self-government."[33] The South, burned by the defeat of the Confederacy, felt like the punishment being meted against them was too severe. The Fourteenth Amendment fed their ire, as it "made virtually the entire political leadership of the South ineligible for office. The eleven states, already being charged with tasks to complete in order to be readmitted to the Union, were especially hard hit by Section 3 of the 14th Amendment, which prohibited anyone from holding a civil or military office who 'shall have engaged in insurrection or rebellion against the same [the Union], or given aid or comfort to the enemies thereof.'"[34]

While Blacks were giving credit to God for the war and its outcome, whites were unhappy with both government and religion
because they felt that the Bible and the Constitution had let them
down. The God of their Bible had allowed them to be defeated, and
the government which decided the fate of all Americans was writing
into its sacred document words that would only further stymie their
lives. Whites were bitter about having lost their power over enslaved
Black people. As Blacks celebrated their freedom, whites grumbled
that Blacks were neglecting their labor as they observed them at-
tending political rallies to obtain information and to feed their newly
ingested freedom of spirit. In 1867, "Richmond's tobacco factories
were forced to close because so many laborers attended the Republican state convention."[35] For a time, Blacks even sidelined God, so
busy were they celebrating their freedom. "Politics got in our midst
and our revival or religious work for a while began to wane," said
one Black who had been a minister to enslaved people.[36]

The Fourteenth Amendment was ratified in 1868. The Fifteenth Amendment gave Black people the right to vote at a time
when white lawmakers all over the United States were reluctant to
do so. As late as 1868, says Eric Foner, "only eight northern states
allowed Blacks the right to vote."[37] To Southerners, "the Fifteenth
Amendment was the most revolutionary measure ever to receive
Congressional sanction, the 'crowning' act of a Radical conspiracy
to promote Black equality and transform America from a confederation of states into a centralized nation."[38]

The passing of the Fifteenth Amendment in 1870 felt like a
God-sent victory to Black people, even though it said nothing
about the right of Black people to hold office; more importantly,
the amendment failed to set uniform eligibility voting standards for
the entire country. It also said nothing about the right of women to
vote. America's sacred document was still suffering from an inca-
pacity to consider all humans as important to the nation's life. As
politicians worked to make life easier and more equitable for Black
people in this country, the churches held onto their practice of racial denigration. Biracial congregations decreased after the war, but
in white churches where Blacks remained, whites still refused to
"offer them an equal place within their congregations."[39]

Foner says, "The end of slavery does not appear to have altered the views of many white clergymen as to the legitimacy of

the peculiar institution or the desirability of preserving unaltered Blacks' second class status within biracial churches."[40] White preachers in the South would not subscribe to the idea that slavery in and of itself was a sin, or that those who engaged in slave trading were committing a sin, so their churches kept the races separated by designating some pews for whites and others for Blacks. Black churches sprang up regularly, as Black people refused to endure the humiliation of racist oppression in the institutions which were supposed to represent God. Their God wasn't like the white God, and they were finally able to act on what they believed. They would worship the God of freedom, the God of justice and community, and would abandon the God who had apparently guided white people to treat them so poorly. By the end of 1877, more than ten years after the end of the Civil War, the "vast majority of Southern Blacks had withdrawn from churches dominated by whites."[41] While Southern white Protestant churches steadily lost Black members in the years after the Civil War, Black membership in Roman Catholic churches in the South remained steady, partly because "they did not require Black worshippers to sit in separate pews."[42]

After passage of the Reconstruction Amendments, Blacks moved away from white churches and from the so-called biblical sanction of slavery and racism, and the Black God whom Blacks chose to worship emerged ever more clearly, although they did not call their God "Black." It is just that the God that Black people worshipped was so different from the white God of their former masters. Even during slavery, their conception of God had met their great need to remain hopeful in spite of racism and white supremacy. Their religious convictions "profoundly affected the way" they "expressed aspirations for justice and autonomy," says Foner, who continues, "Blacks inherited from slavery a distinctive version of Christian faith, in which Jesus appeared as a personal redeemer offering solace in the face of misfortune, while the Old Testament suggested that they were a chosen people, analogous to the Jews in Egypt, whom God, in the fullness of time, would deliver from bondage."[43]

Blacks were as intent on placing God in the center of their cultural beliefs as were whites. Puritans had viewed their safe passage to the new world as evidence of God's favor while Southern whites, after losing the war, felt that God had let them down.

Blacks, however, looked to God for justification and evidence of God's presence in their lives. The beginning of the war and its outcome were seen by Blacks as messianic and as proof of how much God abhorred slavery. "God," they said, "had scourged America with war for her injustice to the Black man, had allowed his agent Lincoln, like Moses, to glimpse the promised land of universal freedom," and then mysteriously removed him before he "reached its blessed fruitions."[44]

Black people knew they would need God—a different God of a different ilk than the God who had stood silently by for hundreds of years as they suffered. They forgave God for not delivering them because they developed such a strong belief that God would in fact deliver them in God's own way and in God's own time. They staunchly believed the stories of deliverance found in the Book of Daniel in the Hebrew Scriptures. They were convinced that they, too, had been in a sort of lions' den, as had been Daniel, and a fiery furnace, like the three Hebrew boys—Shadrach, Meshach, and Abednego. They were certain that their faith in their God was as intentional as had been the faith of those four biblical characters, and that it had saved them. They knew that faith in a God who was able to save and deliver them was the reason why they had not been obliterated as a people in spite of the conditions under which they lived.[45]

Blacks realized that it was their duty and call to "make freedom a full-blown institution, just as slavery had been an institution."[46] They leaned on their God, even as Southern whites leaned on their God. Both races had issues with the Divine—Blacks wondering why God had allowed slavery, and whites questioning why God had not given them victory in the Civil War. Charles Reagan Wilson, in *Baptized in Blood*, says that observers and scholars identified what they called the "South's two civil religions—one Black and one white," showing how these "two groups advanced differing understandings of American providential destiny."[47]

Southern whites wrestled with understanding God, and they moved ever more closely to the ideology of white supremacy, believing that they may have "lost the military battle but won the spiritual victory."[48] The South, says Wilson, wanted a separate political identity, a dream that was defeated during the war but that did not die. "The cultural dream replaced the political dream; the South's kingdom was to be of culture, and not of politics."[49] After the war, what is now referred to as a "Southern civil religion" developed, tying together Christian churches and Southern culture. Both God and the Bible became tools used to sanctify and justify Southern culture and values, and the Constitution was viewed as a tool which could help develop and maintain the cultural religion and political system that the South was creating. Southern religion would create its own moral codes and accepted modes of behavior, and the things that occurred, even the lessons preached, seemed as far away from the Christianity of Jesus as could be.

Epigraphs

Vincent Harding, *There Is a River: The Black Struggle for Freedom in America* (Orlando: Harcourt Brace & Company, 1981), 209–10. Charles Langston, the grandfather of poet Langston Hughes, was born a free man to a mulatto mother who was enslaved and a white father. Langston helped rescue an escaped enslaved man, John Price, from federal authorities in 1859 and was arrested.

Katherine Stewart, *The Power Worshippers: Inside the Dangerous Rise of Religious Nationalism* (New York: Bloomsbury Publishing, 2019), 107. The words were spoken by a white "Baptist of Georgia," not identified as a preacher.

NOTES

1. Rita Nakashima Brock and Rebecca Ann Parker, *Saving Paradise: How Christianity Traded Love of This World for Crucifixion and Empire* (Boston: Beacon Press, 2008), 398.

2. Brock and Parker, 400.

3. Katherine Stewart, *The Power Worshippers: Inside the Dangerous Rise of Religious Nationalism* (New York: Bloomsbury Publishing, 2019), 106.

4. Stewart.

5. Vincent Harding, *There Is a River: The Black Struggle for Freedom in America* (Orlando: Harcourt Brace & Company, 1981), 197.

6. Harding, 199.

7. Harding, 201.

8. Harding.

9. Harding, 202.

10. Harding, 206.

11. Harding.

12. Harding, 213.

13. Harding, 216.

14. Jon Meacham, *American Gospel: God, the Founding Fathers, and the Making of a Nation* (New York: Random House, 2007), 118.

15. Meacham, 125.

16. Meacham, 143.

17. Meacham, 144.

18. Meacham.

19. Andrew Seidel, *The Founding Myth: Why Christian Nationalism Is Un-American* (New York: Sterling Publishing, 2019), 16.

20. Seidel, 3.

21. Jeff Schweitzer, "Founding Fathers: We Are Not a Christian Nation," February 26, 2015, updated April 28, 2015, HuffPost, https://www.huffpost.com/entry/founding-fathers-we-are-n_b_6761840, 1.

22. Harlow Giles Unger, "The U.S. a Christian Nation? Not According to the Founders!", History News Network, https://historynewsnetwork.org/article/172973.

23. Larry R. Morrison, "The Religious Defense of American Slavery Before 1830," https://www.kingscollege.net/gbrodie/The%20religious%20justification%20of%20slavery%20before%201830.pdf, 20.

24. Morrison, 27.

25. Peter Gomes, *The Scandalous Gospel of Jesus: What's So Good about the Good News?* (New York: HarperCollins, 2007), 20.

26. Gomes.

27. Gomes, 23.

28. Edward Wilmot Blyden, *Christianity, Islam, and the Negro Race* (Mansfield Centre, CT: Martino Publishing, 2016), 35.

29. Blyden, 36.

30. Words in the Emancipation Proclamation, passed January 1, 1863.

31. Doris Kearns Goodwin, *Team of Rivals* (New York: Simon & Schuster, 2005), 686.

32. Special Field Order No. 15 provided for the confiscation of 400,000 acres of land along the Atlantic coast of South Carolina, Georgia, and Florida, dividing it into parcels of not more than 40 acres on which about 18,000 formerly enslaved families would be allowed to settle.

33. Eric Foner, *Reconstruction: America's Unfinished Revolution, 1863–1877* (New York: Harper & Row, 1988), 259.

34. Foner, 253.

35. Foner, 282.

36. Foner.

37. Foner, 443.

38. Foner, 446.

39. Foner, 89.

40. Foner.

41. Foner, 91.

42. Foner.

43. Foner, 93.

44. Foner, 94.

45. The story of Daniel in the lions' den and the three Hebrew boys in the fiery furnace, surviving in spite of grave injustice, was a story to which enslaved Africans turned for proof and evidence of God's ability and willingness to free and save those who were under the yoke of slavery.

46. Harding, 260.

47. Charles Reagan Wilson, *Baptized in Blood: The Religion of the Lost Cause* (Athens: University of Georgia Press, 2009), xv.

48. Wilson, xvi.

49. Wilson, 1.

10
The State Over God

The integration movement . . . is one very important
facet of a world-wide, highly-organized, centuries-old
assault on mankind's greatest treasure—our faith in
Jesus Christ.
      —Father T. Robert Ingram, Episcopal priest, 1956

We already have seen how many people believed that Thomas Jefferson's declaration that "all men are created equal" had no basis in fact. They were willing to argue that God had never intended for everyone to be equal. Even before the Declaration of Independence was written, there seemed to be a basic agreement that such a thought defied credulity, and it would seem that Jefferson did not believe his own rhetoric, for he owned slaves, human beings whom he clearly believed to be inferior to him and to white people in general. If it is deemed true that his belief in equality extended only to wealthy and white Protestant males, then we can safely surmise that he didn't believe in equality for women, Native Americans, or even poor whites.

As we have seen, Jefferson sought true religious pluralism, believing that adherents of all religions, including Islam and Judaism, also had the right to worship freely in this nation.[1] But the burgeoning American capitalist system was clearly not interested in pushing egalitarianism as an American or religious value. The United States was on a mission to become an empire, and its wealth was being built on the backs of enslaved Africans. A theology already had been formed and propagated that claimed that God ordained that some people would forever remain inferior to whites. If God said it, no person could go against it. The state and the church bonded with one another to form an airtight defense against the argument that slavery was wrong.

White supremacy ideology permeated the fabric of Southern religion and became, in effect, the foundation for its theology. Losing the Civil War caused Southern whites to become nostalgic and yearn for what Charles Reagan Wilson describes as "cultural nationalism" and a "homogenous people," meaning people of the same blood and lineage.[2] Individuals within religious denominations were conflicted over the issue of slavery, and denominations split as the arguments for and against it increased. Southern religion was tenacious in its criticism of abolitionism. Southern pastors preached that slavery was of a divine nature and that it needed to be protected from those who would abolish it. These pastors believed they were uttering a holy cause, given to them directly by God as they "interpreted battle victories as God's blessings, and defeats as God's punishments for their failings."[3] Even before the Civil War, Southern preachers had called for secession, and during the war, they encouraged their members to be willing to go onto the battlefield for God and for the saving of the Southern way of life. Such a "path to victory may be through a baptism of blood,"[4] said one preacher, but it was a journey that all Southerners should be willing to undertake.

In spite of the divine urging of Southern preachers, however, the South lost the war, which made Southerners angry. Not only were they angry that they had lost the war, but also they were angry and disappointed with God. They remembered the words of Psalm 110:1, "The LORD says to my lord, 'Sit at my right hand until I make your enemies your footstool.'" There could have been no greater enemy than the Union, which had had the audacity to interfere with their Southern way of life. The Confederate cause was God's cause, they believed. Why, then, had God not given them the victory? The preachers, even more so than the Confederate military leaders, had worked hard to instill and maintain in the soldiers their truth that God was on their side. At every opportunity that they were afforded, these zealous preachers had gone out to the battlefields to baptize, confirm, serve communion, hand out Bibles, and teach Bible study lessons. The Confederates had welcomed and invited chaplains to aid in keeping up the soldiers' morale and will to fight. Believing that they were fighting for God, nothing less than their full commitment to God could be tolerated. How is it, they wondered, that the state, that is, the Union, had emerged from the Civil War ahead of the ultimate will of God?

It is not as though the church had not fought against the state during the war. Southern preachers held revivals in the height of the war, encouraging men and women alike to take up the cause of God, which was, they preached, the preservation of slavery. The government had no right to infringe on their rights. What the preachers were doing was helping to create a civil religion; Wilson says "the antebellum and wartime religious culture evolved into a Southern civil religion, based on Christianity and regional history."[5] In spite of the religious presence in the ranks of the Confederate military operations, however, the God that they preached and who they believed wanted this war, lost, and God's South lost. Southerners began to mourn what would become known as the Lost Cause, so it became necessary to remind them that although they had lost the war, their belief in the rightness of slavery was a solid one. Preachers drummed into the minds of Southerners that they were good people, virtuous, chosen by God. They must never forget that. Samuel S. Hill, a historian of Southern religion, said that "many southern whites . . . regarded their society as God's most favored,"[6] and they were taught this in spite of the outcome of the war.

Still, Southerners were angry. It was bad enough that the Emancipation Proclamation had ended slavery, and now free Blacks were not doing the bidding of white men but were forging a life for themselves (for they, too, believed that the hand of God had been shown in the outcome of the Civil War, a divine hand of mercy and justice rather than one of punishment). As the president and the Congress worked to figure out how to live in the new reality and passed the Reconstruction Amendments, angry Southern whites only became angrier. No matter what the state said, they continued to believe that God had made Black people inferior to white people and had determined that Blacks would be so forever. Southerners united in their belief that racial integration and equality "represented a heinous moral evil,"[7] and "they refused to believe that the Gospel required them to dismantle segregation."[8]

Only their religion and white supremacist beliefs about what the Bible said could help the defeated soldiers, in spite of their feeling that God had deserted them. Wilson reports that more than ten thousand Southerners went into exile after 1865, moving to places like Canada, Mexico, Brazil, and even Europe.[9] "Racial traditions and practices" served as the "cement for the South's cultural cohesion," and white supremacy was cemented as the "primary component of Southern culture."[10] According to Wilson, the civil religion of the South was "clearly differentiated from what Christianity may have at one time meant . . . civil religion, by definition, centers on the religious implications of a nation. The Southern public faith involved a nation—a dead one, which was perhaps the unique quality of this phenomenon."[11] He continues:

> One of the central issues of the American faith has been the relationship between church and state, but [ever] since the Confederate quest for political nationhood failed, the Southern faith has been less concerned with such political issues than with the cultural quest of identity. Because it emerged from a heterogeneous immigrant society, the American civil religion was especially significant in providing uprooted immigrants with a sense of belonging. Because of its origins in Confederate defeat, the Southern civil religion offered confused and suffering Southerners a sense of meaning, an identity in a precarious but distinct culture.[12]

The Lost Cause civil religion was homogeneous—all white—and while holding onto some of the "Christian concepts including the belief in heaven and hell, depravity, redemption and atonement, God and Satan, they put into their religion their own denominational attributes and ideas."[13] In effect, this civil religion represented a new Christian sect, born in the aftermath of the Civil War. The religious interpretation of the Lost Cause could be called the myth of the "Crusading Christian Confederates," says Wilson,[14] for at the center of their belief system was a strong idea of the virtue and importance of holding onto "Southern values." Instead of concentrating on the words of the gospel, the civil religion of the South focused on naming and maintaining Southern values and what they called virtue. Those values remain in place today. In "I Still Believe in Traditional Southern Values," Alyssa Michelle Hoover wrote in 2016:

> The South is not just a place to live. It's a way of life. We are
> known for our strong accents and even stronger values. To
> some, these values may be outdated or too conservative, but
> to me these values are what have always guided my life. . . .
> I believe in holding open doors, blessing people when they
> sneeze, and saying "excuse me" when you pass by someone. I
> believe saying "please" and "thank you" should be a habit. There
> is no such thing as being too polite in the South.[15]

The preachers preached virtue and values, even as they vilified
the Union and considered their treatment of Black people to be
within the will of almighty God. They believed they had fought for
freedom just as the soldiers of the Revolutionary War had done,
claiming a nobility that was beyond reproach. The Yankee was a
"monster" who "symbolized a chaotic, unrestrained Northern society which had threatened the pristine, orderly, Godly Southern
civilization."[16] One minister said that the "behavior of the Union
soldier was a gross violation of the moral law."[17] If God was angry,
it was with the Union soldiers, and with Southerners for having
"violated the rules of virtue, including callousness, covetousness,
greed, and worldliness."[18] But the Southerners did not include on
their list of offenses toward God the debacle called slavery. They
"refused to admit that God's displeasure with the peculiar institution was the cause of the Confederate defeat."[19] In defiance of the
federal government, Southerners who called themselves Christian
remade their religion to one that was "divinely suited for white
supremacy."[20] Carolyn Renée Dupont said they rejected the commands of God as having been fixed in stone.[21] The Union might
have won the battle, but Southern Christians, armed with their Bibles and their interpretation of their Bibles, were determined to win
the war for divine favor in their quest to preserve white supremacy.
Wilson says that in 1875, "Confederates met for a celebration, not
of the American nation; they celebrated ritualistically the Confederate nation that still lived in their minds."[22]

Not only had the Union ravaged their land, it had also des-
ecrated their sacred icons. Robert E. Lee was practically a god; in
their grieving the loss of the Civil War, Southerners compared him
with Christian saints. Wilson says he was compared with Moses

as one who had led his people through the wilderness but had not been allowed to cross over into the Promised Land.[23] Lee was called by many Southerners a "perfect man," compared unabashedly with Jesus the Christ.[24] Southerners thought of themselves as chosen people who had been maligned, as badly as had been the Israelites who had been led through the wilderness by Moses; they were the victims of this debacle called the Civil War; they were the chosen people, and they would never, ever forget. The state would have to repent for its violence against the will of God; the Civil War had been a "holy war," according to Wilson. The "Lost Cause jeremiad" perpetuated the belief in "the wickedness of the Yankees" and therefore of the federal government.[25]

It seems that in the minds of many Southerners, the state had created a breach that could never be fixed. Their belief in the holiness of their cause resulted in a mindset that lent itself to intractability. If they were the chosen people, and the Union had fought against them, then almighty God would be the final arbiter of their fate. Of that they were clear.

Civil Religion Battles the State

And so the South, in rebellion against the state, perpetuated its fight for the survival and perpetuation of white supremacy. The church, says Dupont, played an active role in creating and sustaining the system of oppression,"[26] and Southern Christians saw nothing wrong with it. Their bigotry was laced with resentment of having lost the war, and not even God or the words of the Bible could dilute it. As the state pushed laws and policies that would give Americans of African descent full citizenship and rights, white Southerners fought back, in some ways more vehemently against the state than against Black people themselves. To them, African Americans were a problem, but the state was more of a problem, because it used its power to try to make Southerners go in a direction they clearly believed was against the will of God and was certainly against the Southern way of life.

Their resentment infiltrated the state. In spite of the passage of the Reconstruction Amendments, Eric Foner writes that there were contentious fights in the Congress, and even after Reconstruction, when the Thirteenth, Fourteenth, and Fifteenth Amendments were passed, the United States Supreme Court, on which sat Southern men who were not divorced from their culture, ruled against the laws that were meant to right the wrongs of a democracy which had never lived up to its stated ideals. Foner writes that "the Court, over time, played a crucial role in the long retreat from the ideals of Reconstruction."[27] The court took issue with each of the amendments and engaged in "a long process of definition," according to Foner, and "even though alternative understandings were readily available, in almost every instance, the Court chose to restrict the scope of the second founding."[28] It was in the court that the state was taken to battle over and over. Though it was the job of the court to "fix . . . the national doctrine and policy," lawmakers would complain in later years that "thanks to the Supreme Court decisions, the federal government had been deprived of the power to protect southern Blacks against the 'outrages' committed by individuals and mobs."[29]

Angry and religious Southern whites engaged in a reign of terror during Reconstruction. By 1877, they had had enough of allowing Black people freedom the likes of which they had never had in the United States. To their repulsion, sixteen Blacks had been elected to Congress and more than six hundred Blacks had been elected to state legislatures. Beginning in 1865, during what Foner calls a period of "presidential reconstruction," Blacks were attacked for minor things, like not tipping a hat to a white person or not stepping off a sidewalk to let a white person pass. The dehumanization of Blacks, which had been extant from the moment they were jammed onto ships and brought to the Americas, increased, violently working to make sure they would not become confused as to who they were in this country.

It would take more than a war to uproot the will of God. *United States v. Cruikshank* was a case brought after the 1873 Colfax Massacre resulted in the murder of hundreds of Black men by a ninety-eight-member white mob. Although all ninety-eight were indicted, only a few stood trial, charged with conspiracy to deprive the victims of their constitutional rights, a violation of the Fourteenth Amendment. Three men were convicted, and the case went all the way to the US Supreme Court, where Justice Joseph Bradley ruled that "rights" were "only given or granted under the purview of the federal government," but that ordinary crimes such as murder were state crimes and therefore not protected. The white men went free.[30] There was enough racial animus on the court that even justices who were not from the South ended up supporting racist policies and laws. Southerners did not have to worry about having enough support in federal government to help them seek vengeance for what they believed the state had done to them.

Southerners could and did consider themselves to be living within the will of God in spite of how their treatment of Black enslaved people played out in a number of ways over the years. One stark example, chronicled years after the Civil War, depicts the religious life of Sam Bowers, who was the Imperial Wizard of the Ku Klux Klan in 1957. At that time, Bowers "had been sitting atop the FBI's most-wanted list for several years. He was suspected of plotting nine murders, seventy-five burnings of Black churches, and three hundred assaults."[31] But he was a good church man. He joined Hillcrest Baptist Church, where he served as a deacon and taught a men's Sunday school class.

Bowers knew the Bible. One of his heroes was Elijah, who slaughtered the prophets of Baal at the Kishon Brook (1 Kings 18:40). There, the prophet gets the go-ahead from God to slaughter more than four hundred people. After Elijah lets his soldiers see a miracle performed by God (something they needed to see in order to know their actions were approved by God), Elijah says to them, "Seize the prophets of Baal; do not let one of them escape." Bowers referred to this biblical story to energize value and virtue-filled white Christian men to "purge Mississippi of the invading infidels."[32] For Bowers, being a good Christian man meant to kill people "with no malice, in complete silence and in the manner of a Christian act. . . . Catch them outside of the law . . . then under Mississippi law, you have the right to kill them."[33] He would tell his followers to fast and pray as they prepared to engage in heinous and violent acts against Black people. Yet, he believed that his Christianity was intact and that his actions were sanctioned by God.

Some Tenets of Southern Christianity

It might be said that Blacks were perceived by some whites as not honoring the Southern way of life, not being polite as Southern culture demanded. The offenses of Black people were minor, yet the violence meted against them was accepted and ignored by law enforcement. What whites wanted to do was force Black people back into labor, so laws were made that were sure to be violated by unassuming Blacks, leading them into courtrooms that were as unsympathetic to justice for them as they were sympathetic to protecting the desires of white people. Foner says that for Southerners, "custom became law":

> If employers could no longer subject Blacks to corporal punishment, courts could mandate whipping as a punishment for vagrancy or petty theft. If individual whites could no longer hold Blacks in involuntary servitude courts could sentence freedmen to long prison terms, force them into labor without compensation on public works, or bind them out to white employers who would pay their fines. . . . The convict lease system was expanded so as to provide employers with a source of cheap labor.[34]

Later came what Foner describes as "radical Reconstruction," where violent, organized groups, including the Ku Klux Klan and the Knights of the White Camelia, were formed solely "to obstruct and destroy Reconstruction government, to assassinate or intimidate Black and white Republican officials, [and] to use violence to prevent people from voting. According to historians Foner and David Blight, the KKK felt emboldened enough to take Black people out of their houses in the dead of night and "strip them out on a road, make them run down the road, make them sometimes lie on a rock where they would be whipped, where men would line up to whip them. Sometimes they would burn parts of their bodies."[35] White Southern virtue demanded that white men protect the Southern way of life by keeping Black people in their place, and it demanded that they minimize or eliminate the Black presence in the political sphere. Violent whites also attacked whites who were sympathetic to Black people. It was a brutal time for Black people, with neither the Bible nor the Constitution protecting them. Neither the government—federal, state, or local—nor the Bible was able to stop the wave of violence that was responsible for the death and destruction of individual Black people and entire Black communities.

Bible-reading whites who called themselves Christian resented the mere presence of Black people in the country in general, but in the South in particular. Wilson reports that Robert Lewis Dabney warned that "the Black presence is an eating cancer that imperiled the South."[36] Southerners also held deep anger against the North, mocking its "advanced Christian civilization." Further, they accused the North of "trying to provoke slaves into a bloody rebellion," concluding that the effort failed, as Blacks proved themselves to be "more civilized than their instigators."[37]

How could one God and one Constitution be so differently understood by white people in general and Southern white people in particular? In his second inaugural address, President Abraham Lincoln noted that the large number of "colored slaves . . . constituted a peculiar and powerful interest. All knew that this interest was, somehow, the cause of the war."[38] He continued:

> To strengthen, perpetuate, and extend this interest was the cause for which the insurgents would rend the Union, even by war; while the government claimed no right to more than to restrict the territorial arrangement of it. Neither party expected for the war, the magnitude, or the duration, which it has already attained. Neither anticipated that the cause of the conflict might cease with, or even before, the conflict itself should cease. Both looked for an easier triumph and a result less fundamental and astounding. Both read the same Bible and pray to the same God; and each invokes His aid against the other.[39]

The Christianity which Southern whites claimed, even as they dealt with their anger at having lost the war, was different from what Wes Howard-Brook called the "religion of creation" and what Edward Blyden called the "Christianity of Christ." The religion of the Southern Christians was what Jon Meacham labeled "civil religion," a practice based on their culture and on their desire to honor, elevate, and restore what they called Southern values, although its proponents and followers claimed Christianity as their religion. By the early 1800s, Southern religion was being called "conservative," and by 1850, Wilson notes that Southern leaders "began more consciously drawing from European ideas. Southerners came to believe in cultural nationalism," which did not ascribe to the concept of equal justice for all people, especially Blacks.[40]

Following the Civil War, Southern whites believed there needed to be what they called a "manly Christianity," meaning that they were duty-bound to protect white women. Manly Christianity, a great contradiction in principle and practice, was seen as another Southern virtue and was promoted even as white men continued to rape Black women at will. Whites used the Bible to describe their heroes.

Part of Southern Christianity was the rejection of Northern industrialism, which was making many persons wealthy. This is particularly interesting as the South's agrarian economy had likewise made many people wealthy and had put the United States on a trajectory of financial greatness. In the aftermath of their losing the war as well as the free labor that had built their economy on the backs of enslaved Africans, Southerners grew to despise the wealth they saw burgeoning in the North and warned their fellow Southerners not to fall into the trap of materialism. The North was materialistic, they proffered, whereas the South was deeply spiritual, and they preached that Southerners should never forget that core Southern value. Ascribing to tenets of the Southern jeremiad, Southern preachers cautioned their own to repent for coveting wealth and materialism in order to prevent further punishment,[41] which revealed their sense of guilt at having become comfortable with wealth. Part of the reason they had lost the war, some Southern preachers believed, was because they had become greedy, so they were called to repent to avoid repeating their behavior and incurring further punishment. They clearly understood their having lost the war to be God's judgment on them and punishment for the sin of greed.

Conflicting Interpretations of the Bible

The devotion to the idea of Southern virtue and values, however, did not keep Southerners from being angry at the outcome of the war, angry at the loss of their source of labor, and angry at what they believed to be the audacity of Northerners to claim moral superiority. None of their preoccupation with Southern virtue and values led them to believe, however, that Black people should be free or that they were human because white supremacy was a Southern value, too, even if no one used those words. After the war, the Ku Klux Klan and other racist groups emerged, determined—in the name of their God and their Bible—to make sure they did the work of making the South the way they wanted it to be. They made conscious decisions to challenge the state which had dared to challenge them.

Christian nationalism grew. The Constitution did little to nothing to make life fair or just for Black people (or for women, Native Americans, and other ethnic groups). Wilson says the KKK was "the most passionate organization associated with the highly ritualized civil religion."[42] Black people, some believed, posed a threat to the salvation of a "virtuous Southern civilization,"[43] so the KKK felt no compunction about waging acts of violence against them, which they did with little if any resistance from the state. Southern virtue meant that everyone understood that, in spite of the outcome of the war, African Americans were still inferior and still inhuman. There was not the slightest consideration of the message of Jesus the Christ, who said, "Come unto me, all ye that labour and are heavy laden, and I will give you rest" (Matthew 11:28, KJV), nor any concern with the Great Commandment. Those words were meant for white humans, they believed, and not Black people, of whom they had doubts as concerned their humanness.

Southerners continued to quote the Bible to justify their views, reminding people that the Bible was the literal word of God, and they became more and more skilled at interpreting verses to accommodate their white supremacist views. They believed they were doing justice, and rebuking the oppressor—that is, the state—as directed in Isaiah: "Learn to do good; Seek justice, Rebuke the oppressor; Defend the fatherless, Plead for the widow" (Isaiah 1:17, NKJV). They identified the North and those who believed in the abolition of slavery as the oppressor, even as Blacks, believing that this same verse was a call to fight white supremacy and slavery, identified those whites who pushed slavery as the oppressor. Southerners would use the words of the prophet Joel to describe their situation following the war:

> Awake, you drunkards, and weep; and wail, all you drinkers of wine, because of the new wine, for it has been cut off from your mouth. For a nation has come up against My land, strong, and

> without number; his teeth are the teeth of a lion, and he has the
> fangs of a fierce lion. He has laid waste My vine, and ruined My
> fig tree; he has stripped it bare and thrown it away; its branches
> are made white. Lament like a virgin girded with sackcloth. . . .
> Consecrate a fast, call a sacred assembly; gather the elders and
> all the inhabitants of the land into the house of the LORD your
> God, and cry out to the LORD. Alas for the day! For the day
> of the LORD is at hand; it shall come as destruction from the
> Almighty. (Joel 1:5-8a,14-15, NKJV)

Enslaved Blacks would have interpreted those same words differently, in accordance with their beliefs, needs, and situations.

In the end, the Bible was too open for interpretation; it was used by both oppressed and oppressor. For the former, it defended white supremacy and slavery; for the latter, it provided evidence of God's displeasure with what their oppressors were doing to them. There was no solid, undeniable, "fixed" word of God, not from the Bible. All of its words, it seems, were open to interpretation.

One Road, Two Conflicting Directions

Thus, if one was going to live according to the will of God, the Bible was the roadmap that showed one road heading in two opposite directions at the same time. White Southerners, consumed with civil religion and the recovery and salvation of Southern values and virtue, felt the same as Blacks felt, that they honestly were doing God's will. There was little to no intersection of beliefs. The Constitution had been written in such a way to favor slave holders, and its amendments did not help the cause of Black freedom. It gave courts much leeway in interpreting laws which adversely affected Black life, leaving "good, Christian men" feeling little angst about their actions.

Even if they didn't say it out loud, everyone knew and believed that the preamble to the Constitution applied only to white people. Furthermore, the document omitted a clear distinction between people and property, allowing Southern whites to view enslaved Africans as property who were therefore incapable of experiencing human emotions. Howard Thurman tells the story of how a little white girl once stabbed him with a pin, and when he cried,

"Ouch!" she shrank back, surprised. "That did not hurt you—you can't feel!" he quotes her as saying.[44]

So the pain that whites inflicted on Black people did not make them worry about what God would think. Their bypassing and ignoring the laws of the federal government and the words of the Constitution did not bother them. Black people (including Muslims from Africa), fought in every war of this country, beginning with the Revolutionary War (on the side of the British) and including the War of 1812, the Civil War, and both World Wars (although they were never respected by either Southern or Northern whites), so it is troubling that law enforcement knew, ignored, and in many cases participated in the violence meted against Blacks in the South during and after Reconstruction. The state was weak against the ravages of white violence against Blacks. Black soldiers reported being treated more humanely by Germans during World War II than by white law enforcement officers, especially in the South, where Germans soldiers were held as prisoners of war and treated better than Blacks. These Southerners were religious, law-abiding people, yet history is cluttered with stories of how they killed people and entire communities because of their color, and neither the federal Constitution nor the laws of Southern states did anything to stop them. America was still touting its belief in its exceptionalism, even while it made race laws that were studied, copied, and used by other countries. Because many white Americans did not believe that God had made Black people, they were able to brutalize them without much worry that they were displeasing God.

A case in point was the brutalization of Isaac Woodard, a Black man who fought in World War II and continued to wear his uniform after completing his tour of duty and returning home. Blacks in uniform were common irritants for some whites, who believed that the Black soldiers had grown "uppity" and had forgotten their place. In 1946, hours after coming home from a war in which American soldiers fought for our freedom against Nazi terror, Woodard, who was on a bus in South Carolina, asked the bus driver to stop because he had to use the restroom. The white driver did not appreciate his asking the question and called friends to meet the bus at the next stop. The police chief of that city, along with others, met the bus, and they beat Woodard before taking him to jail. During the beating, the police chief jammed his night stick into Woodard's eyes, effectively blinding him, and left him bleeding on the jail floor, where he lay for several days. He lost his sight. The police chief was tried but acquitted because the brutality of violence against Blacks was common and condoned by white supremacists. These were "good, Christian men" who, like Sam Bowers, may very well have been leaders in their churches. But they believed in whiteness. As far as they were concerned, neither the Bible nor the Constitution told them not to be violent against Black people.

White preachers helped stoke the protesting hearts and spirits of Southern whites who, though they believed that Blacks were inferior, felt that they themselves were under attack because they were critical of the cruel treatment of Blacks. Following the historic *Brown v. Board of Education* case, which ruled that "separate but equal" was unconstitutional, many white preachers urged their members to ignore the ruling, which many of them did. One such preacher was W. A. Criswell, who was the pastor of one of the largest churches in the Southern Baptist Convention. He launched an attack against the forces of desegregation, calling ministers who supported it cowards who "refused to speak up and against this thing called integration."[45] In a sermon entitled "Never Had I Been So Blind," Criswell railed against government interference with the Southern way of life and said that "mandated integration [was] a denial of everything we believe in."[46] He hated even the thought of integration, as much as many whites hate the thought of diversity training today. In his sermon, he argued that integration was "not the ultimate will of God" and preached that integration was undemocratic and unchristian.[47] Southern whites were inspired by Criswell's sermon; Senator Strom Thurmond was so moved that he encouraged his fellow lawmakers to pass a resolution "asking the United States Attorney General to put the NAACP on the Justice Department's subversive list, and to ban members of the NAACP from public employment."[48]

Some Southern pastors and white religious leaders, including Billy Graham, criticized Criswell for his comments. Graham said, "My Pastor and I have never seen eye to eye on the race question."[49] But many white pastors and churchgoers did see eye to eye. Years later, Pastor Bob Marsh, the preacher and father of author-historian Charles Marsh, faced his own struggle with race and God. According to his son Charles, the elder Marsh had "not been convinced by the Civil Rights brass that God was on their side."[50] Rev. Marsh preached a sermon entitled "The Sorrow of Selma," in which he explained that his sorrow was grounded in the South's dignity, which had been stolen and mocked "in the media's portrayal of our region as a society of barbarians, heartless, anti-God people."[51] In that sermon, Marsh criticized those who criticized whites struggling with the whole idea of civil rights for Black people, and proclaimed:

> You can be an unbathed beatnik, immoral kook, sign-carrying degenerate, a radical revolutionary who treats the sacred with disdain and you can have no regard for decency and honesty. . . . But if you dare stand for the principles of righteousness and morality which made this nation great, if you love individual initiative and freedom, if you think that our nation is great because it has been established within the framework of Theistic principles and must remain that way, and that the ideals of Marxism and Fabianism are dangerous . . . if this is what you believe, then the guns of public opinion are turned [on] you to mock you as a reactionary, to brand you as antiquated, and destroy you as a member of the fanatical, radical right.[52]

The Bible, the church, and the Constitution protected white supremacy. Some whites recognized the contradictions in their "worshiping a Jew who broke all the rules, who showed us the grace in the unclean and the hypocrisy of the pure, the Lord of beggars and whores, enemy of the righteous. No, maybe our problem was not too much Jesus, but too little."[53]

An Obsession with Whiteness

Since Christianity and the Constitution were infected, so was the US government. White people were obsessed with whiteness and with keeping it in its proper place. They had always been convinced of the sacredness of whiteness, and the loss of the Civil War only made their obsession greater. They were afraid they would lose their berth of superiority, which explains much of the violence they committed against Black people after the Civil War. They believed that things between the races had been good when slavery existed because Blacks knew their place and whites could maintain theirs.

But the Civil War and the freeing of the slaves changed the landscape and caused both Northern and Southern whites to worry that the Black race would infect the white race and destroy that which God had created. "Race," wrote Madison Grant in *The Passing of the Great Race*, "implies heredity, and heredity implies all the moral, social, and intellectual characteristics and traits which are the springs of politics and government."[54]

The obsession with whiteness was national, not regional, and it was so virulent that it caused an American president to rename the nation's residence for presidents after he made what turned out to be a grievous mistake. Everyone knew that enslaved Africans had built the mansion and office and that the staff of the house was almost exclusively Black. Slave-owning presidents, aware of the hypocrisy of owning slaves while leading what was supposed to be a free country, ignored the fact that human beings in their home were being exploited because their color marked them as being deserving of nothing better.

In 1901, President Theodore Roosevelt invited Booker T. Washington to dinner at the Executive Mansion, the name of the presidential home at that time. Washington was a known Black leader whose message to Blacks to pull themselves up by their bootstraps was appealing to whites. President Roosevelt admired Washington and did not think the invitation would cause a stir though he, too, was a racist who believed Black people were lazy and intellectually inferior to whites. In spite of his beliefs, however, he thought Washington's message was a good one for both the Blacks and the country. A press release was issued announcing that Washington had been invited to dinner at the president's house. The lightning-speed white backlash that followed the news surprised the president. The vitriol was brutal and hostile. According to an account by historian Clarence Lusane, one Mississippi senator said, "The Executive Mansion was so saturated with the odour of the nigger that the rats have taken refuge in the stable."[55] Another white person said that the president's act was "the most damnable outrage which has ever been perpetrated by any citizen of the United States."[56]

The backlash was so severe that the day after the unfortunate dinner, the staff denied that the dinner had taken place and said it had not been dinner but only a lunch to which the Black man had been invited. This untruthful disclaimer was needed because a dinner meant that Washington not only would be in the president's house but also that he would be seated with the president's wife and daughter. This scenario appalled whites who believed the sanctity and purity of white women would be threatened by the presence of a Black man at the dinner table. Later that day, the president issued an official letter on stationery which was headed "the White House" as opposed to the Executive Mansion. His intent seemed clear; the house of the presidents would be forever known as the White House, indicating the belief that it was a house for presidents—who should forever be white.

The Constitution could not disinfect and eliminate the disease called white supremacy from the American people, and the Bible as the handbook of the Christianity of Christ was safely kept out of the fray and mainly used to support the cultural trends set and followed by the state. The infection was everywhere; the good news of the gospel was not even considered as an antibiotic to be used to make America well, but the determination of those who believed in the superiority of white people manifested itself in the systematic manipulation of the state to honor the presence and the power of the South. The state would not be able to erase the presence, the desires, and the politics of the Southern God, its victory in the Civil War notwithstanding.

Epigraph

Charles Marsh, *The Last Days: A Son's Story of Sin and Segregation at the Dawn of a New South* (New York: Basic Books, 2001), 22.

NOTES

1. Refer to chapters 6 and 9 for a discussion on the Treaty of Tripoli.
2. Charles Reagan Wilson, *Baptized in Blood: The Religion of the Lost Cause* (Athens: University of Georgia Press, 2009), 3.
3. Wilson, 4.
4. Wilson, 5.
5. Wilson, 8.
6. Wilson, 7.
7. Carolyn Renée Dupont, *Mississippi Praying: Southern White Evangelicals and the Civil Rights Movement, 1945–1975* (New York: New York University Press, 2013), 2.
8. Dupont, 3.

9. Wilson, 63.

10. Wilson, 11–12.

11. Wilson, 13.

12. Wilson.

13. Wilson, 37.

14. Wilson.

15. Alyssa Michelle Hoover, "I Still Believe in Traditional Southern Values," March 27, 2016, Odyssey, https://theodysseyonline.com/traditional-southern-values.

16. Wilson, 40.

17. Wilson.

18. Wilson, 68.

19. Wilson.

20. Wilson.

21. Dupont, 7.

22. Wilson, 18.

23. Wilson, 48.

24. Wilson, 49.

25. Wilson, 80–81.

26. Dupont, 7.

27. Eric Foner, *The Second Founding: How the Civil War and Reconstruction Remade the Constitution* (New York: W. W. Norton, 2019), 127.

28. Foner, 29.

29. Foner, 130.

30. Foner, 145.

31. Charles Marsh, *The Last Days: A Son's Story of Sin and Segregation at the Dawn of a New South* (New York: Basic Books, 2001), 37.

32. Marsh, 39.

33. Marsh.

34. Eric Foner, *Reconstruction: America's Unfinished Revolution, 1863–1877* (New York: Harper & Row, 1988), 205.

35. "Southern Violence During Reconstruction," *American Experience*, PBS, https://www.pbs.org/wgbh/americanexperience/features/reconstruction-southern-violence-during-reconstruction/, 2.

36. Wilson, 107.

37. Wilson, 104.

38. "Transcript of President Abraham Lincoln's Second Inaugural Address (1865)," https://www.ourdocuments.gov/doc.php?flash=false&doc=38&page=transcript, 1.

39. "Transcript."

40. Wilson, 80.

41. Wilson, 80.

42. Wilson, 100.

43. Wilson.

44. Howard Thurman, *The Luminous Darkness: A Personal Interpretation of the Anatomy of Segregation and the Ground of Hope* (reprint; Richmond: Friends United Press, 1980–1981), 7.

45. Curtis W. Freeman, "'Never Had I Been So Blind': W. A. Criswell's 'Change' on Racial Segregation"; Freeman's article is in *The Journal of Southern Religion* 10 (2007), http://jsr.fsu.edu/Volume10/Freeman.pdf.

46. Freeman.

47. Freeman.

48. Freeman.

49. Freeman.

50. Marsh, 45.

51. Marsh, 46.

52. Marsh.

53. Marsh, 106.

54. Madison Grant, *The Passing of the Great Race* (New York: Scribner & Sons, 1916), vii.

55. Clarence Lusane, *The Black History of the White House* (San Francisco: Open Media Series, 2011), 231. See also Simon Mann, "The White House's Ugly Secret," *Sydney Morning Herald*, February 26, 2011, https://www.smh.com.au/world/the-white-houses-ugly-secret-20110225-1b8kq.html.

56. Lusane.

11
With Liberty and Justice for Some

Slavery never ended; it just evolved.
—Bryan Stevenson, Equal Justice Initiative

Confronted with the grave crises precipitated by racial discord within our state in recent months, and the genuine dilemma facing persons of Christian conscience, we are compelled to voice publicly our convictions. Indeed, as Christian ministers and as native Mississippians, sharing the anguish of all our people, we have a particular obligation to speak.
—"Born of Conviction" Statement, January 2, 1963

Neither the Bible nor the Constitution protected—or in many instances yet protects—people of color, and most specifically, Black people.

It is significant that Thomas Jefferson, who penned the words of the Declaration of Independence that all Black people have held onto, owned 600 slaves at the time he wrote those words. It is equally significant that George Washington, the nation's first president who helped America free itself from the religious and political tyranny of England, owned 317 slaves.[1] Our founders talked about freedom while they practiced subjugation and did all they could to protect the rights of those who actively worked to keep freedom from enslaved Africans and their children born in this country.

As noted in the previous chapter, in the aftermath of the Civil War—fought because the South wanted to keep its slaves—white resentment and anger against the federal government flared. Congress passed the Civil Rights Act of 1866, which declared Americans of African descent to be full citizens, entitled to full civil rights, but that did not matter. Good, God-fearing white people who called themselves Christian began a reign of physical and political terror on Black people, and no state or federal laws were effective in stopping that violence. In fact, law enforcement officers were often active participants, even if that participation amounted to their acting as if the violence and murders of innocent people were not happening.

Black people were not safe, the law notwithstanding.

Worshipping the white God became too much for Black people over time. Who was this God who allowed them to be so poorly treated? White Christianity seemed to be on the side of white supremacy and all but ignored the humanity of Black people, doing nothing to stop the brutality that they suffered. Even if in their churches not a word was spoken about this strange and painful dilemma that they faced, they still rejected that God. While both Northern and Southern white Christians adopted and practiced a civil religion based on white supremacist ideas of virtue and values, Black Christians adopted a religion based on Jesus.

Maybe Black Christians didn't know what God was doing, but they did know that God had sent Jesus to this earth to save them, just as God had saved the Israelites. Black Christians were clear: they would call on the name of Jesus until Jesus heard them. While white Christians seemed to go to church to be affirmed in their religious complacency and their acceptance of a God who supported their culture, Black Christians went to church to hear that God, through the delivery of "the word," saw them, understood their plight, and was working on their behalf. Jesus was their redeemer, their savior, and their friend, and Jesus was coming for them. Black people feasted on the words found in the second chapter of Philippians, especially the proclamation that Jesus:

> made Himself of no reputation, taking the form of a bondservant, and coming in the likeness of men. And being found in appearance as a man, He humbled Himself and became obedient to the point of death, even the death of the cross. Therefore God also has highly exalted Him and given Him the name which is above every name, that at the name of Jesus

> every knee should bow, of those in heaven, and of those on
> earth, and of those under the earth, and that every tongue
> should confess that Jesus Christ is Lord, to the glory of God the
> Father. (Philippians 2:7-11, NKJV)

One of the reasons that Black people could withstand the treatment they received from church and state was because they worshiped a God based on the gospel. For them, this was not only the Good News, but the only news that sustained them. Through the years, Blacks had struggled to hold onto the hope that Jesus offered. Though they might politely listen to Black or white preachers espouse the words of the Pauline epistles as the word of God which seemed to cement their place as second-class citizens, they moved those words aside as they called on the name of Jesus to make it through each painful day. Years later, James H. Cone, the father of Black liberation theology, would say that he was "fed up with white theologians writing about the gospel as if it had nothing to do with Black Power and Black people's struggle for cultural identity and political justice."[2] Cone continued, "I was fed up with liberal white ministers condemning riots instead of the social conditions that created them. I was fed up with conservative Black churches preaching an otherworldly gospel as if Jesus had nothing to say about how white supremacy had created a world that was killing Black people."[3]

Black people had been struggling merely "to be," especially after the Civil War and moving forward. Poet Paul Laurence Dunbar wrote that Blacks wore a mask that made it easier for white people to believe that Black people were doing just fine. What seemed most important to the white church and to government was that the spirits of white people be protected at all cost, something that had been a part of everything America had done since its inception. Dunbar wrote in his poem "We Wear the Mask".

We wear the mask that grins and lies,
It hides our cheeks and shades our eyes,—
   This debt we pay to human guile;
With torn and bleeding hearts we smile,
   And mouth with myriad subtleties.

Black people were the stepchildren of white, male American patriots who believed in their rights and their freedom. Howard Thurman called Black people "the disinherited" and said that for those who need "profound succor and strength to enable them to live in the present with dignity and creativity, Christianity has often been sterile and of little avail. The conventional Christian word is muffled, confused, and vague."[4] He wrote that for some, "the Christian movement in its formal expression must be on the side of the strong against the weak,"[5] a characteristic of what Wes Howard-Brook described as the "religion of empire" (an assessment with which Reinhold Niebuhr might agree). American Christianity, that is, the Christianity adhered to by many whites, said Reinhold Niebuhr, is a religion of power, driven as much by a belief in the sacredness of economic power as by a conviction in holding onto white (Southern) values and virtue.[6]

White Christianity, or the religion of white Christians from the South and less obviously from the North, was a religion which "enshrines the belief that violence saves, that war brings peace, that might makes right," according to theologian Walter Wink, and its foundational belief is that of redemptive violence.[7] Relying on the Babylonian creation story, the *Enuma Elish*, white Christians believed violence was necessary to keep order, to keep people in their places. Black Christians did not agree.

Black people were the disinherited and read the Bible in a way that affirmed them and their condition in life, for like them, Jesus was oppressed economically, politically, and socially. To Thurman, the Christianity of Christ, which became the religion of Black people, was "born of a people acquainted with persecution and suffering," living in a world where the positions of those in charge have been "too often secured by a ruthless use of power applied to weak and defenseless peoples."[8] White Christians claimed this same man, Jesus, as their leader, but communities, said Niebuhr, "cannot distinguish between a criminal and a Savior because each violates the laws and customs which represent some minimal order, too low for the Savior and too high for the criminal."[9]

Is there any way that the two groups, oppressor and oppressed, would have been able to worship the same God? Would they have been able and willing to adopt the same message from the Bible?

Hardly. The savior of each group of people represented two entirely different worldviews based on the culture and position of both. Even for Southern white Christians who decried the rise of materialism in the North after the Civil War, the acquisition of power and money was the sure sign that God was on their side. The Puritans believed that God had shown them favor by leading them across the Atlantic to a place where economic growth and opportunity seemed endless. But their prosperity was attained at the expense of others, who they said had been put in place to maximize their lives of blessing. Their God said that these others were meant to be used in the way that they were. Thurman says, correctly, that "the masses of men live with their backs constantly against the wall": "They are the poor, the disinherited, the dispossessed. What does our religion say to them? The issue is not what it counsels them to do for others whose need may be greater, but what religion offers to meet their own needs. The search for an answer to this question is perhaps the most important religious quest of modern life."[10]

Discrimination and Violence against Black People

In spite of the Bible and the Constitution, which some people say makes this a nation of laws, racial violence against Black people flourished after the Civil War, through Reconstruction, and beyond. God allowed it, said more than one slave interviewed for the Works Project Administration put into place by President Franklin Delano Roosevelt. All they could do, as they were beaten and raped, and as they watched others being murdered without anyone ever being held accountable, was believe that the God who saw all, who had sent God's Son Jesus, was hearing their cries. Historian Leon F. Litwack wrote that it is impossible to know precisely how many Black men, women, and children were beaten, flogged, and murdered in the first years of emancipation,[11] and yet, they held onto their God. They worshipped with passion, emotion, and enthusiasm. White missionaries from the North came to the South to minister to the newly freed African Americans, but they were appalled by what they saw. They declared that the greatest need of these Black people was "orderly Churches under the care of educated men."[12] The white visitors noted the difference in the way they and Blacks approached worship: "They believe simply in the love of Christ and they speak of Him and talk to Him with a familiarity that is absolutely startling," said one.[13] The freedmen were not about to give up their God. "What the well-intentioned northern missionaries failed to appreciate was how precisely the degree to which the freedmen considered the emotional fervor inseparable from worship because it brought them that much closer to God," Litwack wrote.[14] They did not want to ever get "too far removed from God's presence," white disapproval of their worship notwithstanding. Their freedom did not save them from the ruthlessness, emotional and physical, of white people. They were going to hold onto the God who they believed had engineered their freedom.

And they had to hold onto God in the way they did. The violence meted out against them was nonstop. Examples of the slaughter of Black people are as heartbreaking as they are tragic, all the more so because both religion and government have ignored them and have refused to take responsibility for the damage they did to Black people politically, physically, and spiritually. In *Lynching in America*, the Equal Justice Initiative (EJI) shares documented instances of horrific violence meted out against Black people by angry whites. White mobs attacked not only individuals but entire cities inhabited by Black people. There was the Colfax Massacre, mentioned earlier in this book; the 1919 Elaine Massacre in Elaine, Arkansas; the Springfield (Illinois) Massacre of 1908; the Rosewood (Florida) Massacre of 1923; and the Tulsa (Oklahoma) Massacre of 1921, to name a few. In all these tragic attacks, neither the government nor divine law served as a guardrail to protect the African Americans under attack.[15]

The EJI has documented nearly four thousand lynchings of Blacks from the end of Reconstruction, in 1877, through 1950. In order to justify their actions, law enforcement agencies, egged on by white society, criminalized Black people so that a reason for their state-sanctioned murders could be given to a gullible public. Many of these cases are described in the EJI report, including the following:

- Keith Bowen in Mississippi in 1889, lynched by an entire white neighborhood because he tried to enter a room where three white women were sitting[16]

- General Lee, lynched by a white mob in 1904 for knocking on the door of a white woman's house in South Carolina[17]

- Thomas Miles, a victim of state-sanctioned murder who was lynched in 1912 for writing letters to a white woman, inviting her to have a cold drink with him[18]

Blacks needed their God, because white resentment against Blacks and the idea that Blacks might even get close to having a status equal to that of whites, coupled with an obsession with their whiteness, increased after the war. The lynchings were only part of what happened. Discrimination against Blacks continued to be unchallenged by church and state, and the subhuman treatment of Blacks did not diminish over time. In her account of the great migration of Blacks from the South between 1915 and 1970, Isabel Wilkerson, author of *The Warmth of Other Suns*, tells stories of the indignities meted out to Black people because of their race, inspiring them to move out of the South. Basketball great Bill Russell, Wilkerson writes, "watched his parents suffer one indignity after another." She writes, "His father once went to a gas station only to be told that he would have to wait for the white people to get their gas first. He waited and waited, and, when his turn seemed never to come, he started to pull off. The owner came up, put a shotgun to his head, and told him he was not to leave until all of the white people had been served."[19]

The evil of white supremacy was deep and wide. Blacks were accosted for merely being alive. Wilkerson describes how in North Carolina, "white and colored passengers could not occupy contiguous seats on the same bench,"[20] and in Georgia, she writes, "the penalty for willfully riding in the wrong seat was a fine of a thousand dollars or six months in prison."[21]

In 1957, a man named Arrington High got into trouble and was placed in the Mississippi State Hospital, an institution for the insane, because he "protested the southern order of things."[22] He had been writing a weekly newsletter for fourteen years, documenting the base treatment of Black people. Wilkerson says that "what got him declared insane . . . was exposing the segregationists who were consorting with prostitutes at a colored brothel that catered only to white politicians."[23] At the age of forty-seven, he was given a sentence that would cut him off from the world, including his wife and four children, for the remainder of his life. He escaped from the hospital in 1958, helped by people who knew his situation (including some whites) and who hated the injustice of which they knew High was a victim. His friends, guiding him via a carefully executed plan, put him into a coffin with holes in it for him to breathe and onto a train headed for Chicago. He was forced to lie still for the fifteen-hour ride.[24]

During the time of the Dust Bowl, which began in 1930 and lasted for nearly ten years, whites suffered, but Black suffering was all the worse because of the ever-present white supremacy. One of the states badly affected by the storm was Oklahoma, whose governor, William Henry David Murray, hated Black people, and Jews even more. He "believed Blacks were inferior to whites in all ways and said [they] must be fenced from society like quarantined hogs."[25] In an account that is difficult to read, Timothy Egan tells the story of two Black men who were arrested in the city of Dalhart, Texas, after they emerged from a train looking for food and a warm place, as the dust caused wild fluctuations in temperature. While looking for food, they were arrested and detained for a week before they appeared before a judge who ordered them to dance once they were summoned to court. Dumfounded and humiliated, they paused when they heard what they had been asked to do. But the judge was serious; he believed that they were "good for nothing but toe-tapping," and he insisted that they dance. They complied with the order, thinking it would lead to their release. It did not. They danced, "forcing silly grins on their faces," after which, the judge "banged his gavel and ordered the men back to jail for another two months."[26]

In April, they were brought back to the courthouse for trial. Their crime had been that they were looking for food and warmth, and they admitted to going into the train depot and taking what food they could find. They were then found guilty of criminal trespassing and were sentenced to 120 days in jail. Before heading back to their cells, the judge again ordered them to dance.[27] An appeal to the Bible, or to the Christianity of Christ, would not have worked because the judge was a part of the justice system which on the state level got its authority to discriminate against Blacks from the words of the Constitution—written, unwritten, and implied. These men were denied due process, in complete violation of the Fourteenth Amendment, but it did not matter.

The men danced.

Finding Balm in the Christianity of Christ

The oppressed always look for God, but frequently they cannot find God in the way they need. In their space of suffering, they often feel alone, so they latch onto the God they create in order to give them strength to fight the brutality they suffer. Just as the Thirteenth Amendment outlawing slavery was ignored while Blacks continued to be sold to whites, the Fourteenth Amendment, guaranteeing Blacks due process under the law, was violated as well, and continues to be violated.

While the instances of Black people being denied due process are many, there are a few cases which stand out, such as the so-called Central Park Five, in which five young Black teens were accused of raping a white female jogger in Central Park in 1989. The teens were coerced to confess the crime, which they did not commit, resulting in their receiving prison sentences from five to fifteen years. The murderers of Emmett Till, a Black youth from Chicago who was fourteen when he was accused of flirting with a white woman in Money, Mississippi, were acquitted of the crime by an all-white, all-male jury after deliberating for only sixty-seven minutes. The murderers confessed to the crime after they were acquitted in an article which appeared in *Life* magazine.

The American legal legacy is filled with cases of Blacks who have been accused and convicted of crimes that they did not commit, and in which the real perpetrators have been known to be white and who frequently have not been indicted, much less convicted for their crimes. A case in recent history was the murder of Trayvon Martin by George Zimmerman, who was acquitted, and Michael Brown, shot to death by Officer Darren Wilson in Ferguson, Missouri, who was not indicted for the shooting.

The Fourteenth Amendment did not guarantee a method by which Blacks would be protected from false charges and false imprisonment. In another recent case, Khalief Browder spent three years in Rikers Island prison, much of it in solitary confinement, after being accused of stealing a backpack, which, from the time of his arrest, he said that he had not done. He was sixteen years old at the time of his arrest, but his case never went to trial in spite of the Fourteenth Amendment and the promise that all American citizens were entitled to due process. He could have been released had he confessed to taking the backpack, but he never wavered in his proclamation of his innocence and never took the plea deal he was offered. The experience robbed him of his youth and shattered his spirit; shortly after he was released, he committed suicide.

The criminalization of Black people, which began in earnest during Reconstruction, has continued, feeding the white supremacist belief that Black people are criminals. Not much is ever said, about how white anger after the Civil War led whites to criminalize Blacks in order to find ways to arrest them and keep them working—re-enslaving them via the convict leasing program. Whites consistently ignored the law even as they declared the United States to be a nation of laws.

White outrage following *Brown v. Board of Education* was swift to erupt and long-standing. In the Southern Declaration of 1956, also known as the Declaration of Constitutional Principles, one hundred senators, led by Senator Strom Thurmond, objected to the decision, writing, "The unwarranted decision of the Supreme Court in the public school cases is now bearing the fruit always produced when men substitute naked power for established law."[28] They wrote:

> The Founding Fathers gave us a Constitution of checks and balances because they realized the inescapable lesson of history that no man or group of men can be safely entrusted with unlimited power . . . We regard the decision of the Supreme Court in the school cases as a clear abuse of judicial power. It climaxes a trend in the Federal Judiciary undertaking to legislate, in derogation of the authority of Congress, and to encroach upon the reserved rights of the States and the people. The original Constitution does not mention education. Neither does the 14th amendment or any other amendment . . . In the case of *Plessy v. Ferguson*, in 1896, the Supreme Court expressly declared that under the 14th amendment no person was denied any of his rights if the states provided separate but equal facilities . . . This unwarranted exercise of power by the Court,

> contrary to the Constitution, is creating chaos and confusion
> in the States principally affected. It is destroying the amicable
> relations between the white and Negro races that have been
> created through 90 years of patient effort by the good people of
> both races.[29]

Whites not only protested the Supreme Court decision but also ignored it for years, pulling their children out of public schools and either home schooling them or forming private institutions.

The Constitution was clearly not respected enough to force white people to abandon their white supremacist beliefs. Thurman's "disinherited" have been abandoned by the government, even as that same government has protected the rights and interests of white people. The American empire worked, and has worked as empires throughout history have worked, favoring some citizens at the expense of others. Though there is resentment at the term, white Americans have guarded their status as privileged citizens. In antiquity, "the favored . . . idealized the position of the Roman in the world and suffered the moral fate of the Romans by becoming like them."[30] Whites in this country did the same, even as Blacks fought against mischaracterizations of themselves from the late nineteenth century to the present. Thurman, in describing how the Jews and other subjugated peoples dealt with the oppression of the Romans in Jesus' day, observed that "Jesus had to resent deeply the loss of Jewish national independence and the aggression of Rome. . . . Natural humiliation was hurting and burning. The balm for that burning humiliation was humility."[31] Black people, as well, knew and still know about burning humiliation with humility; to do otherwise was too often a death sentence.

Thus, according to Thurman, the Christianity of Jesus, the source of hope for Black people, became a "technique of survival." Blacks had to practice humiliation and forgiveness, even if it went against their human will. While Thurman says that Christianity became "a religion of the powerful and the dominant, used sometimes as an instrument of oppression," it might be more correct to say it branched off, resulting in the development of a Christianity of the dominant and a Christianity of the oppressed. Many Blacks rejected this Christianity of the oppressed and saw it as a "betrayal of the Negro into the hands of his enemies by focusing his attention upon heaven, forgiveness, love, and the like,"[32] but those who held onto the hope that they saw in Jesus made their Christianity one of strength. Importantly, their Christianity did not have as its seedbed the words of Paul; rather, it had the words of Jesus which convinced and convicted them that, through and because of Jesus, they mattered to God.

Because they had to find a way to stand and to survive, their Christianity became otherworldly, characterized by their belief in and yearning for heaven. They faced the inescapable truth that their oppressors had what seemed to be absolute power on earth, which led them to adopt and nurture the belief that they would soon be done with the troubles of the world. Their oppressors, like the rich man Dives in the Bible who oppressed the poor man Lazarus, would meet their fate before the very face of God.[33] God would come through for them. They knew and believed Jesus' words that said "not everyone who says to me, 'Lord, Lord,' will enter into the kingdom of heaven" (Matthew 7:21). It was from that belief came the words of the great Negro spiritual, "Everbody talkin' 'bout heb'n ain't goin' dere." God, their God, was righteous and good and fair to them, even if the white folks were not.

In the biblical story, a rich man named Dives dies. (He is unnamed but is called Dives in the story because that is the Latin term for "rich man.") After his burial and placement in Hades, he looks up and sees a poor man named Lazarus, who also had died. While the two men were alive, they had interacted. Dives, who the Bible says "dressed in purple and fine linen and feasted sumptuously every day," was able to look out of a window and see poor Lazarus, covered with sores, sitting at the gate to his home. Lazarus was so hungry, says the story, that he "longed to satisfy his hunger with what fell from the rich man's table." He was so covered with sores that nearby dogs would come and lick them.

In Hades, Dives sees Lazarus in the bosom of Abraham, and calls out, "Father Abraham, have mercy on me, and send Lazarus to dip the tip of his finger in water and cool my tongue, for I am in agony in these flames." But Father Abraham, who is God in this story, remembers how Dives lived when he was alive and says to him, "Child, remember that during your lifetime you received your good things, and Lazarus in like manner evil things; but now he is comforted here and you are in agony. Besides all this, between you and us a great chasm has been fixed, so that those who might want to pass from here to you cannot do so, and no one can cross from there to us." Dives, accustomed to being in control because of his great wealth, decides to try to use Lazarus in another way and says, "Then, father, I beg you to send him to my father's house . . . that he may warn them, so that they will not also come into this place of torment." God again refuses, reminding Dives, a Jewish man who had attended synagogue throughout his life, that he and his family had been given the word and will of God concerning compassionate treatment of the poor while he was alive. Furthermore, they had Moses and the prophets as examples for direction in life. Lazarus will not be doing Dives's bidding now. Dives has missed his opportunity to "do justice, and to love kindness, and to walk humbly with your God" (Micah 6:8). For Black people suffering under the hand of white supremacist oppression, this was good news. Trouble would not last "always." It was their ingestion of the Good News, the gospel, found in the Bible, which this work calls the Christianity of Christ, that equipped Black people—enslaved and free—to endure in a country which did not want them, at least not as human beings.

The "Born of Conviction" Statement

It is important to note that though there were two Gods—one for Black people and another for whites—there were and are white people who historically have latched onto the gospel as opposed to biblical Christianity, also referred to as Christian nationalism, and conservative Christianity. These whites have worked, in spite of great risk to themselves, their reputations, and families, to get people to understand that being a Christian involves a cost. It is difficult, if not impossible, to read the words of Jesus the Christ in the Bible and not be moved to act and think in a way that is different than the status quo. In effect, ingesting the words of Jesus can and often does lead people to do things which are considered to be counter-culture, works whose goal is to bring the kingdom of God, as Jesus taught us to pray, "on earth, as it is in heaven."

White Southerners' anger after the Civil War was primarily directed at the federal government because they believed that Abraham Lincoln had overstepped his authority. In their opinion, the federal government had no right to tell the states how to live their lives, so after the war the states' rights outcry grew in earnest. Whenever the federal government did something that seemed to make life easier for the country's Black people, whites' resentment bubbled over. In protest, their civil religion was formed and oozed out over everything—laws, elections, and attitudes. They grew more and more comfortable with their God, who seemed to sanction bigotry and racism, and continued to believe and teach that being concerned with equal treatment of and for Black people was against the will of God.

Carolyn Renée Dupont wrote in *Mississippi Praying* that white Southerners believed "racial integration represented a heinous moral evil."[34] White Christians possessed an "ardent devotion to the Christian Gospel and an equal zeal for what can only be called white supremacy."[35] It was an impossible combination. Martin Luther King Jr. commented on his disappointment with Southern white Christian churches which "stand on the sideline and merely mouth pious irrelevancies and sanctimonious trivialities."[36] Not only did white Christians in both the North and the South fail to fight for Black equality, says Dupont, but they actively fought against it.[37]

In their quest to protect and preserve their culture and the Southern way of doing things, Southern white Christians almost completely abandoned the gospel, all the while continuing to call Christianity their faith. Audaciously, from the very pews on which they sat, these Christians "served as serious obstacles to the aspirations of Black Americans because they regarded their quest for freedom and dignity as being *un*christian."[38] Whites in the South worked for segregation to "advantage whites in every facet of their lives and to saddle Blacks with corresponding and unyielding disadvantage."[39]

Such was the atmosphere in Mississippi. It was a spiritual gumbo in which love of God as a principle was mixed with love of God as a white Southern creation, or re-creation, of the God of the Bible. It was a gumbo in which white Christians manipulated the gospel in such a way that their effort to preserve white culture was done in lieu of the direction of the words of the gospel. It was a gumbo to which all white Christians were expected to contribute and to keep warm, for they believed it had been prepared in spite of a culture which was hostile to everything they stood for.

Their anger was never far from the surface. The mere thought of white and Black children being together roiled their spirits, causing riots when Black students integrated Central High School in 1957. The entire world saw on television the angry mob, yelling and jeering at the students as they walked calmly into the school. The anger hadn't abated five years later when James Meredith, a US Air Force veteran who also was a Black man, applied to the University of Mississippi, or Ole Miss, a public state university. The year was 1962, eight years after *Brown*.

Though Ole Miss was not affected by the *Brown* ruling, which applied only to grades K–12 in public schools, Southern whites resisted integration at any level in public education. Meredith was accepted into Ole Miss, but his acceptance was revoked when the university found out that he was Black. He didn't have the support of the South, but to the chagrin and disappointment of the South, he did have the federal government on his side. A federal court order had been issued, requiring the university to honor his acceptance and to allow him to register. Governor Ross Barnett vowed that "schools in Mississippi would remain segregated" as long as he was governor.[40] That included Ole Miss. Barnett said that he was "prepared to suffer imprisonment for this just cause."[41]

On September 30, 1962, white Mississippians got word that Meredith, accompanied by federal marshals, was on his way to Ole Miss. Meredith arrived at the campus and was ushered into his dorm secretly as angry whites gathered with the fury and passion of a lynch mob and began to riot on the campus. Three hundred federal marshals surrounded the Lyceum Building in the center of the campus as the mob began rioting, throwing bricks, bottles, rocks, and iron pipes, among other weapons. When the violence quelled later that night, the toll was significant: 2 men were dead; the riot had required the presence of more than 3,000 federal marshals, 160 of whom had been injured, 28 by gunfire.[42] In spite of the violence, however, the goal of keeping Ole Miss a whites-only institution failed. The following morning, October 1, 1962, Meredith registered for classes.

While many white clergy were as incensed as were the masses, there were some white clergy who were disturbed not because of the integration of the university but because they had seen their fellow clergymen violate what they believed to be the letter and the spirit of the gospel. Their relationship with the gospel haunted them; they could not and would not believe that the Jesus of the Gospels was pleased with the raw racial hatred that had been at the root of the riot and of so much more that happened in the South because white people did not want Black people infecting and affecting their way of life. A particular pastor, who would later become one of twenty-eight pastors who wrote and signed what became known as the "Born of Conviction" statement, recalled some years later how he felt as he watched what was happening at Ole Miss on television. He stood, watching, and found himself saddened as "The Star Spangled Banner" was played at the end of the viewing day. With tears in his eyes, he says he thought, "I'm an American first; this is my country. I cannot agree with what's happening up there in Ole Miss and where the leaders of this state are taking us."[43]

When the riot was over and Meredith's status as a student had been cemented, segregationists began to blame "the brutal tyrants in Washington" for what had happened. They might have claimed to love Jesus, but they refused to show respect for the federal government or its Constitution. When President John F. Kennedy was assassinated in 1963, some white children cheered, notes Joseph Reiff, and concerning the intrusion of the federal government into Mississippi's affairs, one churchgoer wrote:

> Could it be that the Methodist people should repent because we object to having Negroes attend our churches . . . and because we don't want them to enroll in the University and our public schools and intermarry with our young people and thus mongrelize the race? It would seem to me that the repentance should be on the part of the Federal Government that has laid aside the constitution and run rough-shod over our Governor and our State.[44]

The silence of white Christians, and especially of white Christian pastors, was too much for some of those pastors to bear. Two weeks after the riot, four young white Methodist ministers—Jerry Furr, Maxie Dunman, Jerry Trigg, and Jim Waits—were so troubled that they agreed that, whatever the cost, they had to say something. The gospel mandated it: "For whosoever will save his life shall lose it; but whosoever shall lose his life for my sake and the gospel's, the same shall save it" (Mark 8:35, KJV). The pastors, says Reiff, took their "bibles and a copy of the 1960 *Book of Discipline*" and used those two tools to write a statement which they hoped would be a "theological proclamation as an alternative to the dominant white Mississippi rhetoric."[45] After writing it, the four sought other white Methodist pastors who would lend their signatures, and the statement was published in the *Mississippi Methodist Advocate* on January 2, 1963. Only four paragraphs long, the statement included these words:

> Confronted with the grave crises precipitated by racial discord within our state in recent months, and the genuine dilemma facing persons of Christian conscience, we are compelled to voice publicly our convictions. Indeed, as Christian ministers and as native Mississippians, sharing the anguish of all our people, we have a particular obligation to speak. Thus understanding our mutual involvement in these issues, we bind ourselves together in this expression of our Christian commitment. We speak only for ourselves, though mindful that many others share these affirmations.
>
> Born of the deep conviction of our souls, . . . We affirm our faith in the official position of The Methodist Church. . . . "Our Lord Jesus Christ teaches that all men are brothers. He permits no discrimination because of race, color or creed."[46]

The backlash was swift and violent. The following Saturday, Rev. Lampton "awoke to find his car tires slashed" and decided not to hold service on that Sunday after being warned that some of his church members "threatened violence to the church and parsonage."[47] He never returned to that pulpit.

Straying from the civil religion called Christianity, which supported white supremacy and segregation, was difficult even before the "Born of Conviction" statement was written. One pastor, in response to the turmoil going on at Ole Miss, wrote in the fall of 1962 that "true followers of Christ" are always "disturbers" in keeping with "the tradition of speaking against injustice." He said, "Our point is that Christ is the social conscience of our time just as He has always been accepted as the personal conscience of man. It is a painful thing to be disturbed; the pain may very well be a blessing and it surely is a necessary thing."[48]

Jerry Trigg, one of the four writers of the "Born of Conviction" statement, preached a sermon on the Lord's Prayer on September 30, just before the riot that began at Ole Miss that night. In his sermon, he described how in a certain location "there was a rise of a segregationist party whose leader surrounded himself with police and declared that only whites were acceptable."[49] He told how the leader decried what he considered to be inferior races and how his nation was meant to be the superior nation of the world. The more Trigg preached, the more uncomfortable his congregation became because they were convinced that he was talking about the governor of Mississippi. As he continued to preach, some of his members walked out, missing the end of the sermon when Trigg revealed that the leader he had been talking about was Adolf Hitler. He was trying to warn them, says Reiff, that they could be setting themselves up to face "the same issues that German Christians had faced."[50] It turns out that Germans—Christian and not—were in fact watching America and emulating some of America's race laws. Trigg was not that far off.[51]

Thus, God, the creator of all, was being second-guessed, and humans were deciding which of God's creatures were worthy of life and rights. The capacity of white people to manipulate, terrorize, and exploit Black people and other people of color was seemingly endless. In an attempt to help his nephew understand what his life as a Black person in America would be like, James Baldwin wrote to him, "This innocent country set you down in a ghetto in which, in fact, it intended that you should perish. . . . You were born where you were born and faced the future that you faced because you were Black and for no other reason."[52] Black people were forced to function in the white man's world, and neither the Constitution nor the Bible was successful in making that functioning any easier. Neither document provided safety for Black people, and the word of a liberating, loving, and inclusive God was all but erased from the religion of the oppressors, who happened to be white.

The world knew what white people were doing to Black people in America. The Nazis knew and taught that "the southern states of North America maintain the most stringent separation between the white population and coloreds in both public and personal interactions."[53] The Prussian Memorandum, the principal statement of German eugenics that marked Germany's march toward the Nuremburg Laws, revealed that Nazis "cited the example of Jim Crow, . . . and that they treated Jim Crow as *more* radical than what the Nazis themselves envisaged."[54]

America, for all its desire to be the most moral nation the world had ever known, fell miserably short as it continually worshipped whiteness as an entity to be protected at all costs. The suffering that America's obsession with whiteness caused Black people was immeasurable, a pain expressed by the poet Countee Cullen, who wrote in his poem "Yet Do I Marvel":

> I doubt not God is good, well-meaning, kind,
> And did He stoop to quibble could tell why
> The little buried mole continues blind,
> Why flesh that mirrors Him must some day die,
> Make plain the reason tortured Tantalus
> Is baited by the fickle fruit, declare
> If merely brute caprice dooms Sisyphus
> To struggle up a never-ending stair.
> Inscrutable His ways are, and immune
> To catechism by a mind too strewn
> With petty cares to slightly understand
> What awful brain compels His awful hand.
> Yet do I marvel at this curious thing:
> To make a poet Black, and bid him sing!

African Americans indeed gained strength from their God to sing and to stand in spite of their condition.

Epigraphs

Equal Justice Initiative, *Lynching in America: Confronting the Legacy of Racial Terror* (Montgomery: Equal Justice Initiative, 2015).

"Born of Conviction" Statement, January 2, 1963; see Joseph T. Reiff, *Born of Conviction: White Methodists and Mississippi's Closed Society* (New York: Oxford University Press, 2016), 289.

NOTES

1. See "A Decision to Free His Slaves," George Washington's Mount Vernon, https://www.mountvernon.org/george-washington/slavery/washingtons-1799-will/.
2. James Cone, *Said I Wasn't Gonna Tell Nobody* (New York: Orbis, 2018), 9.
3. Cone.
4. Howard Thurman, *Jesus and the Disinherited*, foreword by Vincent Harding (Boston: Beacon Press, 1976), 11.
5. Thurman.
6. Reinhold D. Niebuhr, *The Irony of American History* (Chicago: University of Chicago Press, 1952), 55.
7. Walter Wink, *The Powers That Be: Theology for a New Millennium* (New York: Doubleday. A Galilee Book, 1998), 42.
8. Thurman, 12.
9. Niebuhr, 160.
10. Thurman, 13.
11. Leon F. Litwack, *Been in the Storm So Long: The Aftermath of Slavery* (New York: Vintage Books, 1980), 276–77.
12. Litwack, 459.
13. Litwack.
14. Litwack, 460.
15. Equal Justice Initiative, *Lynching in America* (Montgomery: Equal Justice Initiative, 2015).
16. Equal Justice Initiative, 31.
17. Equal Justice Initiative.
18. Equal Justice Initiative.
19. Isabel Wilkerson, *The Warmth of Other Suns* (New York: Random House, 2010), 186.
20. Wilkerson, 113.
21. Wilkerson.
22. Wilkerson, 351.
23. Wilkerson, 352.
24. Wilkerson.
25. Timothy Egan, *The Worst Hard Time* (Boston: Houghton Mifflin, 2006), 109.
26. Egan, 177.
27. Egan, 183.
28. "The Southern Manifesto," http://americanradioworks.publicradio.org/features/marshall/manifesto.html.
29. "Southern Manifesto."
30. Thurman, 24.
31. Thurman, 27.
32. Thurman, 29.
33. This story is found only in Luke 16:19-31.
34. Carolyn Renée Dupont, *Mississippi Praying: Southern White Evangelicals and the Civil Rights Movement, 1945–1975* (New York: New York University Press, 2013), 2.
35. Dupont.

36. Martin Luther King Jr., "Letter from a Birmingham Jail"; see the letter and other resources at Stanford University, The Martin Luther King, Jr. Research and Education Institute, https://kinginstitute.stanford.edu/king-papers/documents/letter-birmingham-jail.

37. Dupont, 5.

38. Dupont, 7.

39. Dupont, 8.

40. Joseph T. Reiff, *Born of Conviction: White Methodists and Mississippi's Closed Society* (New York: Oxford University Press, 2016), 58.

41. Reiff.

42. Reiff, 59.

43. Reiff, 60.

44. Reiff, 61.

45. Reiff, 83.

46. Reiff, 289–290.

47. Dupont, 127.

48. Reiff, 65.

49. Reiff, 66.

50. Reiff.

51. See James Whitman, *Hitler's American Model: The United States and the Making of Nazi Race Law* (Princeton, NJ: Princeton University Press, 2017), xi. Jerry Trigg's comparison of segregationist leaders with Hitler in relation to America was not a new thing; others had done it and still continue to do so. Whitman poses a relevant question: "How can it be that America has both so much democracy and so much racism?" (xi). The issues now are not that much different than those in 1930, Whitman says, and certainly are not that much different than the issues of the 1960s (Ibid., xi). America's total commitment to the principles of white supremacy had caught the attention of Hitler and others in Germany who were seeking to create a master race. While they rejected some of America's race laws, they in fact did borrow much of what they saw in America as they constructed the infrastructure and the rationale for what would become the Holocaust. They believed in and accepted the idea that some people were more worthy of life than others. America, the land of liberty and justice for all, had given them solid direction in their own quest for racial purity.

52. James Baldwin, *The Fire Next Time* (New York: Vintage International, 1993), 7.

53. Whitman, 86.

54. Whitman, 66–67.

12
Moving On

Finally, brothers and sisters, whatever is true, whatever is honorable, whatever is just, whatever is pure, whatever is pleasing, whatever is commendable—if there is any excellence and if there is anything worthy of praise—think about these things.   —Philippians 4:8

In a conversation I had with the late Rev. Dr. James H. Cone, he expressed how he had to write his second-to-last book before his passing, *The Cross and the Lynching Tree.* "I couldn't get past what I was thinking," he said. "I kept thinking about lynching and that 'old rugged cross' and I couldn't get away from the thought that I had that the cross *was* a lynching tree—that Jesus had been *lynched!"*

In Dr. Cone's eyes as well as in his voice, I could see and hear the agony he must have carried with him for a long time. Lynching was and is one of the most heinous atrocities carried out against Black people in this country. In church we had always lifted up the cross as the symbol of salvation, but never had we—or at least never had I—even thought that the Messiah had been lynched. Lynching was brutal and barbaric. It was so accepted that the US Congress refused to pass laws to get rid of it. It was the embodiment of the intersection of God and country, the Bible and the Constitution, with little pushback. Cone noted:

> The claim that whites had the right to control the Black population through lynching and other extralegal forms of mob violence was grounded in the religious belief that America is a white nation called by God to bear witness to the superiority of "white over Black . . ." Even prominent religious scholars in the North, like . . . church historian Philip Schaff . . . , believed that "The Anglo-Saxon and Anglo-American, of all modern races,

possess the strongest national character and the one best fitted
for universal dominion." Such beliefs made lynching defensible
and even necessary for many whites. Cole Blease, the two-time
governor and U.S. senator from South Carolina, proclaimed that
lynching is a "divine right of the Caucasian race to dispose of
the offending blackamoor without the benefit of jury." Lynching
was the white community's way of forcibly reminding Blacks of
their inferiority and powerlessness.[1]

That during the time of Jesus, the state used crucifixion as the
way to punish—humiliating people as well as hanging them up as
public spectacles so as to intimidate others—was a narrative lost in
the celebration of Jesus' dying on the cross as the way to salvation.
It became, noted Cone, "the great symbol of the Christian narrative
of salvation,"[2] and "during the course of 2,000 years of Christian
history, this symbol of salvation has been detached from any reference to the ongoing suffering and oppression of human beings."[3]

Cone and others came to a painful revelation about and understanding of the Bible: it had been written by and interpreted from
the perspective of the dominant class in Israel.[4]

Even as he grew up in Arkansas, Cone realized that something
was awry; while he was being taught about the inclusive love of
God, the white people who lived around him and others in the South
"tried to make us believe that God created Black people to be white
people's servants."[5] Cone said that "their affirmation of faith in Jesus Christ was a source of puzzlement to me because they excluded
Blacks not only socially but also from their church services."[6] When
it came to religion, specifically Christianity, to help people understand life, Christianity failed at a basic level because, Cone concluded, white Christianity doesn't understand that "the answer cannot
be the same for Blacks and whites who do not share the same life."[7]

Long before Cone, W. E. B. Du Bois, who condemned "white
religion" as an "utter failure,"[8] concluded much the same thing.
Du Bois said that "a nation's religion is its life and as such white
Christianity is a miserable failure."[9] He said the white Christ
was not the biblical Christ: "Yet Jesus Christ was a laborer
and Black men are laborers; He was poor and we are poor; He
was despised of his fellow men and we are despised; He was
persecuted and crucified, and we are mobbed and lynched. If

Jesus Christ came to America He would associate with Negroes
and Italians and working people; He would eat and pray with
them, and He would seldom see the interior of the Cathedral of
Saint John the Divine."[10]

The disconnect between the God of white religion and that of
Black religion only became more stark and more painful to endure
as the United States grew as a nation. The dehumanization of Black
people was done almost without thinking. James Baldwin noted
that in spite of this being called a Christian nation, "one must face
the fact that this Christian nation may never have read any of the
Gospels, but they do understand money."[11] Baldwin says that it is
the American republic "which created something which they call a
'nigger.' They created it out of necessities of their own."[12] Baldwin
continued that, as some neighborhoods in this country looked like
"a concentration camp," one would wonder how that happened
to be, and he concluded that "is not an act of God. It is an act of
the nation, and it began not quite a hundred years ago when the
North signed a bargain with the South. . . . Now we are here not
only to mourn . . . We are here to begin to achieve the American
Revolution."[13]

But white Christianity's idea of how to honor the intentions of
the founders and support the American Revolution came from an
entirely different angle; as clergy, they lifted up the names of George
Washington and Robert E. Lee as "the highest products of Southern
civilization" precisely because they were thought to "share deep
religious faith, [and] moral character."[14] Southern white clergy "believed that the Confederates had struggled for the same principles
of the Americans of 1776."[15] The Civil War had been a moral war,
Southern clergy believed, fought "to maintain the supremacy of the
word of God."[16]

The quest of Southern confederate religion, which has morphed
into what is today known as Christian nationalism, was to bring
God back into the country, as God, they believed, had been there
from the beginning. Adherents of civil religion believed that the
fight against slavery had resulted not only in the defeat of the Confederacy in the war, but also in the dilution of biblical principles
in Christianity, which they defined not so much from the Bible as
from their cultural perspectives. In their interpretation of the Bible
and understanding of the revolution, God was a warrior who had

sought justice. God ordained the separation of the races, as well as the place of other non-white men. Howard Thurman said that there has always been a unique moral climate in which Blacks and whites have lived together, yet separately, in the United States. Here, he said, "the Christian ethic has been deeply influenced . . . For a long time, the Christian Church has profoundly compromised with the demands of the Gospel of Jesus Christ, especially with respect to the meaning and practice of love."[17] The ethic of love, however, does not seem to be part of the theological structure of Christian nationalism. Violence, however, is. In a 1981 interview, the Rev. Carl McIntire said, "Separation involved hard, grueling controversy. It involves attacks, personal attacks, even violent attacks . . . Satan preaches brotherly love in order to hold men in apostasy. Aggression is an expansion of Christian love."[18] A biblical passage used to support such an ideology is highlighted in an essay by James B. Jordan entitled "Pacifism and the Old Testament":

> That it is a privilege to engage in God's wars is clearly seen in the Psalms, perhaps nowhere better than in Ps. 149:5-7, where the saints sing for joy on their beds while they contemplate warring against God's enemies, or Ps. 58:10, "The righteous will rejoice when he sees the vengeance; he will wash his feet in the blood of the wicked." Those who cannot say "Amen" to such sentiments have not yet learned to think God's thoughts after him . . . We have no problem rejoicing in His judgments, or in seeing it a privilege to be called to execute them . . .
> The righteous . . . are called by God's law to exercise a holy "violence" against certain of the wicked, thereby manifesting God's wrath.[19]

The Bible, thusly interpreted, leaves the concept of liberty, fairness, peace, and egalitarianism out of the picture.

Jesus as Liberator

The Constitution did not contain the words "God" or "slave," and yet the government, by its failure to address the problem of slavery head-on, did much to support those who believed that the Bible ordained it, just as the Bible's failure to say explicitly that racism is a sin allowed bigots to restructure and redefine religion—which they called Christianity—to suit their purposes.

The fact that African Americans saw God and specifically Jesus as one who valued them made white supremacists angry, for not only did African Americans object to the way God had been presented to them, but also they were able to win some battles against the government, using God as their strength, in their fight against racial oppression.

That African Americans saw God and Jesus as liberators allowed them to survive and even to exude joy in their worship services. If worship was a celebration of their survival, it was also a time to release and relieve the grief and the stress which they carried with them on a daily basis. It was only their belief that God heard them and loved them that made them able to get up even as the government and the church knocked them down, over and over. With hope and power they would sing the words of Fanny Crosby:

Pass me not, O gentle Savior,
　　Hear my humble cry!
While on others Thou art calling,
　　Do not pass me by!
Savior, Savior!
　　Hear my humble cry!
While on others Thou art calling
　　Do not pass me by!

The founders were religious men, in that most had grown up in the church and most claimed to be a member of a specific denomination, but most, by their own admission, were not Christian. They had no allegiance to the concept of egalitarianism, to the Great Commandment, or to the concept of racial equality, and they did not accept the mystical aspects of Jesus. They bowed to the whims and desires of the Southern states and Southern clergymen as they created the Constitution. What was most important to them was to create a nation that was not an autocracy and which would create and sustain an economy that would help them reach that goal. They claimed to be moral men, if not religious, but being moral did not include humanizing human beings for their own economic purposes.

Fear and Resentment

What was fertilized in the creation of our white supremacist government, supported as much by the silence of the founders as by those who bellowed their racist rants, was a group of people who began to believe in their invincibility, over and above the Constitution and the Bible. They realized that they were the group of people in power, and they enjoyed it and wanted to hold onto it. When reports came out in the 2000s that by 2034 America would be a non-white majority country, fear, which has always been a component in maintaining white supremacy, took on a new energy. Howard Thurman notes that when the Japanese bombed Pearl Harbor, one of the biggest reactions from whites was resentment and fear that their race, for the first time, had been challenged by a non-white people. "The control of white power over most of the earth was challenged by nonwhite power," he said.[20] The ultimate privilege of white people in this country was that their power had gone unchallenged, showing up in church but also in the courts and in the world. Their God and their government protected them, and that protection felt invincible until the attack on Pearl Harbor. White fear and resentment also rose to the surface after the September 1, 2011, attacks on the World Trade Center and the Pentagon by al-Qaeda. The belief in white supremacy had made government officials ignore warnings that these attacks would occur, but when they did, there was a deep terror that roiled in the spirits of those who felt that their race, their government, and their God would always protect them. Those attacks were as consequential for the white mind as had been the defeat of the Confederacy in the Civil War.

When Barack Obama was elected president, that fear—and not a small amount of resentment—was stoked yet again. Believing in their ultimate support and protection by God and law, the minds of many of the men and women in power were jostled into recognizing that in the end, all human beings desire and deserve freedom, dignity, and power and will not stop working for it until they get it.

Those in power know that instinctively, and that is why they work so hard to keep non-white people and others who do not meet their standards of worthiness in their place. Voter suppression will only increase as the number of people of color in this country increases. The essence of this government, which was pushed out of a womb of white supremacy, is one of control, or, as those who use the Bible to explain their ideas, one of domination. In order to maintain control, whites believe they have to keep people of color under their control. According to Carol Anderson, author of *White Rage*, the Great Migration happened in two phases; during the first phase, which went from 1915 to about 1940, a recorded 1.6 million people migrated north. It was during and after World War II, from the mid-1940s to the 1960s, says Anderson, that many more Blacks migrated north, bringing the total of migrants to 6 million.[21]

> Migration is the story of America. It is foundational. From Pilgrims fleeing oppression in Europe, to the millions who took advantage of the Homestead Act to "go West," to the erection of the Statue of Liberty in New York's harbor, all the way up to the U.S. Congress tying Most Favored Nation status to the human right of Soviet Jews to emigrate, the movement of people fleeing tyranny, violence, and withered opportunity is sacrosanct to Americans . . . Yet, when more than 1.5 million African Americans left the land below the Mason-Dixon Line, white southern elites raged with cool, calculated efficiency. There was no lynch mob seeking vengeance; rather, these were mayors, governors, legislators, business leaders and police chiefs who bristled at "the first step . . . the nation's servant class ever took without asking."[22]

A Cultural Divide

Americans, white and Black, don't like to talk about racism. The complaint of many whites is that we talk about it too much, that we should leave it alone. A Black woman recalled her father telling her how his father had sought to find out more about his enslaved family:

> My grandfather went to the folks who had owned our family and asked, "Do you have any documentation about our history during the slave days? We would like to see it, if possible." The man at the door . . . said, "Sure, I'll give it to you." The man went into his house and came back with some papers in his hands. Now, whether the papers were trivial or actual plantation records, who knows? But he stood in the door, in front of my

grandfather, and lit a match to the papers. "You want your history? Here it is . . . take the ashes and get off of my land."[23]

Senate Majority Leader Mitch McConnell recently dismissed the need for reparations for African Americans: "None of us currently living are responsible," he said. "I don't think reparations for something that happened 150 years ago is a good idea."[24] And some years ago, the evidence of there being a different way of interpreting the Bible—in essence, a different Bible for a different group of people—was made evident by a remark made by Robert Byrd, the late Democratic senator from Virginia. He and other senators, mostly from the South but not all, were fighting to keep the Voting Rights Act of 1965 from becoming law. The fights had been long and vicious, but the Southern senators held onto their determination to make the bill fail. Taylor Branch writes in *Pillar of Fire* that Byrd "turned to religious themes" as he spoke throughout the night of June 10, 1965. Branch says that Byrd offered his observations: "I have attempted to reach some understanding as to the Scriptural basis upon which we are implored to enact the proposed legislation, and I find none . . . Shall responsible men and women be persuaded that throughout the religious history of this country, that they failed to preach the truth? . . . If so, I might say to Christians that Christ died in vain."[25]

Branch goes on to illustrate how Byrd expounded on the biblical "curse of Noah" and cited verses from Leviticus. He "cited the parable of vineyard laborers" and said Jesus not only condoned employment discrimination but endorsed a property-owner's right to "do what I will with mine own."[26] Byrd ploughed on, using the Bible—his Bible, the Bible of white supremacist ideology—to prove God's approval of racial discrimination. Branch says Byrd was pressed on the Parable of the Good Samaritan, and the Great Commandment to love one's neighbor as oneself, and Byrd struck back with a fury: "But the scriptural admonition does not say that we may not *choose* our neighbor!"[27]

And that response is a perfect illustration of the impotence of the Bible and the Constitution to end racism. Both texts are embraced by two groups of people with radically different experiences, cultures, and worldviews. As long as the cultural divide remains in this country, the clash between the two will never end. If there is to be liberty and justice for all, and not for some, "the least of these" will have to stay on a battlefield made uneven by the weight of two sacred documents weighted in favor of the powerful.

In spite of the Bible and the Constitution, we, at this time in our history, are in trouble as a nation. With the election of Donald Trump to the presidency, the weakness of American politics and religion could no longer hide under or behind the myth of being a nation dedicated to "liberty and justice for all." By now, one hopes that point has been made clear, but if there was any doubt, this presidency has erased it. Not only has our political system had the blanket of protection ripped off of it, but also the concept of American Christianity has taken a seat front and center.

The truth of the matter is that neither sacred text—the Bible or the Constitution—has ever been strong enough or respected enough to force people to honor and respect Black lives, or the lives of indigenous Americans before Black people were herded into this country. When the Black Lives Matter movement was birthed after the murder of Trayvon Martin by George Zimmerman, many whites objected, responding with the refrains "all lives matter," and more specifically, "blue lives matter," referring to police officers.

But the history, which too many do not know, of Black lives not mattering is too revelatory, too stark in its honesty to try to pretend that Black lives have ever mattered to this country except as tools to be used to build white wealth. The power of the lynching of Emmett Till in 1955 was that in spite of local officials wanting to hurry and bury his mutilated body, his mother, Mamie Till, refused to let that happen. She wanted for the world to see what hatred based on racism had done to her only child. People reacted at seeing his body, and the civil rights movement of the 1960s was birthed largely because of Till's death; it opened a window of opportunity for Black people to speak out and have a modicum of support from the white world, which historically had been dubious of the cries of racial terror committed on Blacks by whites.

But Till's murder, preceded by *Brown v. Board of Education* in 1954 and followed by the Montgomery bus boycott which began in December 1955, and then the sit-ins, Freedom Rides, and the fight for the right to vote were not enough for the words of Jesus in the Gospels to take hold. A large segment of religious people who called themselves Christian and an even larger segment of people who called themselves patriots remained unconcerned with the lives of people whom they had been taught were inferior to them. Windows of opportunity to force awareness and change came and went; those windows closed after allowing baby steps of change for African Americans.

That positive change has come for African Americans only in bits and pieces, making way for activists to push through those open windows, says much for the tenacity of spirit of African Americans, but it also forces us to look, once again, at how the Bible and the Constitution are failing the cause of justice for African Americans. Neither the God of religious people in power nor the Constitution of this country can be depended upon to protect the rights of Black people. State-sanctioned killings of Black people are still being committed, and the offending officers are still being set loose by police departments and the justice system. The murder of George Floyd in May 2020 set off demonstrations in this country and around the world. The image of the white officer with his knee on the neck of Floyd, even as he begged for his life, has been as jarring for people to see as was the image of Till, but even as the hearts of people have been disturbed to the point of leading them to protest, the questions remain. How long will the window of opportunity stay open? How long will people who say they believe in the Bible and the Constitution stay on a battlefield for racial justice which has only gotten bloodier with each battle fought so that there might be liberty and justice for all in this country?

Clearly there is a difference in the way Blacks and whites see both documents. Both the late Rev. C. T. Vivian and Congressman John Lewis, who died on the same day, said that their work was based on and driven by the words of Jesus the Christ found in the Gospels. The movement for justice for Black people, they said individually at different times in their lives, was driven by Jesus' words, just as was their determination to get justice nonviolently and by leaning on the truth of the Constitution. While people in power espouse that they believe in the rule of law, what civil rights activists realized was that their definition of that rule of law was different than it was for Black people. While, as has been discussed in this book, Jesus and Christianity in general were weaponized to assure the preservation of white power, Black people have relied on Jesus' words, not the mere saying of his name, to guide them in their quest for justice.

The struggle to remain true to the gospel and to the Constitution is not an easy one, but it seems that belief in the ultimate power of both documents has been what has kept Black people sane in their quest for justice and equality. Negro spirituals and hymns speak to the hope that the gospel and the Constitution give to Black people; there had to be a God who heard, listened, and cared. Without that hope, the pressure of being oppressed so completely would have caused Black people to give up long ago.

It is that hope and faith in both of America's sacred documents, combined with the words of Jesus the Christ, which have been the glue which has held Black spirits together There is no way one can read the words of Jesus and not be compelled to take inventory of one's heart and actions. The central message of the gospel is that all lives, including Black lives, the lives of women, and the lives of other marginalized people, matter. Those who have grown up studying the Gospels have felt the sting of Jesus' commands: to love one another no matter what. Those same lessons drilled in the message that whatever people may do to you, we are compelled to forgive each other, not once, but seventy times seven (Matthew 18:21-22). That is why so often, to the astonishment of those who have not internalized the Gospels, some family members of people killed because of racism say they forgive the assailants. To the ones who have studied Jesus' words, it is a lesson that has at least stymied the human tendency to hate those who have hated them; the words of Jesus are much like a perpetual itch of the soul. The parents of slain children remember those words and recall the hope that is communicated in the Gospels, even through their tears and grief as the murderers of their children are set free. For Black people, there is nowhere to go but to the gospel and to the Constitution. The parents and families of not only George Floyd, but also of Eric Garner, Trayvon Martin, Breonna Taylor, Sandra Bland, Jordan Davis, Armaud Arbery, Elijah McClain, Freddie Gray, and so many others, have to lean on a hope and faith which seems irrational in the face of such deep tragedy. And yet, it is what has kept them alive and determined to fight for the truth of the documents on which they lean.

It is troubling to learn the depth of white supremacist thinking. I was shocked when I read that President Abraham Lincoln blamed Black people for the Civil War. It was disappointing to learn how racist was President Woodrow Wilson. It has been disturbing to learn about the deep racist beliefs of some of the justices on the United States Supreme Court. Many judges, including some on the Supreme Court, do not believe that racism exists, when history shows a pattern of racist decisions, including *Plessy v. Ferguson* (1896), *Dred Scott v. Sandford* (1856), *Cummings v. Richmond* (1899), and *Lum v. Rice* (1927). The Fourteenth Amendment was intended to protect the full citizenship claims by people of color but consistently ruled against people of color in cases where they argued their rights as American citizens had been violated. Some justices, historically and even now, believe that there is no more racism. Justice Samuel Alito, who sits presently on the Supreme Court, is but one of justices past and present who do not believe that racism exists.

So, where are we? What can we do and what can we use to end racism if neither the Bible nor the Constitution are respected by many whites, especially and including white evangelicals, to be a guide away from practicing racism? Matthew Avery Sutton, in *American Apocalypse*, said that "government by anything other than white Protestant males who lived up to evangelicals' litmus tests proved threatening" in Harry Truman's day, and that appears to be the reality in the present day.[28] As President Trump makes statements feeding the racist paranoia that many whites still harbor, he is echoing sentiments which have been longstanding in this country. When the US Supreme Court has made rulings that seem to grant human and civil rights to Blacks, it has been white evangelicals who have protested most loudly. After *Brown v. Board of Education* was decided, many white preachers declared that the country was declining and heading toward mass immorality and lawlessness, and many evangelicals feel the same way today. Too many white people ignored the gospel and the law—which is telling, since they claim to believe in the rule of law.

Sometimes a system or an institution is so broken that it cannot be fixed; it must be dismantled and rebuilt. Because America has never owned its racism, causing its core to rot, it seems highly unlikely that racism will be dismantled as a social cancer unless and until the foundation is replaced. Even as the racial, ethnic, and religious diversity of this country increases, the number of people who use both the Bible and the Constitution to hold onto racial bigotry threaten America's survival. In the 2016 election, the Russians used America's racism to bait people one way or another, and today, the president, losing support because of his mishandling of the coronavirus pandemic and its subsequent effect on the American economy, is using our foundational racism as a life jacket for his faltering presidency. As hundreds of thousands of people are getting COVID-19, and thousands are dying, this president is counting on allegiance to American white supremacy to do as it has always done—divide people and impede progress, rather than calling on their allegiance to the Bible and the Constitution. He has enough support in the Senate, in the courts, and in some churches to do what he is doing, and he knows it.

The prayer has to be that there are enough people who will read the history of how the church and the government have worked together over the four hundred years since Africans were brought to this country to block people of African descent from receiving fair treatment. The prayer is that more churches will look at and practice the Gospels and specifically, the words of Jesus, if they are in fact going to call themselves Christian. The country is slipping into an abyss, led by this president, and it is slipping largely because racism still exists and too many churches are still more aligned with the state than they are with a God of equality and egalitarianism, even as governments are still influenced by people who say their concept of a God who sanctions white supremacy is the only God.

It is the premise of this writer that that concept is wrong, and the hope is that enough people will save this country from a descent into tyranny by standing up for the truth of the Jesus of the Bible and the words of the Declaration of Independence: that all people are indeed created equal and are endowed by their creator with certain unalienable rights. Unless and until our sacred texts are honored and respected, the American experiment will continue to be attacked by those who have seen through the veneer of American exceptionalism all along, and we the people of this country, with the exception of the very few who have money and who are in power, will suffer for it.

Surely, that is not the will of God, nor was it the vision of our founding fathers.

NOTES

1. James H. Cone, *The Cross and the Lynching Tree* (Maryknoll, NY: Orbis, 2011), 7.

2. Cone, *Lynching Tree*, xiv.

3. Cone, *Lynching Tree*.

4. James H. Cone, *God of the Oppressed*, rev. ed. (Maryknoll, NY: Orbis, 1997), xii.

5. Cone, *God of the Oppressed*, 2.

6. Cone, *God of the Oppressed*, 3.

7. Cone, *God of the Oppressed*, 9.

8. Cone, *Lynching Tree*, 102.

9. Cone, *Lynching Tree*.

10. Cone, *Lynching Tree*, 103.

11. James Baldwin. "We Can Change This Country," in *The Cross of Redemption: Uncollected Writings* (New York: Vintage International, 2011), 59.

12. Baldwin, 60.

13. Baldwin, 62–63.

14. Charles Reagan Wilson, *Baptized in Blood: The Religion of the Lost Cause* (Athens: University of Georgia Press, 2009), 40.

15. Wilson.

16. Wilson, 42.

17. Howard Thurman, *The Luminous Darkness: A Personal Interpretation of the Anatomy of Segregation and the Ground of Hope* (reprint; Richmond: Friends United Press, 1980–1981), 2–3.

18. Katherine Stewart, *The Power Worshippers: Inside the Dangerous Rise of Religious Nationalism* (New York: Bloomsbury Publishing, 2019), 125.

19. James B. Jordan, cited in Walter Wink, *The Powers That Be: Theology for a New Millennium* (New York: Doubleday. A Galilee Book, 1998), 59.

20. Thurman, *Luminous Darkness*, 53.

21. Carol Anderson, "The Black Codes & The Great Migration," https://www.youtube.com/watch?v=-GCb87uCHM0.

22. Carol Anderson, *White Rage: The Unspoken Truth of Our Racial Divide* (New York: Bloomsbury Press, 2016), 42.

23. Edward Ball, "Retracing Slavery's Trail of Tears," *Smithsonian*, November 2015, https://www.smithsonianmag.com/history/slavery-trail-of-tears-180956968/.

24. Ted Barrett, "McConnell Opposes Paying Reparations: 'None of Us Currently Living Are Responsible' for Slavery," June 19, 2019, CNN, https://www.cnn.com/2019/06/18/politics/mitch-mcconnell-opposes-reparations-slavery/index.html.

25. Taylor Branch, *Pillar of Fire: America in the King Years: 1963–65* (New York: Simon & Schuster, 1998), 335.

26. Branch, 336.

27. Branch.

28. Matthew Avery Sutton, *American Apocalypse: A History of Modern Evangelicalism* (Cambridge, MA: Belknap Press, 2017), 307.

Bibliography of Online Sources

Alger, William A. "Come, Let Us Go Up to the House of God and He Will Teach Us." WallBuilders. https://wallbuilders.com/sermon-civil-war-1861/.

"An Appeal from the Colored Men of Philadelphia to the President of the United States." https://static1.squarespace.com/static/590be125ff7c502a07752a5b/t/5eb4b69a05feaf0320dcf4a3/15889 01531735/Gibbs%2C+Jr.%2C+Jonathan+Clarkson%2C+An+Appeal +from+the+Colored+Men+of+Philadelphia+to+the+President.pdf.

Balmer, Randall. "The Real Origins of the Religious Right." May 27, 2014. Politico Magazine. https://www.politico.com/magazine/story/2014/05/religious-right-real-origins-107133?o=1.

Banks, Adelle M. "Museum Highlights 'Slave Bible' That Focuses on Servitude, Leaves Out Freedom." November 27, 2018. Religious News Service. https://religionnews.com/2018/11/27/museum-highlights-slave-bible-that-focuses-on-servitude/.

Barnhart, Dave. "Reading a Pro-slavery Sermon from 1863." August 6, 2015. https://davebarnhart.wordpress.com/2015/08/06/reading-a-pro-slavery-sermon-from-1863/.

Bump, Philip. "Why Are Evangelical Americans So Loyal to Trump? Because They're Heavily Republican." April 10, 2019. *Washington Post*. https://www.washingtonpost.com/politics/2019/04/10/why-are-evangelical-americans-so-loyal-trump-because-theyre-heavily-republican/.

Burst, Todd. "Benjamin Franklin's Racist Project for the Future of America in 'Observations Concerning the Increase of Mankind, Peopling of Countries,&c.'" May 31, 2018. Medium. https://medium.com/@tsrub88j/benjamin-franklins-racist-project-for-the-future-of-ameri ca-in-observations-concerning-the-7ee76e4e7474.

Camacho, Daniel José. "On the Brutal, Violent History of Racism in the U.S. Church." May 9, 2019. Sojourners. https://sojo.net/articles/brutal-violent-history-racism-us-church.

Clark, Emily Suzanne. "Religion and Race in America." February 2017. Oxford Research Encyclopedia. https://oxfordre.com/american history/view/10.1093/acrefore/9780199329175.001.0001/acrefore -9780199329175-e-322?rskey=h6efMs.

Cline, Austin. "Insightful Thomas Paine Quotes on Religion." December 28, 2018. Learn Religions. https://www.learnreligions.com/top-thomas -paine-quotes-on-religion-4072775.

"The Constitution and Slavery." Constitutional Rights Foundation. http://www.crf-usa.org/black-history-month/the-constitution-and-slavery.

"The Constitution of the United States: A Transcription." National Archives. https://www.archives.gov/founding-docs/constitution-transcript.

"The Constitution of the United States, The Bill of Rights and All Amendments." https://constitutionus.com/#n2.

Douglass, Frederick. "The Constitution of the United States: Is It Pro-Slavery or Anti-Slavery?" BlackPast. https://www.blackpast.org/global-african-history/1860-frederick-douglass-constitution-united-states-it-pro-slavery-or-anti-slavery/.

Fea, John. "Religion and Early Politics: Benjamin Franklin and His Religious Beliefs." *Pennsylvania Heritage* 37, no. 4 (Fall 2011). http://www.phmc.state.pa.us/portal/communities/pa-heritage/religion-early-politics-benjamin-franklin.html.

————. "Why Do White Evangelicals Still Staunchly Support Donald Trump?" April 5, 2019. *Washington Post*. http://pleacher.com/forwards/politics/chright.html.

Finkelman, Paul. "Three-Fifths Clause: Why Its Taint Persists." February 26, 2013. The Root. https://www.theroot.com/three-fifths-clause-why-its-taint-persists-1790895387.

Freeman, Curtis W. "'Never Had I Been So Blind': W. A. Criswell's 'Change' on Racial Segregation." *The Journal of Southern Religion* 10 (2007). http://jsr.fsu.edu/Volume10/Freeman.pdf.

Gardiner, William J. "Reflections on the History of White Supremacy in the United States." March 2009. https://www.uua.org/sites/live-new.uua.org/files/documents/gardinerwilliam/whiteness/white_supremacy_us.pdf .

Garnet, Henry Highland. "Let the Monster Perish." January 28, 2007. BlackPast. https://www.blackpast.org/African-american-history/1865-henry-highland-garnet-let-monster-perish/.

Harvey, Sean P. "Ideas of Race in Early America." April 2016. Oxford Research Encyclopedia. https://oxfordre.com/americanhistory/view/10.1093/acrefore/9780199329175.001.0001/acrefore-9780199329175-e-262?rskey=FF6ogN&result=1.

Historic Ipswich. "The Great Dying 1616–1619, 'By God's Visitation, a Wonderful Plague.'" https://historicipswich.org/2017/09/01/the-great-dying/.

History.com editors. "Articles of Confederation." October 27, 2009, updated September 27, 2019. History. https://www.history.com/topics/early-us/articles-of-confederation.

————. "Constitution." October 27, 2009, updated September 27, 2019. History. https://www.history.com/topics/united-states-constitution/constitution.

————. "Manifest Destiny." April 5, 2010, updated November 15, 2019. History. https://www.history.com/topics/westward-expansion/manifest-destiny.

Holmes, David L. "The Founding Fathers, Deism, and Christianity." Encyclopedia Britannica. https://www.britannica.com/topic/The-Founding-Fathers-Deism-and-Christianity-1272214.

Hossain, Shah Aashna. "Scientific Racism in 'Enlightened Europe.'" January 16, 2008. Serendip Studio. https://serendipstudio.org/exchange /serendipupdate/scientific-racism-enlightened-europe.

"How Many of the Signers of the Declaration of Independence Owned Slaves?" http://mrheintz.com/how-many-signers-of-the-declaration-of -independence-owned-slaves.html.

"How the Romans Used Crucifixion—Including Jesus's—as a Political Weapon." April 4, 2015. *Newsweek* [special edition]. http://www .newsweek.com/how-romans-used-crucifixion-including-jesus-political -weapon-318934.

Irons, Charles F. "Religion During the Civil War." Encyclopedia Virginia. https://encyclopediavirginia.org/religion-during_the_civil_war#start_.

"Is Jesus God? Asked the Council of Nicea." Christianity.com. https: //www.christianity.com/church/church-history/timeline/1-300/is-jesus -god-11629651.html.

King, Martin Luther, Jr. "The Death of Evil Upon the Seashore." Stanford University. The Martin Luther King, Jr. Research and Education Institute. https://kinginstitute.stanford.edu/king-papers/documents/death -evil-upon-seashore-sermon-delivered-service-prayer-and-thanksgiving.

———. "A Realistic Look at the Question of Progress in the Area of Race Relations." Stanford University. The Martin Luther King, Jr. Research and Education Institute. https://kinginstitute.stanford.edu/king-papers /documents/realistic-look-question-progress-area-race-relations -address-delivered-st.

Little, Becky. "Why Bibles Given to Slaves Omitted Most of the Old Testament." December 11, 2018, updated April 3, 2019. History. https: //history.com/news/slave-bible-redacted-old-testament.

Lyman, Brian. "'Where Was the Lord?' On Jefferson Davis' Birthday, Nine Slave Testimonies." *Montgomery Advertiser.* June 3, 2019. https: //www.montgomeryadvertiser.com/in-depth/news/2019/06/03 /alabama-state-holiday-jefferson-davis-birthday-where-lord-9-slave -testimonies/3740398002/.

Mann, Simon. "The White House's Ugly Secret." *Sydney Morning Herald.* February 26, 2011. https://www.smh.com.au/world/the-white-houses -ugly-secret-20110225-1b8kq.html.

Massey, Wyatt. "'We Are Therefore Demanding . . . ' Reparations in the Christian Church." *The Frederick News-Post* [Frederick, MD]. March 29, 2019. https://www.fredericknewspost.com/news/lifestyle/religion /we-are-therefore-demanding-reparations-in-the-christian-church /article_c396439b-5929-5685-ac5a-40f31c12353e.html.

Mattson, Stephen. "The False and Idolatrous Narrative of American Christianity." May 13, 2019. Sojourners. https://sojo.net/articles /false-and-idolatrous-narrative-american-christianity.

"A New Version of the Lord's Prayer." Founders Online. https://founders .archives.gov/documents/Franklin/01-15-02-0170.

Norton, Quinn. "How White People Got Made." October 14, 2017. The Message. https://medium.com/message/how-white-people-got-made-6e eb076ade42.

Palmer, Benjamin Morgan. "Thanksgiving Sermon." https://civilwarcauses. org/palmer.htm.

Patrick, Leslie. "African American and Civil Rights in Pennsylvania." *Pennsylvania Heritage* (Spring 2010). http://www.phmc.state.pa.us /portal/communities/pa-heritage/african-americans-civil-rights -pennsylvania.html.

Prentiss, George L. "Some of the Providential Lessons of 1861." Wall-Builders. https://wallbuilders.com/sermon-new-year-1861-1862/.

Ramsey, Sonya. "The Troubled History of American Education after the *Brown* Decision." February 9, 2017. Process: A Blog for American History. http://www.processhistory.org/american-education-after-brown.

"Richard Furman's Exposition." Furman University. http://history.furman. edu/~benson.docs/rcd-fmnl.htm.

Robinson, Jeffery. "Five Truths about Black History." American Civil Liberties Union. https://www.aclu.org/issues/racial-justice/five-truths -about-black-history.

Schweitzer, Jeff. "Founding Fathers: We Are Not a Christian Nation." February 26, 2015, updated April 28, 2015. HuffPost. https://www .huffpost.com/entry/founding-fathers-we-are-n_b_6761840.

Semuels, Alana. "The Founding Fathers Weren't Concerned with Inequality." April 25, 2016. The Atlantic. https://www.theatlantic. com/business/archive/2016/04/does-income-inequality-really-violate --principles/479577/.

Serwer, Adam. "White Nationalism's Deep American Roots." April 2019. The Atlantic. https://www.theatlantic.com/magazine/archive/2019/04 /adam-serwer-madison-grant-white-nationalism/583258/.

Shelly, Bruce L. "325 The First Council of Nicea." Christian History. October 1, 1990. https://www.christianitytoday.com/history/channel /utilities/print.html?type=article&id=3745.

"Signers of the Constitution." United States History. https://www.u-s -history.com/pages/h1027.html.

"Signers of the Declaration of Independence." US History.org. http://www .ushistory.org/declaration/signers/index.html.

Sorkin, Amy Davidson. "In Voting Rights, Scalia Sees a 'Racial Entitlement.'" February 28, 2013. *The New Yorker*. https://www.newyorker.com /news/amy-davidson/in-voting-rights-scalia-sees-a-racial-entitlement.

"The Southern Declaration on Integration (1956)." https://wwnorton .com/college/history/archive/resources/documents/ch33_03.htm.

Taylor, Alan. "The New Nation: 1783–1815." The Gilder Lehrman Institute of American History. https://ap.gilderlehrman.org/essay/new -nation-1783%C3%A2%E2%82%AC%E2%80%9C1815.

"Teddy Roosevelt's 'Shocking' Dinner with Washington." May 14, 2012. *Talk of the Nation*. NPR. https://www.npr.org/2012/05/14/152684575 /teddy-roosevelts-shocking-dinner-with-washington.

"Virginia Slave Laws." Digital History. http://www.digitalhistory.uh.edu /disp_textbook.cfm?smtID=3&psid=71.

Wade, Lisa. "Whites, Blacks, and Apes in the Great Chain of Being." July 12, 2012. Sociological Images. https://thesocietypages.org /socimages/2012/07/12/whites-blacks-apes-in-the-great-chain-of-being/.

Warinner, Andrew. "How Many of America's Founding Fathers Were Slave Owners?" September 9, 2011. Quora. https://www.quora.com /How-many-of-Americas-founding-fathers-were-slave-owners.

White House Historical Association. "How Did the White House Get Its Name?" https://whitehousehistory.org/questions/how-did-the-white -house-get-its-name.

Williamson, Vanessa. "When White Supremacy Came to Virginia." August 15, 2017. Brookings. https://www.brookings.edu/blog/fixgov/2017/08 /15/when-white-supremacy-came-to-virginia.

Wulf, Andrea. "Thomas Jefferson's Quest to Prove America's Natural Superiority." March 7, 2016. The Atlantic. https://www.theatlantic.com /science/archive/2016/03/jefferson-american-dream/471696.

Zinn, Howard. "The Scourge of Nationalism." June 1, 2005. Howard Zinn.org. https://www.howardzinn.org/the-scourge-of-nationalism/.